THE PARADOX OF CHANGE

The Paradox of Change

AMERICAN WOMEN
IN THE 20th CENTURY

William H. Chafe

OXFORD UNIVERSITY PRESS
New York   Oxford

Oxford University Press

Oxford   New York   Toronto
Delhi   Bombay   Calcutta   Madras   Karachi
Petaling Jaya   Singapore   Hong Kong   Tokyo
Nairobi   Dar es Salaam   Cape Town
Melbourne   Auckland
and associated companies in
Berlin   Ibadan

Library of Congress Cataloging-in-Publication Data
Chafe, William Henry.
The paradox of change : American women in the 20th century /
William H. Chafe.
p.   cm.   Rev. ed. of: The American woman, 1972.
Includes bibliographical references and index.
ISBN 0-19-504418-5
ISBN 0-19-504419-3 (pbk.)
1. Women—United States—History—20th century. 2. Women's
rights—United States—History—20th century. I. Chafe, William
Henry. American woman. II. Title.
HQ1426.C45 1991   305.42'0973'0904—dc20   90–43457

2 4 6 8 10 9 7 5 3 1
Printed in the United States of America

For L.J.W.C.—feminist, companion, partner

Preface

WHEN *The American Woman* was first published nearly two decades ago, the field of women's history had just begun to achieve legitimacy and popularity. Although such scholars as Julia Cherry Spruill and Mary Beard had pioneered work in the discipline during the 1930s, their efforts were soon dwarfed by the emergence of the "consensus" school of the 1940s and 1950s, with its focus on prominent American men. By the 1960s, however, writers such as Eleanor Flexner, Anne Firor Scott, Gerda Lerner, and Aileen Kraditor had begun to blaze a new trail. During the early 1970s, they were joined by scores of graduate students and younger colleagues inspired by the challenge and excitement of writing a different kind of history, one that would literally re-vision the past. For the first time, those who comprise the majority of hu-mankind would occupy center stage in the story of our collective experience.

The results of these past twenty years of scholarship have been nothing short of astonishing. Together with labor history and Afro-American history, women's history has helped to transform our sense of what the discipline of history is all about. In 1965, most books began with male politicians and focused on events where men—usually white and upper class—played the primary roles. Today, the majority of history books begin with the experi-ences of people who are not famous, who may not have wielded power, yet whose day-to-day lives illuminate, as much as any president's life, the strug-gles and triumphs of given moments in time. New questions have been asked—about control of the workplace, relations in the home, the political uses of education, the sometimes insidious impact of socialization, and the ability of people to resist oppression; the evidence developed in response to those questions, in turn, has drastically altered our sense of the historical landscape.

One of the reasons I have decided to rework *The American Woman* is to acknowledge the impact of this scholarship and incorporate at least some of its discoveries. Countless books and articles have been written since 1972 about 20th-century American women. Historians have explored the powerful, but previously hidden, subject of sexuality; the fabric and texture of communities of women who joined together to pursue various objectives, reactionary as well as progressive; the differences that divided women of different classes and ethnic groups; and the powerful forces of occupational segregation and structural inequality that generated certain commonalities of treatment by gender, regardless of these differences. At least some of this new research occurred in response to my own thesis about the significance of World War II for 20th-century women's history; while I have not accepted here all the revisions suggested by my colleagues since 1972, I have benefited enormously from their work.

A second reason for this new edition is my own desire to understand better the patterns and themes of 20th-century women's history. Those of us who wrote in the late 1960s and early 1970s carried our own conceptual and theoretical baggage. Models of social change were implicit, and sometimes explicit, in our writing. Yet in contrast to how the field has developed in more recent years, we were relatively unsophisticated in our theoretical understanding. Since then, women's history has advanced even further in conceptual clarity than it has in empirical discoveries. As a consequence, we now have the opportunity for greater precision and analytical insight in the conclusions we reach. As I have rethought the arguments set forth in the original version of this book, I have often wished that ideas I believed were *implicit* in my narrative had been made *explicit*. Now, with all the work that has been done in more recent years, it makes sense to try to recast the evidence on 20th-century women's experience within a more up-to-date conceptual framework.

Here, it is appropriate to identify some of the conceptual categories that are most helpful in sorting out the patterns and themes to be found in women's history during the last century.

The first, and most basic, flows from the simple question of how different women are from men and the extent to which that difference is a product of natural causes or, by contrast, a product of imposed segregation and discrimination. Clearly, one of the sources of women's oppression (legally, politically, and economically) is the degree to which women have been treated as a class, or caste—different from and lesser than men. But does that mean that all treatment of women as different is inherently invidious and oppressive? Does equality require or presume sameness; or can there be equality *with* difference?

In this context, a direct relationship seems to exist between one's diagnosis of the problem and one's prescription for its solution. If separate roles, activities, and values are, *prima facie*, a source of inequality, then anything that hints of sanctioning or reinforcing a "separate sphere" for women needs to be abolished. On the other hand, if women *are* different from men, such differences should be a source of strength and a cause for celebration, not an obstacle to be eliminated. In such a case, only the invidious treatment that accompanies difference should be attacked, while the principle of difference itself should be upheld and defended.

Those who argue on behalf of difference are sometimes accused of being "essentialists." According to their critics, they believe that women—*all women* —have different values, temperament, and concerns than men have and that they cannot and should not be treated as identical with men. Essentialists believe that women of all classes, races, and backgrounds share certain tendencies, such as nurturance and cooperation, that predispose women to a common approach to each other and to social problems. For such people, "sisterhood" is a powerful and global phenomenon, rooted in the natural differences that separate women from men and that unite women of all backgrounds.

The argument for difference and essentialism often coincides with the argument that a separate "women's culture" exists. According to this analysis, women's "separate sphere" provides a basis for sharing strengths and values that comprise a distinctive cultural worldview. When women unite around these values and concerns, they represent a powerful force for social change and transformation, significantly improving the world they live in by acting on their distinctive qualities. Were women to sacrifice this distinctiveness by becoming "imitation men," they would both lose their own identity and vitiate their capacity to change the world.

Those who believe in difference are also more likely to endorse what Karen Offen has called "relational feminism," a commitment by women to act as a collective body on behalf of a more humane and just world. Feminism of this kind values interdependency and community rather than individualism and isolation. It is also more likely to recognize the value of separatism as a strategy for change and the value of pluralism as a positive goal. (Contemporary radical feminists also emphasize separatism as a strategy but believe in a more confrontational approach to men.) Rather than seek integration or assimilation—which, in most cases, means adapting to the values and characteristics of the dominant group (in this case, white males)—women would defend their own culture and values and seek to build from that homebase a society more consistent with women's basic concerns. Arguably, a culture based on such collective action would produce greater justice and a social order significantly different from that which prevails today. Whatever their disagreements, then, those who are associated with arguments for essentialism, difference, a women's culture, separatism, and universal sisterhood participate in a set of worldviews that have internal consistency and far-reaching implications for how women see themselves and are seen by others.

A dramatically different worldview is held by those who choose the other side of these issues. Acting within the liberal, natural-rights philosophy associated with John Locke, John Stuart Mill, and Mary Wollstonecraft, these women's rights activists see all treatment of women as a separate or different class of people as inherently contradictory to the idea of self-determination and equal opportunity. According to this view, women and men should be treated the same, as identical under the law and within the social and economic structure. Within this framework, separate treatment means unequal treatment, as the Supreme Court ruled in 1954 when, on the issue of racial separation, it declared in *Brown v. Board of Education* that segregation of the races automatically entailed and produced inequality. There may be individual differences between *people*, but not categorical differences between sexes or races. Hence, all notions of a separate women's sphere should be abolished, because admitting even the possibility of a *positive* separate sphere sanctions the likelihood of a *negative* separate sphere. Once the concept of separateness is sanctioned, according to this argument, inequality is the natural result. Any effort to distinguish between "good" separation and "bad" separation is inherently flawed and dangerous, since separation itself is the problem, destroying *individual* rights by making the category of sexual difference primary.

As a natural corollary, natural-rights adherents dismiss "women's culture" as a by-product of segregation and oppression, therefore something that should be eliminated, not celebrated. Since separation violates natural-rights philosophy, any institutions or concepts that perpetuate separation stand in the path of freedom and independence. "Women's culture," by this logic, developed as a compensatory mechanism that itself reflected and contributed to inequality. Only when all such categories as "women's place," "woman's culture," and "woman's sphere" become anachronistic can women as individuals be treated as equal in their own right.

Not surprisingly, then, the feminism associated with natural-rights philosophy is one of radical individualism, wherein each human being, regardless of background, will be treated *identically*, with sex or race or class completely removed from the equation.* If the goal is individual freedom and independence, collective concerns, based on a shared sense of values or relationships, become irrelevant and even counterproductive. There is no *women's* interest or point of view, only that of different individuals. Hence, the ultimate purpose of feminism is assimilation or integration of women, as individuals, into the existing society. Social transformation or revolution is not the point, especially if that transformation is premised on an alternative collective set of values. Rather, the desired end is sufficient reform to guarantee that women are treated not as women but as individuals and accepted completely on that basis within existing social, political, and economic institutions.

For those who embrace the ideology of radical individualism, of course, the concept of global sisterhood is a contradiction in terms. The goal, after all, is to set aside such sex-based categories and the implied bonding and relational accountability that they carry with them. Women may need to unite and temporarily form separate political groupings to achieve freedom, but the only purpose in that is to reach the stage where such alliances have no basis for existing and wither away. At that juncture, each woman would be free to pursue her own individual agenda of personal self-realization; all notions of separate spheres or distinctive cultures serve more as reminders of a previous condition of servitude than as rallying points for liberation.

In reality, of course, these positions never existed in such spartan contrast as outlined above. More often than not, women activists adopted a mixture of attitudes. It was not at all unusual, for example, for Elizabeth Cady Stanton to argue for women's rights on the grounds of both natural-rights individualism and women's moral difference and superiority to men. In one context, a person might insist on individual freedom from all sex-based treatment; and in another, insist that women *qua* women deserved special recognition. Such complexity persists to this day.

More important, a discussion of gender difference does not address the most profound conclusion of feminist scholars in recent years, namely, that women, like men, are so shaped by the *intersection* of different variables of gender, class, and race that to attempt a generalization on the basis of gender alone is ludicrous. In her challenging theoretical overview of women's history, Gerda Lerner talks about achieving a "woman-defined" perspective based on values and concerns that are "woman-oriented." Yet Cuban women who are cigar workers in Tampa will have a vastly different concept of family, work,

*There may be a communal organizational base that provides a foundation for seeking such individualism and serves as a means toward that end.

and community than women who are members of the Junior League in Grosse Pointe, Michigan. As Nancy Hewitt has shown so well, it is far easier for working-class ethnic women to join with working-class ethnic men to pursue their common interests than it is for the same women to join with their class enemies and antagonists, rich white women. And while women who are black and struggling to survive may well join in their own "sisterhood" to work for advancement of the race, they do not share this "sisterhood" with upper-class white women who may celebrate their separate "women's" organizations but who, nevertheless, show only condescension toward the black women who work for them. In short, what constitutes "sisterhood" will vary depending on the context, with differences among women a far more salient reality than the common bonds that unite them. Thus, even generalizations about separatism as a strategy and "women's culture" will only be valid within certain ethnic and economic parameters.

All of this helps to explain why Jacquelyn Hall has recently called upon women's historians to concentrate on developing the "partial truths" that compel our attention and to forgo the quest for "total truths" that are both undiscoverable and false. If we recognize how rich the diversity of women's experience is, we can then celebrate the complex analysis that emerges from articulating the "partial truths" we discover; and in the process, we can better appreciate just how textured and fascinating are the insights that come from acknowledging difference rather than denying it.

Much of what follows is identical to what I wrote nearly twenty years ago. But some is different, and throughout these pages, I have tried to keep in mind the conceptual advances that have been achieved over the past two decades. As only the most simple acknowledgment of these changes, the reader will note that part of the book's title has been changed. Reference is no longer to *The American Woman* but is now to *American Women*, for this must be a story of difference as well as of commonality.

Georgetown, Maine   W. H. C.
August 1989

Acknowledgments

I AM DEEPLY INDEBTED to my colleagues in women's history for the support they have given me over the years. An enormous amount of work has been done by scholars during the past two decades. The dialogues that have occurred among historians of women have been no less sharp than in other areas. But as a general rule, I believe there has been a greater sense of community and shared concerns than in other fields in our discipline. In some ways, this is reflected in the "collective" events of women's history, such as the Berkshire conferences; at other times, it simply exists in conversations where criticism is supportive rather than destructive.

The present work has been substantially enhanced by the studies that have been published over the past twenty years. Most of the authors of these works are mentioned in the bibliographical essay which appears at the end of this volume, and to select out any of these would inevitably do injustice to others. But I am particularly grateful for the criticisms I have received from Nancy Cott and Nancy Hewitt, whose wise and acute observations improved this present book significantly. As always, I am also indebted to the community of scholars at Duke and Chapel Hill, especially Anne F. Scott, Jaquelyn Dowd Hall, Jane DeHart, Peter Filene, and others from the board of the Duke–UNC Center for Research on Women. And I am especially appreciative of the help I received on this venture from our graduate student community, most particularly Christina Greene, Gretchen Lemke-Santangelo, and Kirsten Fischer.

Originally, this book was written as a dissertation under the direction of William E. Leuchtenburg. I continue to be grateful for his support in that enterprise and to cherish our friendship, as well as that of my graduate student colleagues at Columbia who helped make all of this possible. The present volume was completed at the Center for Advanced Study in the Behavioral Sciences in Stanford, California. There never was a better place to work. In addition to support from the center, I also received fellowship assistance from the John Simon Guggenheim Foundation and from The National Endowment for the Humanities.

Contents

PART FOUR

THE POSTWAR YEARS AND THE REVIVAL OF FEMINISM

PART ONE

POLITICS
AND IDEOLOGY,
1848–1940

CHAPTER 1

1920: A Beginning, a Middle, or an End Point

HISTORIANS, by virtue of their focus on recognizable events and dates, sometimes become captives of a chronology that deceives more than it informs. Such may be the case in the natural tendency of women's historians to zero in on victory for woman suffrage as a benchmark in women's political and social experience. Because the Nineteenth Amendment was so long in coming and required such extraordinary struggle, it almost immediately assumed near mythic proportions. Friends and foes alike ascribed a significance to the victory that generated expectations for women's voting that may have borne no relationship either to what had been achieved or to what might be forthcoming. Using 1920 as a measuring point for women's status in America, therefore, may be more misleading than helpful.

On the other hand, if the battle for the suffrage becomes a window through which to examine the changing roles of different groups of American women over a seventy-five-year period, it can help to illuminate the underlying patterns that shaped women's choices and possibilities. Rather than automatically serving as a terminus, the suffrage can instead reflect what had changed, what was still in process, and what remained unresolved among the major issues uniting, or dividing, American women. It is with the latter frame of reference in mind that this introductory chapter seeks to use women's political activism as a means of understanding some of the themes—both electoral and economic—that defined women's twentieth-century world.

—— I ——

When Woodrow Wilson journeyed to Capitol Hill in the fall of 1918 to address the United States Senate, he came to ask for help in his crusade to "make the world safe for democracy." "The executive tasks of this war rest upon me," he told the lawmakers. "I ask that you lighten them and place in my hands instruments . . . which I do not now have, which I sorely need, and which I have daily to apologize for not being able to employ." The subject of Wilson's appeal was neither guns nor airplanes but woman suffrage. Its enactment, the commander in chief declared, was "vital to winning the war" and essential to implementing democracy. Within a year, Congress voted overwhelmingly to send the Nineteenth Amendment to the states for ratification.

The woman's movement had not always enjoyed such mainstream support. The women's rights advocates who gathered at Seneca Falls, New York, in 1848 were far removed from the centers of power in American life. Many had participated in the abolitionist struggle, demonstrating by their actions the extent to which they deviated from prevailing norms that defined public controversies as beyond women's "sphere." When female abolitionists sought to speak in public or circulate petitions, they were castigated for departing from their proper "place." Even male abolitionists were critical of their activities, and in 1840, women were excluded from a world antislavery conference in London. In response to such treatment, many of the women determined that there was an inextricable connection between their *own* ability to be free and achieving emancipation for black slaves. Bridling at the expectation that men and women should occupy totally separate spheres of activity, they demanded a drastic revision of the values and laws governing relationships between the sexes and forthrightly attacked all forms of discrimination. Their efforts were greeted with derision and contempt. The Worcester *Telegram* denounced the Seneca Falls convention as an attempt at "insurrection," and a Buffalo paper referred to it as "revolutionary." Women's rights advocates were generally dismissed as a "class of wild enthusiasts and visionaries"; they received little popular backing.

The contrast between 1848 and 1918 dramatizes the changes which had occurred not only within the women's rights movement in the intervening years but also in the roles and activities of American women. The woman's movement itself had moved from being an isolated radical group into being a moderate reform coalition. Early women's rights advocates had taken an uncompromising stand on almost all issues and set out to eliminate the rigid division of labor between men and women. Although itself a radical demand, the suffrage constituted only one of a long series of issues raised by women's rights advocates. By the turn of the century, on the other hand, the franchise had been elevated to a position of primary importance, with other demands either jettisoned or de-emphasized. Moreover, proponents now argued that the suffrage was necessary to preserve and enlarge women's "sphere," not abolish it.

In fact, these shifts reflected as much what was taking place in the larger society as they did political strategies and choices. As historians of the 1830s and 1840s have long noted, the age of the "common *man*" that accompanied Jacksonian Democracy was also the age of segregating women—especially middle and upper-class white women—more and more into a sharply limited "women's sphere." It was at least in part as a protest against that change and its manifestation in the discrimination experienced by female abolitionists, that early women's rights activists set out to abolish all such separate treatment. By the late nineteenth century, on the other hand, middle and upper-class white women had so thoroughly expanded and empowered their separate "sphere" that it had become more an instrument for political influence than a barrier to freedom. At the same time, the movement of immigrant and working-class women into cities and factories highlighted the danger that the "public sphere" held for women. Hence, the discourse about suffrage exemplified altered material circumstances as well as changing political ideology.

Still, the radical nature of the early women's rights movement is manifest to anyone who reads closely the Declaration of Sentiments and Resolutions passed by the women at Seneca Falls. In the nineteenth century, married women were not allowed to testify in court, hold title to property, establish businesses, or sign papers as witnesses. Women's rights advocates addressed themselves both to the specifics of such discrimination and to the assumptions underlying it. Beginning with the assertion that "all men and women are created equal," they proceeded to indict mankind for its "history of repeated injuries and usurpations" toward women. The delegates charged that men had denied them political representation, made them "civilly dead," refused them the right to own their property, and "oppressed them on all sides." In marriage, a wife was compelled to pledge obedience and to give her husband "power to deprive her of her liberty." In business, men "monopolized nearly all the profitable employments." And in morals, women suffered from an iniquitous double standard dictated by men who claimed it as their right to "assign for her a sphere of action, when that belongs to her conscience and to her God." Hardly an area existed, the delegates concluded, where man had not consciously endeavored to "destroy woman's confidence in her own powers, to lessen her self-respect, and to make her willing to lead a dependent and abject life."

Clearly rooted in the natural-rights philosophy that had infused the Declaration of Independence that was their model, the Seneca Falls activists were seeking the kind of *individual* self-determination that was the essence of universal human rights. Thus, to counter the oppression they perceived, women's rights leaders proposed the elimination of all barriers separating the activities of the two sexes. Although rooted in their coming together collectively to protest, the program they advocated was for the abolition of mandated separate treatment. Henceforth, they declared, any law which restricted women's freedom or placed them in a position inferior to men had "no force or authority." Proclaiming the "*identity* of the race in capabilities and responsibilities," they demanded the "overthrow of the monopoly of the pulpit"; equal access to education, the trades, and professions; an end to the double standard; and the right to move in "the enlarged sphere" which their Creator had assigned them. God had made men and women equal, the delegates asserted, and the treatment of one sex as different from and less equal than the other ran "contrary to the great precept of nature."

Their declaration boldly challenged every social convention concerning women's proper "place." Although women's rights advocates sought to redress a whole series of specific grievances, the most impressive part of their document was its assault on the web of assumptions that the delegates thought responsible for women's status. Implicit throughout the declaration was the view that as long as society prescribed separate areas of responsibility for each sex, women could never be free. By insisting that men and women were identical in "capacities and responsibilities," women's rights activists attacked the fundamental premise underlying relations between the sexes—the notion of distinct female and male spheres. Once it was established that the two sexes were alike in the eyes of God, there was no longer any basis for treating women as separate and inferior. Demands for equality in the church, state, and family logically followed, as did the plea for the vote. After all, what was more emblematic of the rights of universal citizenship and individual self-determination than the ability to cast a ballot. But this was just one part of a quest for a complete transformation in society's thinking about women.

For at least the next few decades, women's rights leaders continued to emphasize these themes. Just as the abolitionists used a natural-rights commitment to individualism and self-determination as the basis for their demands for emancipation, so, too, did the supporters of women's rights. As the historian Ellen DuBois has shown so well, this dedication to the political rights of citizenship is what made the post-Civil War campaign for woman suffrage so radical. Even when male abolitionists excluded women from the right to vote by inserting the word "male" in the Fourteenth Amendment, women's rights advocates, in the "new departure" campaign of the late 1860s, insisted that the right to vote was inherent in citizenship and, therefore, that women as citizens already possessed the right to vote. Individual rights superseded all categories of social designation, and in a world ruled by the philosophy of natural rights, women were individuals just as men were. (Those activists, including Susan B. Anthony, who sought to cast ballots under this rationale in 1872, were arrested; the Supreme Court also rejected the reasoning in its 1875 ruling in *Minor v. Happersett*.)

The doctrine of radical individualism received perhaps its most thorough exposition at the turn of the century in the works of Charlotte Perkins Gilman. Although Gilman wrote primarily for a twentieth-century audience, she brilliantly articulated many of the arguments against a distinctive "sphere" for women and men that had first been enunciated at Seneca Falls. Her treatise on *Women and Economics* (1898) was hailed by the *Nation* as "the most significant utterance on the subject since Mills' *The Subjection of Women*," and her writings to this day constitute one of the most important feminist assessments of women's position in America.

At the heart of Gilman's analysis was her contention that all the roles a woman was permitted to play derived from her sexual functions. A man might pursue a variety of activities—build a career, enter politics, join a fraternal organization. But a woman could only marry and have children. The cause of this sexual differentiation, Gilman believed, could be traced to prehistoric times when women first became dependent on men for food and shelter. Thereafter, a woman's survival rested on her ability to seduce and hold a husband. In effect, sex became a woman's economic way of life; while "men worked to live . . . women mated to live. . . . " A man might conquer the world in a hundred ways, but for a woman there was only "a single channel, a single choice. Wealth, power, social distinction, fame . . . all, must come to her through a small gold ring."

The pernicious consequences of sexual dependence afflicted everyone. Woman's human impulses to grow and to create were stifled. Men were denied true companions because their wives shared nothing in common with them. And children were psychologically deprived as a result of being dominated by mothers who had never been allowed to develop mental maturity. A nation which expected to maximize the potential of all its citizens depended upon each individual pursuing his or her unique talents. Yet social convention dictated that half the race perform nothing but menial household tasks. The sexual division of labor thus not only dulled women's minds and limited their horizons; it also robbed the country of the full utilization of its human resources.

Pursuing the logic of her analysis, Gilman concluded that women could achieve freedom only when they gained economic equality with men. The suffrage represented one step in the right direction and received Gilman's endorsement. But gaining the vote was incidental in her mind to the primary goal of providing women with the opportunity to leave the home if they wished. The household, in her view, constituted a prison which confined women and forced upon them the role of servant. Since it was women's economic dependence on men that created the chains of their servitude, freedom could come only if wives and daughters went out into the world to earn their own support, thereby neutralizing the chief force which kept them in an abject state. Work, Gilman believed, was "the essential process of human life," and until women shared in that process on an equal basis with men, they would remain "near-sighted," "near-minded," and inferior.

To achieve her goal, Gilman relied primarily on the power of reason and the forces of specialization which were transforming the national economy. The home, she argued, was appallingly inefficient. All women were no more suited or contented to be "house servants and housekeepers than all men would be." The talents of some women qualified them to be specialists in cooking, cleaning, or child care. But the talents of others could be best utilized outside the home in business and the professions. The task of society, Gilman reasoned, was to evolve mechanisms which would allow each *individual* to cultivate his or her own potential. To that end, she suggested the establishment of central kitchens to prepare the community's food, the development of public nurseries to assume responsibility for child care, and the creation of a corps of expert housekeepers to maintain the cleanliness of homes. With most women liberated from domestic chores, marriage would evolve into a partnership of equals; individual human beings would maximize their diverse abilities; and society would be free of the crippling effects of a dual system of labor. The result "would be a world of men and women humanly related, as well as sexually related, working together as they were meant to do, for the common good of all."

As much as anyone else, Gilman understood the radical implications of the Seneca Falls declaration. If women were to achieve equality, they had to dismantle the sexual division of labor, pursue their *individual* desires, and join as equal participants in all areas of life *on the same basis as men*. If that required a social revolution, including the establishment of surrogate institutions like child-care centers and community kitchens—the communal side of radical individualism—so be it. To Gilman's credit, she understood that necessity. In effect, she took the broad goals enunciated at Seneca Falls and developed a blueprint to carry them out.

Despite her brilliance, however, Gilman fell victim to the very power of the ideas she was seeking to counteract. Although she sought a world where women would receive identical treatment with men in the economic marketplace and hence erode the foundation of a sexual division of labor, she assumed that women would continue to hold a monopoly on the domestic virtues of warmth and nurturance—a logical inconsistency given her previous contention that such virtues were primarily a creation of women's economic dependence on men. Ironically, even the social system designed to replace "separate spheres" presumed women's prior commitment to hearth and home.

Prophetic critics like Gilman or Stanton did not find much support for the kinds of changes they were advocating. In criticizing the nuclear family, the church, and marriage, they were attacking institutions to which most people were deeply devoted. Women could not achieve individual self-determination without altering the family and forcing a radical revision of a whole set of social relationships. Yet even friends of women's rights were committed to different values. Emerson, for example, asserted that woman should look to man for protection. "When he is her guardian, all goes well for both." Enemies, of course, were even stronger in their defense of the status quo. Thus, when women sought the right to vote in Washington, D.C., on the basis of a natural-rights argument, Senator Peter Frelinghuysen of New Jersey insisted that women had a "higher and holier" function than to engage in the turmoil of public life. "Their mission is at home," he said, "by their blandishments and their love to assuage the passions of men."

More than anything else, however, what destroyed the credibility of the natural rights argument was the growing indication that most women, at least of the middle and upper class, were committed to the idea of "separate spheres." As historians have looked more carefully at the lives of nineteenth-century women, they have become convinced that "bonds of sisterhood" joined women together, especially well-off women, and that the rewards derived from cultivating the activities of women's domestic sphere made it a reality to be cherished and celebrated, not avoided. For some historians, these bonds led to a "female world of love and ritual," with intimacy available through female bonding that existed nowhere else in Victorian relationships. Carroll Smith-Rosenberg, for example, has shown that many middle-class women shared a physical and emotional closeness that was erotic as well as spiritual. Others have seen fictive kinship networks as women's means of creating stability and security in a world of too frequent mobility and alienation. But almost every scholar now agrees that women's "sphere" became for many privileged women a positive social reality, pivotal both to a harmonious world view and to a growing influence and power for women. Nancy Cott has written that "the doctrine of woman's sphere opened to women . . . the avenues of domestic influence, religious morality, and child nurture. It articulated a social power based on their special female qualities." For some, the gains were sufficient even to warrant the label "domestic feminism."

In summarizing the results of this scholarship, Paula Baker and Suzanne Lebsock have advanced the argument that women used their distinctive sphere to achieve a degree of political influence perhaps never seen before or since. Gender, Baker says, "rather than other social or economic distinctions, [represented] the most salient political division" in nineteenth-century America. Politics, as traditionally defined, was a man's world. Women remained outside of man's political sphere. Yet as they immersed themselves in "feminine" activities of welfare and nurture on the local level, they soon became involved in issues that were public in nature. When these issues, in turn, became central to a whole era of political decision making, women's political culture gradually assumed ascendancy over man's. As a result, Suzanne Lebsock concludes, the years 1880 to 1920 comprised "a great age for women in politics."

The argument begins with the recognition that in early nineteenth-century America, with the advent of industrialism and the political innovations of Jacksonian Democracy, men's and women's spheres became more sharply polarized among the middle and upper classes. The language of republicanism proved consistent with such cultural norms of masculinity as individualism and self-reliance; while some women (such as those at Seneca Falls) wished to share directly in those values, most women accepted the notion that their task of citizenship was to be good mothers and impart moral virtue to their children. Through these distinctions, gender helped to define different political cultures. Men bonded together through the rituals of mass rallies, parades, and other public political behavior. Women, in turn, bonded together around their church and household responsibilities. But as these totally separate activities extended into nurturance and care of the dependent and needy outside of the home, the politics of 'domesticity gradually attained a public dimension, albeit one defined as "feminine." Thus, Paula Baker contends, there developed a "distinct nineteenth-century women's political culture," diametrically different from that of men's, yet significant both in its responsibilities and in its capacity for continued expansion and growth. Women's public involvement in issues related to domestic values accelerated at just the time the Fourteenth Amendment inserted the word "male" to define the prerequisites for *formal* political participation through the franchise, highlighting the extent to which the gender segregation of American political culture was complete.

But if women could not go to the ballot box, they could devote even more of their energies to the local issues that most clearly came within the purview of their "domestic" concerns. Thus, for example, the woman's Christian Temperance Union (WCTU) mobilized thousands of women in local crusades for "Home Protection." A beginner might simply join a group set up to discuss better ways of protecting children from the influences of a corrupt world, but before long, the same person could be involved in organizing campaigns for local option laws or in seeking better conditions for women workers or prison inmates. As Ruth Bordin has shown in her study of the WCTU, "Home Protection" could lead before long to running child-care centers, industrial schools for women workers, shelters for abused or displaced women, or a legislative lobbying office.

Through these connections of home, community, and politics, women quickly expanded their sphere far beyond the confines of their own immediate households. Anne Firor Scott has demonstrated that women's voluntary associations were *everywhere* in the nineteenth-century, building schools, dispensing charity, working for literacy and better living conditions for the poor—in short, developing the social and educational infrastructure of America. Even ventures that began with a relatively narrow focus, such as the literary-club movement, usually carried over at some point to questions more structural or systemic in nature. And although, as we shall see, class limitations prevented many middle- and upper-class women from comprehending or identifying with the struggles of black or working-class women, the politics of domesticity at least nourished a tentative outreach that, however limited, acknowledged the problems of the oppressed more than did most traditional male politics.

The settlement-house movement most clearly illuminates the links connecting the domestic sphere of middle-class women's lives, the informal political influence they were rapidly acquiring, and privileged women's concern for their poorer and less powerful "sisters." Suzanne Lebsock has observed that "settlement workers took the domestic and the public spheres that . . . were cast as mutually exclusive . . . and rolled them into one: settlements were places to live, to work and to agitate for change." Fulfilling their domestic function, the settlements provided a natural location—a "home"—where women could focus their nurturant and charitable energies. Yet they simultaneously served as outposts for political and community activism. In some ways, Hull House and the other settlements represented simply an extension into a new arena of work that more traditional women's organizations had already been doing. The difference was that the settlement-house workers constituted a class with a distinctive experience. Trained at college to use their minds independently, yet frustrated by the constraints of what Jane Addams called the "family claim," they forged their own full-time institution to combine the intimacy of a household community with a mission to transform the health, education, and living standards of their society.

Inevitably, as work on problems of safety, disease, and education occupied more and more energy, the solutions to these "domestic" problems took on more of a public character. Thus, as Florence Kelley saw the unregulated and dangerous factory conditions that threatened the arms and legs of industrial workers, she recognized that only a public law governing factory safety could provide any semblance of security for workers' health. It was only logical, after she succeeded in pushing through such legislation, that she should become the government commissioner in charge of enforcing it. When Julia Lathrop and her co-workers documented the social scandal of the abuse of children in America's new industrial ghettos, it made sense that they should turn to government for protection of the young and that Lathrop should become the first director of the Children's Bureau. Whether the issue was minimum wages, maximum hours, better sanitation, or railroad-crossing safety, it became clear that formal political action was necessary to implement the "domestic" quest for more humane and healthy social institutions. Through all these activities, women's political power and influence became a dominant reality well before the final drive for woman suffrage—and it was a reality rooted in the ideology of a distinctive "women's sphere."

Still, it would be a mistake not to acknowledge the limitations of this sphere. Although the concept presumed that woman constituted a universal category, allowing women, by virtue of their common domestic experiences, to cross class, religious, and ethnic lines, in reality gender solidarity was ephemeral. Priorities of black and working-class women were dramatically different from those of white clubwomen or middle-class reformers. All too often, for example, white clubwomen failed even to consider the plight of their black "sisters." Some actively participated in the effort to disenfranchise blacks or exhibited racist stereotypes in their attitudes toward blacks, including domestic servants in their own households. Similarly, white women of the middle class, however generous they might have thought they were being in their outreach to immigrant or working women, rarely respected or identified with working-class worlds where gender often meant something very different from what it did among the bourgeoisie. "Mother's aid" laws, for example, originated with middle-class reformers concerned about the health and well-being of widows and poverty-stricken mothers. Yet in implementation they often reflected mean-spiritedness, condescension, and class arrogance, providing mere scraps of aid and in the process, imposing a system of investigation that undermined the dignity and self-respect of the beneficiaries by intervening with skepticism and suspicion into their personal affairs. If reaching out to help represented the benevolent gender-based nurturance of "women's sphere," reaching down to intrude and regulate represented the class-limited narrowness of the privileged elite.

In fact, the sisterly alliances of black, Latina, or white working-class women usually took place *against*, rather than in concert with, middle-class reformers. Nancy Hewitt has shown that "sisterhood" ordinarily had a material basis in one's class. Hence, Cuban female cigar workers were more likely to unite with their male co-workers than ally with the wives and sisters of their employers who spoke for their husbands' class interests. Black and working-class women also chose styles of action dramatically different from those of white middle-class women. It was far more likely that working-class women would resort to spontaneous demonstrations—bread riots or wildcat walkouts on behalf of aggrieved workers—than join the hierarchical organizations and structured programs of middle-class reform groups. Thus, in values, goals, and life-styles, women of different backgrounds displayed dramatically different interests and behavior patterns. Sisterhood might exist, but rarely across racial and class barriers.

The rapidly growing female labor force simply highlighted this truth. During the years after the Civil War, millions of women worked for pay; most were single, young, and poor, yet significant differences still existed in the jobs that were accessible to women of different backgrounds. Virtually all black women, for example, toiled either as agricultural workers or as domestic servants. Except for some higher-level positions within a segregated economy (such as school teacher), no other opportunities were available. Poor white women, in turn, occupied positions in the textile mills that flourished throughout the South. Often accompanied by their children, who did even more menial tasks, these women struggled to earn enough to keep a family together. Toward the end of the century, increasing numbers of immigrant women filled the factories of the larger Northern cities. A majority of female garment workers were Italian, and the largest number of women employed in the making of women's clothes were Jewish. Irish women, meanwhile, divided with black women the domestic servant jobs of the Northeast.

The better jobs, not surprisingly, reflected the same kind of ethnic and class distinctions. As the typewriter became more popular and inexpensive, women gradually replaced men as clerks and typists. Most often, these were white, native-born women, either from middle-class families or from those aspiring to that status. Similarly, the growth of large department stores generated increasing demand for salesclerks who could accommodate the new consumers. These, too, were most often white women, usually young, who came from backgrounds at least close to those of the customers they served. Educated daughters of the middle and upper classes, meanwhile, continued to fill the ranks of teachers, while moving as well into the professions of medicine and law and the brand-new field of social work. In every instance, class and race defined the occupation and determined eligibility.

For the vast majority of these women workers, finding a way to secure better wages and working conditions constituted the greatest priority. By the end of the nineteenth century, an annual income of at least $600 was essential for the most minimal family living standard. Yet few working-class families succeeded in earning that much, even with women, men, and children all being employed. Domestic servants worked for as little as three dollars a week; garment workers had to pay for their own needles from their meager wages. The most logical alternative was to organize in collective protest against exploitative employers and use the strength of worker solidarity to secure decent wages and working conditions. Occasionally, such efforts generated substantial support and, as we shall see later, even resulted in dramatic victories (as when the International Ladies Garment Workers Union triumphed in New York City during the great strikes of 1909–1910). Yet for the most part, labor organizing proved unsuccessful, a victim both of employers' success in using class and ethnic splits to divide workers from each other and of organized labor's resistance to investing its resources on behalf of women.

That left the ameliorative efforts of middle-class reformers as the only viable means of securing improvement. As we have seen, middle-class women, no matter how empathetic, rarely shared the perspective of black or immigrant women. "For them," Alice Kessler-Harris has written, "the family, not the job, was central"—hence the focus on modifying the conditions of labor so as to defend women's central task of fulfilling family responsibilities. Protection offered the key. If the situation of employment could be regulated so that women would be better be able to carry forward their distinctive responsibilities to the family, then society would be better off, and women themselves would live safer, more-productive lives. Hence, the emphasis of reform efforts was to secure factory-safety laws, child-labor laws, and—for women especially—minimum-wage and maximum-hour laws that would "protect" women's special role in society and the family.

Nothing illustrated this approach better than the brief of the National Consumers League (NCL) to the Supreme Court in 1908 defending Oregon's ten-hour law for women. The task of women in childbearing and mothering, the NCL argued, required that the state intervene to protect them. "Women are fundamentally weaker than men in all that makes for endurance"; hence, their "special physical organization" necessitated regulation of their work hours, lest their childbearing function be irreparably injured. Agreeing with the NCL, the Court upheld the law, declaring that "women's physical stature and the performance of maternal functions place her at a disadvantage" that the state must correct by sanctioning limitations on women's hours of work. Protection was something that could happen, even if raising wages and transforming labor conditions by organizing workers could not.

Although the emphasis on protective legislation did not eliminate (and may even have underscored) divisions between groups of women based on race and class, the success of social-reform legislation on wages and hours helped forge a link that attracted at least some working-class, immigrant, and black women to the suffrage campaign. If passing better laws would help improve working conditions, even marginally, then factory workers would be for them. And if winning woman suffrage would increase the frequency of such laws, so much greater the reason to be for it as well. For many black women concerned with such issues as lynching and sexual abuse, the same arguments made sense. The suffrage for women might not offer the means for transcending barriers of race and class, but it was at least a step forward that might bring leverage for progress on more immediate concerns later.

Thus, the political posture of middle-class women reformers provided some common ground for women of different backgrounds, notwithstanding how substantial these differences were. Presumably, gaining the vote would redound to the benefit of working women and women who were immigrants or African-American as well. Clearly, the domestic rationale for women acting together served as an argument for suffrage as well as for such specific reforms as maximum-hour laws, city playgrounds, and day nurseries. "Women's place is Home," Rheta Childe Dorr said in 1910. "But home is not contained within the four walls of an individual house. Home is the community. The city fill of people is the Family. The public school is the real Nursery. And badly do the Home and Family need their Mother." Surely, women of all classes and racial backgrounds could agree with such rhetoric.

Adopting the same metaphor, Jane Addams argued that a woman's primary duty was to preserve the health of her children and the cleanliness of her home. In an urban, industrial environment, the fulfillment of her responsibilities depended on the sanitation policies, fire regulations, and housing standards of municipal government. If dirt was to be controlled, garbage collection had to be prompt. If the meat a mother bought for her family was to be free of germs, stringent government inspection was required. And if the clothes her children wore were not to be carriers of disease, government regulation of sweatshops was essential. In short, Addams declared, "if woman would keep on with her old business of caring for her house and rearing her children, she will have to have some conscience in regard to public affairs lying outside her immediate household." Women could preserve the home and remain good mothers, Addams concluded, only if they acquired the vote and through formal political involvement protected the family. The suffrage for women thus became one more extension of all the public reforms that women had become involved with through their "domestic politics"; it also became the final link between the private culture of women's separate sphere and the public culture of traditional politics with its focus on individualist and masculine ideas of citizenship.

The merger of suffragism with Progressivism—and the central role played by women reformers in both—offers a means of answering critical questions about both movements. Historians have long puzzled over three contradictions of this so-called reform period: a) how could it be called "Progressive" when so much of the legislation passed seemed designed to rationalize and systematize the dominance of corporate capitalism? b) what basis is there for attaching a reform label to an era that witnessed the calculated disfranchisement of virtually all black male voters in the South and the rise of racism? and c) what is the justification for seeing as "progress" a series of social-welfare actions that were ameliorative at best?

In effect, a paradigm based on gender, modified by the powerful impact of race and class, helps to explain these contradictions. In reality, there may have been *two* Progressive eras, one based on the cultural politics of men, the other on the cultural politics of women. Thus, railroad laws, trust regulation, and the efforts to rationalize industry and banking reflected traditional political values associated with men and the model of the business corporation. On the other hand, the emphasis on factory safety, child labor, minimum wages and maximum hours, day nurseries, playgrounds, and regulation of sweatshops—all originated in institutions and voluntary associations that were formed, governed, and populated primarily by women (there were some men also) who were dedicated to the "domestic politics" of women's sphere. If the women who supported these programs were victims of the same class and race blinders that operated on men of similar background, however, it becomes more understandable why they did not emphasize solidarity with blacks and workers or identify with their experiences. Using women's politics as a departure point thus helps us to understand the Progressive era's more reformist achievements and simultaneously illuminates the structural shortcomings of those achievements due to class and race limitations impeding women's ability to create a universal gender-based solidarity.

The same insights into women reformers' political culture also help to explain the success and the shortcomings of the suffrage campaign. By using the reform argument of women's distinctiveness as a departure point, suffragists could deflect the primary contention of the opposition that women's rights advocates wanted to destroy the family and make women exactly like men. To the contrary, suffragists now said, women were primarily moral creatures. Hence, their participation in politics would elevate the moral level of government. Men possessed special talents to cope with material problems based on their experience in the business world. But women had special abilities to cope with human problems based on their experience in the home. Each sex occupied its own particular sphere, but the two were complementary rather than incompatible. Just as the creation of a good family required the contribution of both husband and wife, so the establishment of effective government depended upon the equal participation of male and female citizens.

Politics dominated by men alone constituted a half-finished social instrument. Involvement by women was essential to complete it.

By such reasoning, the woman's movement broadened its appeal and helped to identify the cause of suffrage with the larger Progressive coalition and its effort to extend democracy and eliminate social injustice. Both the rhetoric and substance of the suffrage program meshed with the ethos of reform. Women, one suffragist declared, were engaged in "a fight of the home against the saloon; . . . a struggle of justice with greed and prejudice; . . . a long strong battle between the selfish citizens and the patriotic ones." To a remarkable extent, the society at large defined the goals of Progressivism in the same way, and as a result, the suffragists succeeded in making the vote for women a prominent item on the agenda of reform. Indeed, many reformers were convinced that adding women to the electorate would prove decisive in gaining the leverage necessary for enacting far-reaching social-welfare legislation.

The close ties between suffragists and reformers became increasingly obvious as the Progressive period moved on. The number of articles in the *Woman's Journal* advocating reform legislation doubled between 1895 and 1915. More important, an interlocking directorate linked the suffrage movement to other groups in the Progressive coalition. Florence Kelley was vice president of the National Consumers League, a resident of Hull House and the Henry Street Settlement for years, and head of the child-labor committee of the General Federation of Women's Clubs, which in 1914 officially endorsed the suffrage campaign. Jane Addams served as a national officer of the National American Woman Suffrage Association (NAWSA), a board member of the Women's Trade Union League, and an advisor to Theodore Roosevelt. Male reformers like Raymond Robins, Harry Hopkins, Harold Ickes, and Newton Baker worked together with suffragists in many Progressive organizations and sought to achieve the same goals.

On the other hand, suffragists all too often had participated in the same race and class bias that afflicted middle-class women reformers generally. Although the suffrage movement adopted a rhetorical stance that emphasized the universal and eternal nature of "women's sphere," black, poor, and immigrant women had more often than not been left out when it came to specific policies. In 1894, for example, the suffrage leader Carrie Chapman Catt joined those Americans protesting against the influx of foreigners and warned about the effort of undesirables to despoil the nation's wealth. "There is but one way to avert the danger," Catt declared, "Cut off the vote of the slums and give it to women. . . . " A year earlier, the suffrage convention had blatantly appealed to nativist fears by calling attention to the fact that "there are more white women who can read and write than all negro voters; more American women who can read and write than all foreign voters." Woman suffrage, the convention suggested, "would settle the vexed question of rule by illiteracy" and ensure the perpetuation of the American way of life. Thus, notwithstanding its growing identification with a "separate-sphere" rationale for women's political recognition, the suffrage movement made clear that its circle of sisterhood was not inclusive.

Still, at least by the 1910s, large numbers of immigrant, working-class, and black women joined the battle for the suffrage, in part accepting middle-class white women's version of domesticated politics, but also often having their own agenda for improving conditions in their own communities. The Women's Trade Union League (WTUL), for example, hoped that suffrage would lead to legislation protecting the working conditions and well-being of female laborers; anti-lynching associations of black women shared a faith that woman suffrage would promote more humane race relations. And immigrant women saw at least the possibility of more social institutions like day nurseries and playgrounds developing as a consequence of women joining the political process.

In the end, then, the identification of suffragism with women's "domestic political culture" set the stage for moving women's political power from the realm of informal influence to the arena of formal political participation. Judge Ben Lindsey had observed in 1906 that "scarcely without exception it has been the members of the women's clubs who have secured the passage of nearly all the advanced legislation on the statute books for the protection of the home and the child." That political power had been exerted through indirect means, with women still contained within their distinctive sphere. Now, the day was fast approaching when women, supposedly still carrying out their distinctive feminine tasks, would enter directly into men's sphere of politics as well.

—— II ——

The positive consequences of the reform/suffragist coalition became increasingly clear by the second decade of the new century. Significantly, nine of the eleven states that enacted woman suffrage by 1914 had also adopted the initiative and referendum. Suffrage supporters actively supported most pieces of reform legislation, and reformers reciprocated by pressuring political leaders to join the struggle for the franchise. Both major parties responded by moving closer to endorsement of the suffrage, and when the insurgent "Bull Moose" party headed by Theodore Roosevelt met in convention in 1912, it issued an unequivocal call for a constitutional amendment granting women the right to vote. In the past, the woman's movement had suffered from a lack of allies and a dearth of popular support. Now, after repeated rebuffs, it had achieved legitimacy as an entrenched part of a broad-based reform movement.

With the support of leading reformers as an impetus, women activists revived flagging suffrage campaigns in states across the country. In 1910, the state of Washington broke a fourteen-year streak of defeats when its voters approved a suffrage amendment in a popular referendum. Victories followed in Illinois and California, proving for the first time that the vote for women had appeal in areas with large industrial and urban concentrations. In the nation's capital, meanwhile, the militant Congressional Union injected new life into the struggle for a federal amendment. Headed by Alice Paul, a Quaker and veteran of the English suffrage campaign, the Congressional Union was formed in 1913 as the Congressional Committee of the National American Woman's Suffrage Association (NAWSA) and within two months organized a tumultuous parade of 5,000 women to mark the arrival of Woodrow Wilson for the presidential inauguration ceremonies. The Congressional Union insisted that the party in power be made to answer for the failure to approve the suffrage amendment and in 1914 and 1916 mounted a national campaign to defeat Democratic candidates. Both in spirit and tactics, Alice Paul's organization offended the more conservative bent of NAWSA, and by early 1914 the two groups split; but the energy, excitement, and publicity which the Congressional Union generated played a key role in focusing renewed suffrage attention on the necessity for a national constitutional amendment.

Responding to the challenge posed by the Congressional Union, NAWSA reorganized its national office in 1915 and placed Carrie Chapman Catt in charge of the overall suffrage campaign. Catt immediately formulated a "Winning Plan" based on the concept that state and federal efforts should reinforce each other. For every victory won on a local level, she reasoned, additional congressmen and senators could be persuaded to vote for a suffrage amendment. It was especially important, she felt, for suffrage forces to break the solid front of opposition in the Northeast and South. "If New York wins in 1917," she declared, "the backbone of the opposition will be largely bent if not broken." Catt viewed herself as a field commander and brought to the suffrage movement an unprecedented amount of discipline and efficiency. While crucial local affiliates mobilized their energies to achieve state victories, a carefully selected staff of lobbyists cultivated support on Capitol Hill. Catt herself concentrated on President Wilson. Instead of denouncing him as the Congressional Union had done, she solicited his advice, invited him to address suffrage conventions, and in every way possible associated him with the suffrage cause.

Piece by piece, the elements of Catt's "Winning Plan" fell into place. In

1917, the voters of New York passed a suffrage referendum, reversing their decision of two years earlier. A year later Michigan, South Dakota, and Oklahoma joined the suffrage ranks, and in 1919 twenty-six state legislatures petitioned Congress to enact a federal amendment. A previously recalcitrant president himself entered the fray after women had rallied to the support of his war policies. "The services of women during the supreme crisis have been of the most signal usefulness and distinction," he wrote Mrs. Catt. "It is high time that part of our debt should be acknowledged and paid." Although significant battles continued, the suffrage amendment passed the House by a vote of 304 to 90, the Senate by a vote of 56 to 25. Fourteen months later, Tennessee became the thirty-sixth state to ratify. Nearly three-quarters of a century after Seneca Falls, the women's rights movement had reached a benchmark. "How much time and patience . . . how much hope, how much despair went into the battle," Carrie Chapman Catt reflected. "It leaves its mark on one, such a struggle. It fills the days and it rides the nights." And now the fight was over. Women had won the vote.

—— III ——

What the victory actually signified, however, was far less clear. Understandably, suffrage leaders emphasized the continuity of their own cause with that enunciated by the pioneers of the movement in 1848. The woman's movement, Carrie Chapman Catt wrote in 1917, was engaged in a "world-wide revolt against all artificial barriers which laws and customs interpose between women and human freedom." The same purpose had inspired the founders of the women's rights crusade at Seneca Falls. Although a change of tone, style, and philosophy had certainly occurred over the ensuing seventy years, there was sufficient overlap in rhetoric and content to soften the sense of dramatic change. There had been conservatives and radicals in the movement then; there were conservatives and radicals now. The balance of emphasis had shifted heavily toward a focus on women's distinctive "sphere" and away from a natural-rights concern with individualism, yet slogans from both sides could be found intermixed in the speeches of women's rights leaders of both eras.

It also made sense that the suffragists should have ascribed such revolutionary significance to their victory. In the Progressive era, many different groups viewed their particular reform objectives as panaceas for the society's ills. Prohibitionists were convinced that the Eighteenth Amendment would purify the nation's morals. Trustbusters pledged that dismantling large corporations would guarantee economic freedom. And social-welfare reformers contended that woman suffrage would usher in a new age of protection for workers and customers, putting an end to graft and indifference in government. The fact that financiers, railroads, and liquor interests had gone to such great lengths to bankroll the fight against the Nineteenth Amendment encouraged women leaders in their belief that the suffrage would transform society. In effect, the ballot had come to symbolize the entire struggle for equality and to embody all the demands of the woman's movement.

Yet as we have seen, the victory in the suffrage fight was as much a consequence of women's preexisting political power as it was a sign of things to come. Moreover, that preexisting power had explicitly flowed from women's acceptance of a segregated political universe. Men were responsible for the formal processes of politics and for the public world of business, finance, and party ritual. Women, by contrast, developed their own separate institutions, with a set of objectives directly connected to a "domestic political culture" concerned with nurturance, education, morality, and other issues that were part of "women's sphere." Although those concerns led women reformers to enormous influence in shaping the social-welfare apparatus of society, it could be argued that such influence was itself premised on women remaining in institutions and organizations that were separate from men.

But if women had already, in Suzanne Lebsock's words, experienced a "great era" in politics, what would winning the vote achieve? By joining men in the arena of formal political activity, would women lose their distinctive sphere and hence their power and influence? Did having the vote mean that women were citizens, identical to men "in capacities and responsibilities," as the delegates at Seneca Falls had demanded? And if winning the franchise signified a new era of individualism in which each person, male or female, would be accountable for his or her own economic or political actions, what would that do to women's prior reliance on the ideology of sisterhood, however much that ideology had been truncated by considerations of race and class? Would women continue to act collectively, on the basis of a sense of distinctive mission directly tied to their gender; or, now that they had the same legal rights as men in the political process, would they simply be assimilated into existing public institutions, becoming integrated into the larger political process?

In the flush of victory in the ratification fight, Carrie Chapman Catt told a celebratory gathering in New York in 1920 that she had lived to realize the greatest dream of her life. "We are no longer petitioners," she said, "we are not wards of the nation, but free and equal citizens." Only the experience of the next generation, however, could prove whether Catt's words were premature and whether, in fact, the suffrage meant the end, a new beginning, or simply a mid-point in women's experience with politics.

CHAPTER 2

Woman Suffrage and Women's Political Power: The Consequences of the Nineteenth Amendment

IN MANY WAYS, the mood of women activists at the end of the suffrage battle was like that of young idealists forty years later, at the beginning of the 1960s. A new era appeared to be dawning, and nothing seemed beyond the reach of the bold and brilliant reformers who were about to take over. Describing one group of women activists, the intellectual Randolph Bourne wrote: "They have an amazing combination of wisdom and youthfulness, of humor and ability, and innocence and self-reliance. . . . They are of course all self-supporting and independent, and they enjoy the adventure of life; the full, reliant, audacious way in which they go about makes you wonder if the new woman isn't to be very splendid sort of person."

Yet like the idealists of the early 1960s, women activists found the realities of their new world more complicated than they had expected. The right to vote had proven such a transcendent symbol of women's rights that it had successfully muted many of the differences of class, race, and ideology that might otherwise have caused supporters of the suffrage to fragment into factions. But once the Nineteenth Amendment had been ratified, there was no equally dramatic or powerful goal to take its place or to serve the same function of obscuring internal conflict. From Elizabeth Cady Stanton to Carrie Chapman Catt, leaders of the woman's movement had argued for the suffrage on the contradictory grounds that women should both be treated *the same* as men and have the opportunity to act on the values and principles that made them *different* from men. Now, with no transcendent goals uniting them, the same leaders could no longer avoid the conflict between sameness and difference, separatism and integration; they had to face these choices within the context of either joining or remaining distinct from the existing political party structure. The options were not easy, nor the direction clear. Should one work within established procedures or go outside; was accommodation the best path, or critical independence?

There were, in fact, two standards by which to measure the impact of the franchise on women's political influence. One was to use the new criterion of formal electoral participation and trace the extent to which women's exercise of the vote changed the political process. In short, did woman's suffrage make a difference in politics, parties, and elections? The second criterion was to use women's indirect political influence—that which had made middle-class reform women already instrumental to the Progressive era—as an ongoing barometer of their power, focusing on women's traditional reliance on voluntary associations and lobbying as key variables. Here too, the issue was whether suffrage made a difference and whether continuity or discontinuity more accurately described the role of women in pre- and post-suffrage politics. The two questions were intertwined, and each reflected, in its own way, the conflict over sameness and difference. Yet by examining them separately, it may be possible to gain a clearer sense of what did and what did not change as a consequence of the Nineteenth Amendment.

—— I ——

The problem of defining what made women different from or similar to men dominated the discussion of the League of Women Voters (LWV) when it was formed in 1919 as a successor body to NAWSA. The goal of the LWV was to provide organizational leadership for the newly enfranchised citizens. In the tradition of suffragist rhetoric, Carrie Chapman Catt exhorted the delegates to lead "a crusade that shall not end until the electorate is intelligent, clean and American." When it came to specifics, however, the league faced a more difficult task. The central issue was whether it wished to integrate women within the existing political system or segregate them as an independent political force. Both alternatives had support. The whole goal of the suffrage campaign had been to liberate women so that they could join men as equals in the political and social institutions of the country. On the other hand, the fight had been waged on the premise that women had a special set of interests which distinguished them from men and made it necessary for them to have a separate voice. Each position thus represented a powerful segment of the woman's movement. Yet the two were mutually exclusive, or so it seemed.

The debate over league policy toward partisan politics polarized the organization's leadership. Carrie Chapman Catt insisted that "the only way to get things done is to get them done on the inside of a political party." She urged women to participate directly in the political process and to master party techniques. Women would not be welcome, she predicted, but they had to try. "You will see the real thing in the center with the door locked tight. You will have a long hard fight before you get inside . . . but you must move right up to the center." Catt denounced the idea of sex segregation and even suggested that the word "women" be dropped from the league's title.

On the other hand, equally powerful voices eschewed the policy of integration and condemned party politics as the tool of autocrats concerned only with self-aggrandizement. Prominent suffrage leaders like Jane Addams believed that unless women retained their identity as a separate interest group, they would destroy the very principles that made them unique. Women were concerned with public service and high ideals, men with private profit and personal power. Consequently, if women accepted the discipline of regular party membership, they would violate their conscience and compromise their effectiveness.

Although neither Addams nor her allies envisioned a third party of women, anxious politicians interpreted the league's debate as a signal that precisely such a party might be in the offing. President Harding warned against "organizing our citizenship into groups according to sex"; Mrs. Medill McCormick, an Illinois Republican leader, charged that the league was obstructing the enrollment of women into regular-party groups; and the governor of New York denounced the organization as a "menace" to national life, a threat to traditional political allegiances. The very idea of women having a separate set of allegiances by party and platform seemed un-American. Yet the politicians need not have worried. League leaders had neither the will nor the issues to create a third-party movement. Even those members who believed most vehemently in the existence of a separate woman's point of view rejected the idea of establishing an independent political organization. From their point of view, party politics by definition was unsavory.

In the end, the league resolved the conflict over its political role through compromise. Rather than create a new party, it determined to mobilize public opinion behind reform programs and to instruct women in the tasks of citizenship so that they could work more effectively within existing political organizations. "We have got to be nonpartisan and all-partisan," Catt said. Democratic and Republican women would work together for common ends, even while moving to the centers of their respective parties. The problem with this compromise was that its very vagueness prevented the development of a platform of women's concerns that would be cogent and cutting. Indeed, the league totally failed to define the "common ends" that united women. It retained a diffuse belief that women, by virtue of their sex, had a special concern with issues like social welfare and education, but it was unable to give that concern a convincing focus or to provide an institutional means through which women could express their interests in a cohesive way. The suffragists had assumed that women would act together for a common set of principles, but their successors found it almost impossible to provide the means for carrying that assumption into practice.

Still, the notion of women sharing a distinctive set of values created the ideological backdrop for the early response of mainstream politicians to the new voters. Women were so different from men, it was commonly believed, that once they had the vote, the entire political system would be transformed. Pure in spirit, selfless in motivation, and dedicated to the preservation of human life, women voters would remake society and turn government away from war and corruption.

On the face of it, of course, such a literal expectation was absurd. It presumed that women would all vote the same way, regardless of how others in their family voted; it also did not account for the impact of class, region, and race on voting patterns. It presumed that women would demonstrate an explicit and collective allegiance to common ideals, on the basis of their sex, thus creating a separate "bloc" in the electorate. One's sex, in short, would control all political activity, forging a biological alliance that would supercede all other differences.

Yet the argument for women having a "special mission" in politics had occupied a central place in suffragist strategy, and the few instances in which women had played an active role in formal politics prior to 1920 provided some basis for speculation about the development of an independent female constituency. In Illinois, where the votes of men and women were counted separately, women gave the reform candidate for mayor of Chicago in 1915 almost as large a plurality as men gave the machine candidate. Massachusetts suffragists successfully mobilized a nonpartisan coalition to defeat the anti-suffragist Senator John Weeks in 1918. And in Columbus, Ohio, the Franklin County Suffrage Association helped upset the mayor of sixteen years by concentrating five hundred women volunteers in eleven key wards. The women campaigners registered 21,000 new voters, and their candidate won by 19,000 votes.

In addition, enough women leaders rejected the regular party apparatus as a vehicle for expressing their ideals to give male politicians pause. The head of the Illinois Republican Women's Committee bolted her party in 1920 and led a campaign to unseat the Republican mayor of Chicago, William Thompson. Alice Paul actually formed the National Woman's Party to pursue women's rights goals and threatened repeatedly to form an independent female political force for electoral purposes as well. The worst fears of party leaders seemed confirmed when Mary Garrett Hay, national vice-chair of

Republican women, strongly opposed the reelection of New York's Senator James Wadsworth in 1920 because he had been a leader of the anti-suffrage forces in Congress. Hays's action, one reporter wrote, "exemplifies to the doubting element of both parties the dreaded third party, a petticoat hierarchy which may at will upset all orderly slates and commit undreamed of executions at the polls."

Faced with such a specter, politicians moved quickly to win the support of the new voters. The Democratic convention of 1920 incorporated twelve of fifteen League of Women Voters proposals in its national party platform, and the Republic convention endorsed five. The Republican presidential nominee, Warren Harding, invited prominent women leaders to his home and called for equal pay for women, an eight-hour day, passage of maternity and infancy legislation, and creation of a federal department of social welfare. Both parties appointed women as equal members of their respective national committees, and each named women candidates to governmental positions.

State politicians reacted with equal warmth to the potentially powerful new voters. By the end of 1921, twenty state legislatures had granted women the right to serve on juries. Other states passed night-work laws and wage and hour legislation specifically designed to accommodate the wishes of female reformers. Michigan and Montana enacted equal-pay laws, Wisconsin approved a far-reaching equal-rights bill, and lawmakers throughout the South showed a new flexibility toward social legislation. The Georgia assembly treated women lobbyists with unprecedented respect, and the Virginia legislature granted reform leaders eighteen of twenty-four requests, including a children's code, a child-placement bill, and a vocational-education law.

Congress, meanwhile, demonstrated its concern for women by acting expeditiously on maternity and infancy legislation, the primary demand of many women reformers. The Sheppard-Towner bill, calling for an annual appropriation of $1,250,000 for educational instruction in the health care of mothers and babies, stirred immediate controversy when it was introduced in May 1921. Opponents tried to kill the measure by calling it "federal midwifery" and "official meddling between mother and baby which would mean the abolition of the family." Supporters of the bill, however, responded with an impressive display of power. Under the banner "Herod Is Not Dead," *Good Housekeeping* documented the tragic toll in human life caused by maternal and infant illness and secured the endorsements of thirty-four governors. Harriet Taylor Upton, national vice-chair of the Republican party, enlisted Harding's support by repeatedly holding out the threat of retaliation from women at the polls. Representatives of women's reform groups lobbied intensively for the measure and offered dramatic testimony before legislative hearings. No one spoke with more fervor or greater authority than Florence Kelley, executive secretary of the National Consumers League. Citing the fact that a quarter of a million infants died each year in America, she inquired: "What answer can be given to the women who are marveling and asking, 'why does Congress wish women and children to die?'" The *Journal of the American Medical Association* declared that the women had created "one of the strongest lobbies that has ever been seen in Washington."

Faced with the unremitting pressure of women's reform groups, Congress passed the bill. "If the members could have voted in the cloakroom," one backer of the measure asserted later, "it would have been killed." As it was, the act passed with only seven dissenting votes in the Senate and thirty-nine in the House. "The Senators did not quite dare to turn it down," a former suffragist wrote. No other event demonstrated so dramatically the eagerness of politicians to win over the unknown quantity introduced into the electorate by the enactment of the Nineteenth Amendment. The statute represented precisely the kind of protection of human life which the suffragists had talked about as women's special concern. And it indicated the influence which women might exert on a continuing basis if they acted in a concerted way to express their wishes on issues and candidates.

In subsequent years, women reformers enjoyed additional successes. Congress passed the Packers and Stockyards bill in 1921 designed to increase consumer protection; the Cable Act in 1922 reforming citizenship requirements for married women; the Lehlbach Act of 1923 upgrading the merit system in the civil service; and the Child Labor Amendment to the Constitution in 1924. Each bill was strongly supported by the Women's Joint Congressional Committee, an umbrella organization established by various women's groups to coordinate legislative activity. If not every item desired by women activists was enacted, enough received some attention to sustain the hopes of female leaders.

Beginning in mid-decade, however, women's standing in the eyes of politicians dropped precipitously. A congressional supporter urged the Women's Joint Congressional Committee to reduce its pressure for a home-economics measure because Congress was tired of being asked to pass women's legislation. The Child Labor Amendment, which had engaged the energies of so many reform groups, failed ratification in the key states of Massachusetts and New York as Catholic bishops joined the opposition with claims that the amendment would destroy the sanctity of the home. Appropriations for the Women's Bureau and Children's Bureau were cut, and a two-year extension of the Sheppard-Towner Act was secured only by inserting into the new measure a written statement that the act would permanently expire on June

30, 1929. Congressmen seemed as intent on rebuffing the requests of women reformers in the second half of the decade as they had been in granting them during the first half.

The abrupt reversal of fortune bewildered and demoralized women leaders. Just a few years before, their reform coalition had wielded considerable influence over Congress and state politicians. Now they were an embattled minority fighting a rearguard action against the destruction of programs already established. To some extent, the decline could be attributed to a conservative shift in national affairs. In the 1924 elections, the voters had endorsed the candidacy of Calvin Coolidge and rejected the Progressive challenge of Robert La Follette. The Supreme Court cut the ground from beneath many reform proposals by ruling against a federal child-labor law and minimum-wage legislation for women. And a rash of redbaiting attacks had smeared women's organizations as Communist front groups. According to a chart prepared within the War Department, a "spider-web conspiracy" existed among more than twenty women's groups, which were said to be promoting peace and the Moscow party line. In the face of such tactics and the larger conservative milieu, it was difficult for women's issues, or reform generally, to prosper.

Fundamentally, however, women's political standing plummeted in the eyes of male politicians because women failed to vote in the cohesive manner that the politicians had anticipated and feared. The recognition that women had received in the years immediately after 1919 was based in large part on the belief that women would cast their ballots as a monolithic "bloc." When it became clear that no such bloc existed and that women in general voted like men (though in lesser numbers), the basis for such special recognition was gone. "Not one of the disasters has come to pass that four years ago glowered so fearsomely upon the politicians' trade," a reporter wrote in 1924. "Not a boss has been unseated, not a reactionary committee wrested from old-time control. . . . Nothing has been changed." Other observers agreed. "I know of no woman today who has any influence or political power because she is a woman," Democratic Committeewoman Emily Newell Blair declared. "I know of no woman who has a following of other women. I know of no politician who is afraid of the woman vote on any question under the sun."

The low turnout of women voters at the polls constituted the first crushing blow to suffragist hopes. Despite extensive efforts by the League of Women Voters to educate the new members of the electorate, women failed to exercise the franchise in substantial proportions. A low turnout in some states in the 1920 elections could be explained by the fact that the suffrage amendment was not ratified until August 1920. But in New York, where women had been given the franchise in 1917, women cast only 35 percent of the total vote in

1920. In Illinois, where the suffrage had been granted in 1913, the figure was slightly higher, but only 46.5 percent of the women eligible to vote went to the polls in contrast to 74.1 percent of the men. Three years later, in the Chicago mayoralty election, women cast only 36 percent of the vote, and they comprised 75 percent of the eligible adults who were not registered. "Unless they have some personal or family contact with the political questions at issue," the Illinois *State Journal* concluded, "women do not vote."

Equally important was the lack of evidence that women voted differently from men. Instead of becoming more and more solidified, a journalist commented in 1923, "the women's bloc . . . tends to become more and more disintegrated." Occasionally, on issues like Prohibition or corruption in government, women voted in slightly larger proportions than men for the "moral" candidate, but in general, women voted according to their social and economic backgrounds and agreed with the political preference of their husbands rather than according to their sex. Reform leaders had argued "passionately, if ignorantly" that women would use their ballot unselfishly for all mankind, Democratic National Committeewoman Emma Guffey Miller noted, "but our first campaign taught us . . . that women were no more motivated by altruism or sense of historical perspective than men."

In the aftermath of the Chicago mayoral election of 1923, Charles Merriam and Herbert Gosnell attempted to isolate the causes of female nonvoting (and male nonvoting as well) through interviews with those who had failed to go to the polls. Almost a third of the women surveyed pleaded general lack of interest in politics. Immigrant women, in particular, blamed ignorance of the balloting process and fear of embarrassment over language difficulties. The largest specific cause cited, however, was "disbelief in woman's voting." Over 11 percent of those interviewed stated that women should stay at home and leave politics to men. In addition, many of those who had intended to vote explained that they neglected to go to the polls at the last moment because their husbands had failed to remind them. When combined with "lack of interest," such deference to traditional sex roles helped make it highly unlikely that women could play a decisive part in electoral politics, at least in the beginning.

Other observers noted the same tendency of women to continue to defer to men when it came to formal politics. Sue White, a leading suffragist and Southern Democrat, explained that in her region women stayed away from politics because male party members insisted that government was a man's game. The Minnesota League of Women Voters, in turn, reported that women citizens in that state "were too timid to participate in an election where men folks made it plain that they were not wanted." The extent to which political activities were associated in many women's minds with institutions of masculine culture—barber shops and pool halls—simply reinforced the tendency to stay away.

Although much of the discussion of women's voting behavior during the 1920s was impressionistic, subsequent research by political scientists has confirmed the general outlines of the earlier discussion. A high degree of political participation, these scholars have concluded, depends at least in part on the presence of group pressures emphasizing the importance of the ballot and the absence of cross-pressures discouraging political independence. In the case of women, each variable worked against their voting in the same proportion as men. Despite the existence of organizations like the League of Women Voters, most women received little encouragement to vote and even less to stand collectively against men in the way they cast their ballots. The value of the vote, one political scientist has written, corresponds to role beliefs in the general culture, with "man expected to be dominant in action toward the world outside the family. . . ." First-time voters, especially, generally follow the example of an authority figure in the family, and where disagreement exists, the new voter usually decides to abstain from political participation altogether.

Projected backward in time, such observations help to explain why women's political behavior in the 1920s could never match the anxieties of male politicians or the extreme predictions of suffragists and anti-suffragists alike. For women to vote at all required a substantial break with the past. For them to oppose their husbands or fathers in the process entailed a dedication almost revolutionary in nature. As Emily Newell Blair observed in 1925, the very idea of a woman's bloc presumed a man's bloc as well; yet neither the society nor the family could withstand the divisiveness of women fighting for one set of principles and men for another. Some suffragists, Blair noted, had anticipated that "women would organize along sex lines, nominate women, urge special legislation, vote *en masse.*" But such an expectation represented a "hallucination." Like men, they belonged to a variety of social, economic, and cultural groups with different political opinions, and like men, they were more likely to vote their class or race interests than anything else. Black women acted politically to secure measures that would advance the race and immigrant women focused on issues relevant to ethnic communities; however, these concerns were all too often not on the agenda of white, middle-class voters. Thus, race and class differences once again proved more salient than gender solidarity, especially in the absence of a dramatic "woman's" issue of overriding proportions, such as suffrage itself. Yet there was no such issue, and the result, Carrie Chapman Catt noted, was that veterans of the suffrage crusade missed the "exaltation, the thrill of expectancy, the vision which stimulated them in the suffrage campaign."

In retrospect, it seems that the suffragists were caught in a no-win situation when it came to electoral politics. To begin with, they suffered the irony of achieving the right to vote at just the time in our national history when the ballot was declining in importance. Jane Addams noted that during the 1920s, the issue was not whether *woman* suffrage was failing but why *the suffrage itself* was failing. Although women have received much of the blame for the overall decline in voter turnout during the 1920s (down to 50 percent in presidential election years, 33 percent in off-years—nearly as low as turnout became during the 1980s), recent studies by Paul Kleppner, using regression analysis, have shown that much of the fall-off was due to men not voting as well. It appears that the entire political culture was shifting, and even though supposed progress had been made in democratizing the electoral process during the 1910s through direct election of senators, the initiative, referendum and reform, direct primaries, and woman suffrage, the actual value of casting votes at the ballot box had diminished substantially. As scientific efficiency and bureaucratic management models became more important in government, interest-group politics gained a new ascendancy, and direct participation in mass political culture declined. Thus, as Suzanne La Follette observed in 1926, the misfortune of the woman's movement was that "it has succeeded in securing political rights for women at the very period when political rights are worth less than they have been at any time since the 18th Century."

Even if this had not been the case, however, the woman's movement was trapped by the way women's participation in the electoral arena had been defined. Partly due to the inflated rhetoric of suffragists themselves, millions of Americans had been led to believe that women voters would dramatically alter the moral tone and social-welfare policy of American government. Precisely because women were so different from men, their contribution would be to add a whole new dimension to the political process.

Yet how would women accomplish this goal? If they remained outside the established party structures, what difference would it make for women to have the vote. America was a two-party country, and according to the existing rules, women could not be players in the game unless they participated in one of the parties. But if women joined the parties simply as citizens, just like individual men, they would exercise influence only as individuals, not as *women*, who represented a distinctive set of values. Hence, it seemed that the only way women could make an impact on the existing parties was through constituting, *within* the electoral process, a separate bloc or constituency. But that was humanly impossible—first, because of the generic diversity that existed among women based on their different class, religious, and ethnic loyalties; and second, because of the two-party system itself, the lack of single-issue elections, and the entire socialization process which made women more likely to follow the political loyalties of their male-dominated families than to strike out as an independent collectivity.

In short, there was no way out. As Helen Flexner had observed in 1909 in anticipation of this predicament:

> Disillusionment only can result from the claim that women when enfranchised will at once right wrongs, however deep-seated they may be in the body politic, and abolish corruption, though it is intrenched in an established complicated system, and practised by astute and experienced men in the interest of their own personal profit; for such a claim is, in its nature, unreasonable and doomed to disappointment.

Yet by virtue of their own rhetoric and the expectations and fears of male politicians, such claims constituted exactly the unfair measure by which women voters would be judged. Once inside the existing process, women would either have to demonstrate their strength as a collective entity or be discounted. Since it was politically impossible to demonstrate such strength, at least in the 1920s, being discounted quickly became the end result.

The whole enterprise of winning the franchise thus became a paradox. To win the vote meant to join men in the existing parties which, as one woman politico observed, was "exactly where men political leaders wanted them, bound, gagged, divided, and delivered to the Republican and Democratic parties." Yet the other choice—to remain outside—seemed illogical, given the emphasis of the suffrage campaign on joining the game as equal partners. After all, why have the vote if one were not to use it. But if one could not use it as an independent weapon on behalf of a distinctive constituency, what good was it? In the face of such questions, it was not surprising that women could not achieve the goals they had set forth. Party politics *was* still a man's world, and the standards by which women were being judged were male standards.

In this context, it was not surprising that once the specter of a "woman's bloc" was exorcized, the concessions stopped, with men retaining control. Officeholding for women, the reporter Emma Bugbee observed in 1930, was primarily a "widow's game." Two-thirds of those who served in Congress from 1920 to 1930 succeeded their dead husbands, most for only a single term. Of the two woman governors, one—Nellie Ross—took over from her deceased spouse, and the other—"Ma" Ferguson—stood in for her husband in a successful attempt to circumvent a Texas constitutional provision prohibiting the state's chief executive from serving consecutive terms of office. No woman officeholder during the 1920s served with special distinction. Most either accommodated male leaders or remained in office for so brief a time that there was little opportunity for them to build influence.

The career of Mary Norton exemplified the experience of most female politicians during the 1920s. Norton first came to the attention of local Democrats when she approached Frank Hague, mayor of Jersey City, for help in securing public funds for nursery-school education. Two years later, after woman suffrage had passed, the mayor requested her to go on the Democratic state committee to assist in mobilizing women's votes. Norton told Hague that she had no interest in either politics or the suffrage, but her protestations were dismissed as irrelevant. No woman knew anything about politics, Hague said, and in any event, the position of state committeewoman was an empty honor which required no work. Four years later, Norton was handpicked to represent Jersey City in Congress, a position which she held for twenty-six years. She later concluded that the leaders of her party wanted "the honor of sending the first woman of the Democratic party to Congress." More to the point was Mary Dewson's comment to party-boss Jim Farley that "Mayor Hague did not want any rival in his field and felt safer with the Congressman from Jersey City a woman." Although Norton performed with notable distinction in Congress during the 1930s and 1940s, the manner of her selection demonstrated the desire of political leaders to choose women officeholders who were amenable to control by party bosses.

The appointment of Rebecca Felton as the first woman senator highlighted the disparity between the shadow and substance of female power. Mrs. Felton, an octogenarian from Georgia, was named in 1922 to fill a temporary vacancy caused by death. Her tenure lasted for approximately an hour and resulted from a temporary suspension of the rules permitting a postponement of the swearing in of Walter George, the regularly elected senator. For a few short minutes, one commentator wrote, "the woman senator held court . . . on the Senate floor in the midst of flowers and congratulations while national affairs awaited her exit." Once the honorary ritual was concluded, however, the male legislators returned to their seats and Mrs. Felton returned to Georgia. Womanhood had been acknowledged. In contrast, when Eleanor Roosevelt and other women liberals arrived at the 1924 Democratic convention with a series of proposals on the child-labor amendment and other social-welfare measures, they were virtually ignored. Hour after hour, the women sat outside the Platform Committee hearings, hoping in vain that the committee would listen to their plea and reconsider its rejection of a favorable resolution on the child-labor amendment. The party leadership was ever ready with flowery honors. But when it came to the formation of party policy, woman's place remained that of "outsider."

By 1930, therefore, it was understandable that politicians and journalistic observers alike had concluded that woman suffrage would not revolutionize the political process. Rather than doubling the electorate and transforming the way candidates were chosen and parties run, the Nineteenth Amendment produced relatively little change in the political status quo; nor could it have been expected to do so, realistically, in light of the choices available. Women had gained access, as voters and potentially as individual leaders, into a political culture that previously had been completely masculine. But that did not signify the transformation of that culture into one that would become more feminine. By these criteria, then, 1920 did not constitute a turning point.

Yet there are other criteria as well. Prior to 1920, women had always exercised their greatest political influence by operating indirectly through voluntary associations to shape public policy and build social institutions. The suffrage amendment focused the glare of public attention on what happened with the ballot. But what happened to the other instruments through which women expressed their political will, instruments that women themselves controlled? If woman-defined organizations helped to create the truly progressive aspects of the Progressive era, what occurred with those organizations after 1920? And was there a point at which those institutions intersected and overlapped with the still male-controlled political-party process to create a different dynamic than that which prevailed during the 1920s?

——— II ———

One of the issues that most bedeviled historians of a previous generation was Arthur Link's famous query, "What ever happened to the Progressive movement?" By implication, at least, the question suggested that the Progressive movement had ended, brought to a conclusion by the combination of World War I on the one hand and the election of Warren Harding on the other. But that premise, tied as it was to a focus on male political and cultural assumptions, ignored the whole history of small "p" progressivism—that part of the movement focused on humanitarian, social-welfare programs that emanated from women-dominated voluntary associations.

If, in fact, we look at those associations and their commitment to building a social-welfare infrastructure in America, we find that a part of Progressivism not only continued without break into the 1920s and 1930s but also persisted in exercising political influence without regard to the Nineteenth Amendment. This is not to say that members of women's voluntary efforts were indifferent to the vote or to politics, but rather that their concentration on their own voluntary associations permitted them to pursue an independent agenda of social concerns regardless of what the political parties did about women officeholders or women's vote.

Nancy Cott has shown brilliantly in her work *The Grounding of Feminism* that the "domestic political culture" that Paula Baker and Suzanne Lebsock have described so well in the nineteenth and early twentieth centuries remained a thriving entity in the 1920s and 1930s. Women's voluntary associations and women's reform groups did not wither away when women gained the vote; instead, they continued to grow. From local club movements, educational-reform ventures, and traditional social-welfare organizations like the Consumers League, women's groups pushed for incremental reform in the tradition of early twentieth-century settlement-house workers.

Not all women's groups boasted equal success. The new League of Women Voters (LWV), for example, demonstrated little of the popular appeal of NAWSA, its suffragist predecessor. In Dane County, Wisconsin, a thousand women attended a meeting to learn about the ballot, but only eleven joined the league. In Minnesota, league activists complained that few women were willing to accept responsibility as county leaders, and by mid–1921 the organization in South Dakota was almost moribund. Although the LWV claimed to represent all the former members of NAWSA, it retained only 10 to 20 percent of the two million women who had been part of the suffrage mass movement.

But the league was a highly specialized and an overtly political organization. Other groups, more reminiscent of the indirectly political associations of the Progressive era, continued to grow. The Parent Teachers Association (PTA) for example, with its agenda to build more playgrounds, libraries, and health clinics, soared to 1.5 million members in the 1920s. The National Association of Colored Women (NACW) rallied its rapidly expanding membership behind federal anti-lynching legislation; Jewish women, Catholic women, and women who represented various ethnic minorities mobilized to pursue their particular objectives. There may not have been a universal sisterhood uniting behind a common platform, but in their preference for using voluntary associations and the technique of lobbying and in their focus on issues involving health, welfare, and morality, all these groups shared a common *modus operandi*. Indeed, Nancy Cott concludes that by 1930, "the level of organization among women . . . appears to compare very favorably to that at the height of the woman suffrage movement." Although many of these voluntary associations suffered the same hard times during a conservative recrudescence that afflicted more overtly political women, the fact remains that the groups persisted, and even expanded, during a decade when Progressivism was supposedly dead and "reform" a term of nostalgia.

Nothing proves the importance of this persistence better than the role of women reformers during the New Deal. The women who flocked to Washington to build and to manage the New Deal's social-welfare apparatus were frequently the very women who had helped to promote the social-welfare agenda of the Progressive era from their settlement-house bases and their women's voluntary associations. Another favorite historiographical question of the 1960s was whether the New Deal represented continuity or discontinuity with the Progressive period. If we look to women reformers, we have at least one answer, because they constitute a human bridge joining the indirect political influence of the settlement-house generation with the formal political practice of a reform administration in the 1930s.

Perhaps the best way to envision these connections is through the metaphor of a women's community, with interlocking links of personality and common association through shared membership in different voluntary associations. At the heart of the network were a few women who were situated to bring together the constituent parts of the network. By 1932 at the very center was Eleanor Roosevelt, who happened to be the First Lady of the nation.

Discussing this community of women, the historian Linda Gordon has sketched some of the characteristics that bound them together. First, they were a homogeneous group, primarily Protestant, white, and middle or upper class. Second, the vast majority were social workers, part of that new generation of professional women who came out of school at the end of the nineteenth century determined to create their own niche by fusing their education and their commitment to public service through developing a new occupation. Most were also settlement-house veterans. Third, a significant number had never married but rather found emotional as well as professional support through living in communities of women who shared a common lifestyle and set of values. The community, therefore, had a base in women-dominated or sex-segregated organizations and a wealth of experience in developing social programs, at times governmentally funded, to address the needs of women, children, and the poor. Most important, however, their source of influence lay in the separate associations they developed and in the communities that took root there.

A brief look at the life of Eleanor Roosevelt highlights some of the features that made this community so important. Roosevelt was born into an aristocratic family. After a quite unhappy childhood marked by the death of both her parents before she was ten years old, she went off to England to attend an all-girls school run by an extraordinary woman, Marie Souvestre, who provided a powerful role model of intellectual and political independence. As Roosevelt returned to New York for her debutante ball in 1900, Souvestre gave her the trenchant advice not to be seduced by the life of parties and society teas but to keep her mind fixed on the serious issues of life.

Roosevelt took the advice to heart. Shortly after returning to New York, she joined the Junior League, which at the time was engaged in a whole series of charitable activities; she then became associated with the Rivington Street Settlement, where she learned firsthand about the realities of urban and ghetto poverty. Teaching classes at the settlement house, she met several women, among them Mary Rumsey Harriman, who would remain her close friends throughout her life. She also joined the Consumers League, then headed by Florence Kelley, and participated in the efforts of that group to end the evils of sweatshop labor. Roosevelt married her husband Franklin, a distant cousin, in 1902 and temporarily left behind her reform associates in order to raise five children and fulfill the responsibilities of being the wife of a budding politician. But she never forgot the lesson of Souvestre or her years in the New York women's reform movement.

Eleanor started to reimmerse herself in social-welfare activities in Washington during World War I, working with patients at St. Elizabeth's hospital and helping to run the canteen for soldiers at Union Station. Franklin was assistant secretary of the Navy during the war and, in those years, carried on a love affair with Eleanor's private secretary, Lucy Mercer. When she discovered the affair, Eleanor was crushed and, for all intents and purposes, ended her romantic relationship with Franklin. Some have traced Eleanor's subsequent public activity to that private hurt, but in fact, she had recommenced her social-work role well before discovering the affair and continued it when she and Franklin returned to New York after the war. Indeed, her steadily deepening involvement in social-welfare activities did not even end when Franklin contracted polio in 1922. Although Eleanor spent much of her time nursing him back toward a normal life, she persisted in her growing commitment to women and the reform goals that became the centerpiece of her life; now, she simply added to those roles her activity as a political ally and representative of her bedridden husband.

By virtue of her distinctive background and personal situation, Eleanor Roosevelt became the critical link for a network of women reformers who combined the traditional dedication of women social workers to social welfare with a new readiness to act politically as well. Through her own person, Roosevelt showed that direct participation in the formal political process could merge with continued dedication to women's separate and voluntary reform organizations. Although earlier she had opposed woman suffrage, she now joined the LWV and became editor of its newsletter and a lobbyist for its agenda in the state legislature at Albany. She also remained active in the Consumers League; joined for the first time the Women's Trade Union League, in which she learned to overcome some of her earlier anti-immigrant and anti-Semitic prejudices; and walked picket lines with representatives of women's trade unions. During these same years, she became a political spokesperson in her own right, editing the *Democratic Digest,* heading up the women's division of the Democratic party in New York, speaking to countless precinct meetings, and, in the process, keeping the name of Roosevelt before the public. By 1928, when Franklin was ready to run for governor of New York, Eleanor was in charge of the women's division's campaign for Al Smith's presidential candidacy for the entire nation. In her spare time, she owned and with two of her reform and political friends, Nancy Cook and Marian Dickerman, ran a private school for girls in New York.

Significantly, Roosevelt derived both her personal and professional *raison d'être* from this community of women. She met weekly with Esther Lape and Elizabeth Reid of the LWV to talk about the league's agenda and to spend a pleasant evening together. Her friendship with Women's Trade Union League (WTUL) leaders thrived over the years, including personal ties to women like Rose Schneiderman, an immigrant herself, who broadened Roosevelt's social awareness substantially. Molly Dewson, a dedicated reformer in New York's Women's City Club and the National Consumers League, remained a dear and cherished friend with whom Roosevelt sometimes had daily contact. In the meantime, Roosevelt lived with Cook and Dickerman in a cottage she built at the Roosevelt estate in Hyde Park, taking up residence there whenever Franklin was not staying in the main house. Weekends frequently saw large segments of the reform-political community of women gather at Eleanor's cottage as old friends came together around her own house and swimming pool to share their personal and professional concerns.

When Franklin Roosevelt was elected president in 1932, Eleanor believed that the gratifying life she had lived during the previous decade was over and that she would now be tethered by the inhibiting role of First Lady. Instead, she discovered that she could move her community with her to the nation's capitol. The crisis of the Depression compelled a response by the government that inevitably made social-welfare measures a top priority. Programs were devised that in many ways seemed a direct translation into public policy of ideas and objectives that had long preoccupied women's voluntary associations and reform groups. Who better, then, to administer and implement these programs than women from those groups—the same women who had comprised Eleanor Roosevelt's community in New York.

Within a few months, the administration witnessed an influx of women reformers that signified what Molly Dewson called an "unbelievable" change in the status of women in government. Mrs. Roosevelt herself led the way in focusing attention on women's issues, calling a White House conference in November 1933 on the Emergency Needs of Women in an effort to force government agencies to take women seriously. Through her constant concern and omnipresent intelligence network, she discovered where women associates would be most useful and when vacancies occurred that women could fill. She held special press conferences for women reporters in order to give the female press corps increased status and to guarantee attention to stories, often involving women, that would otherwise go unreported. Her close friend, Lorena Hickok, operated as Works Progress Administration (WPA) Director Harry Hopkin's eyes and ears as she toured relief projects throughout the country, sending her memos back both to Hopkins and to Roosevelt. Other women associates occupied policy-making positions in the WPA, the Social Security Administration, and the Labor Department. At times, Washington seemed like a perpetual convention of social workers as women from the National Consumers League and other reform groups came to Washington to take on government assignments. Mary Anderson, director of the Women's Bureau in the Department of Labor, recalled that in earlier years, women government officials had dined together in a small university club. "Now," she said, "there are so many of them they would need a hall."

Nowhere was the Roosevelt fusion of women's reform and politics more manifest than in the work of Molly Dewson, head of the Women's Division of the Democratic party from 1932 to 1937. Second only to Roosevelt herself as a connecting link for women reformers from various women's organizations, Dewson set out to show that women could, and should, play a major role in the very center of party councils. Combining impeccable reform credentials with brilliant political instincts, she succeeded—with Mrs. Roosevelt's help—beyond her fondest expectations. The question was whether she succeeded too well. Like most female reformers, Dewson was convinced that women differed fundamentally from men. Women wanted a better-ordered society and cared primarily about the "security of the home," she believed; men, on the other hand, sought power and individual distinction. In contrast to most reformers, however, Dewson placed her instincts about women's special nature at the service of a specific party. The political organization which first recognized the inherent differences between the sexes, she asserted, would benefit immeasurably. In the past, women politicians had failed to make any impact because they had aped men. The parties, in turn, had failed to recruit female supporters because they had not appealed to women's distinctive interests. Dewson intended to correct that error by treating women as a special class and directing her attention to issues such as public welfare in which women had a particular interest.

Education constituted the heart of Dewson's political strategy. "In 1932 we did not make the old-fashioned plea that our nominee was charming," she told an interviewer after the election. "Instead, we appealed to the intelligence of the country's women." Relying on what she called the "endless chain principle," Dewson urged women party members to be the "mouth to mouth, house to house interpreters of the New Deal" and its programs. Under her Reporter Plan, women party workers in each community were deputized to become expert on a New Deal program, such as social security, and to inform the electorate on a door-to-door basis of its importance for their lives. By 1936, about 15,000 women Reporters were carrying the information they received from Washington to their local communities, ringing doorbells, explaining federal policies, and converting doubtful voters.

In four years, Dewson transformed the Women's Division from a useless appendage of the Democratic party into a vital element in its continued success. When Jim Farley tried to cut the division's program in an economy move, the president enlarged it instead and gave Dewson added powers. The chief executive's vote of confidence paid off in the 1936 election when over 60,000 women precinct workers canvassed the electorate. Local women's committees sponsored Radio Parties focusing on broadcasts by the president, and the Women's Division Rainbow Fliers—one-page pastel fact sheets on major New Deal accomplishments—constituted the principal literature distributed by the national party. Over 83 million fliers were circulated by the end of the campaign, each emphasizing how the New Deal helped average citizens to save their homes or families.

Through her efforts, Molly Dewson contributed significantly to the broadening of the Democratic constituency which occurred in the Roosevelt administration. She directed her efforts not at solid party followers but at voters without a party affiliation. "There is a big group of people who are interested in issues and these are the ones that I want telling about what the New Deal is doing," she wrote. Despite Jim Farley's objections, she dedicated herself to winning over intellectuals and independents. To widen the party's appeal, she secured the president's approval of an Advisory Commission of New Dealers to be comprised primarily of independents, and in her own division, she established special committees to deal with blacks, educators, social workers, and writers. At a time when many party leaders still emphasized reliance on the old political machines, she helped to spearhead the New Deal's attempt to reach out beyond the established political structure and build new loyalties based on the issues.

As a result of Dewson's achievement, women gained new recognition in party ranks. The 1936 Democratic convention passed a rule requiring that each delegate to the Platform Committee be accompanied by an alternate of the opposite sex, thereby ensuring fifty-fifty representation on the committee which had excluded Eleanor Roosevelt twelve years before. A *New York Times* reporter described the new rule as "the biggest coup for women in years," and Emily Newell Blair told a nationwide radio audience that for the first time, women delegates were being treated as equals with men. Each day of the convention, the Washington *Times* noted, "the party leaders have recognized in some way the ability of women, and their value to the party." Seven of eight planks desired by the Women's Division were incorporated into the party platform, and Jim Farley named eight women as vice-chairs of the Democratic National Committee in an effort to establish parity with men. In addition, women's patronage increased dramatically. Dewson later claimed that she "never cared much about the machinery of politics," but she knew enough to ensure that her own workers were rewarded for their efforts. Women party members were placed in nearly every department of government, and women's share of postmasterships shot up from 17.6 percent in 1930 to 26 percent from 1932 to 1938.

The relevance of New Deal programs to the home and family clearly contributed to the increase in women's political activity. Throughout the 1920s, with the exception of the Sheppard-Towner bill and the Child Labor Amendment, politics had been dominated by issues essentially unrelated to women's primary sphere of responsibility. With the coming of the Great Depression, however, the actions of government affected every household in the land. Political decisions determined whether children would have new shoes, whether a mortgage would be foreclosed, whether a mother could feed her family. Government ceased to be extraneous to the concerns of the family but instead provided school lunches, aid to dependent children, and relief checks that helped the family to survive. Mary Dewson—and the women she helped bring to Washington—had devoted their entire lives to such welfare measures, and with the encouragement of the president, Dewson sought in every way possible to identify national politics with the "bread-and-butter" priorities of women in the home.

In all of this, of course, the direct ties of women reformers to the White House were crucial. Dewson was the first to acknowledge the importance of her relationship with the Roosevelts. She had experienced no difficulty in getting started in politics, she recalled, "because FDR backed me." He alone among modern politicians had recognized that women had a contribution to make to politics. Dewson corresponded almost daily with Mrs. Roosevelt, and when questions of great urgency arose, the First Lady seated Dewson next to the president at dinner so that she could persuade him to her point of view. Women's Division requests for help went in duplicate to the White House, often to be followed up by a personal note of endorsement from the president or his wife to the appropriate government or party official. Dewson succeeded in implementing her educational program because at a every critical juncture the president and Mrs. Roosevelt supported her.

Yet if the success of Dewson and other reformers in the New Deal reflected, on the one hand, the continuity of women's political influence from the Progressive era through the 1930s, it also carried with it the danger that once institutionalized in government programs, that influence would come to an end. Using the work of Paula Baker and Suzanne Lebsock as a frame of reference, a strong argument can be made that women's greatest political power occurred through *indirect* activity, carried out by voluntary associations of women reformers who organized in separate groups based on a self-perception that women had distinctive interests and values—a special "sphere" of responsibility. Whatever the impact of the Nineteenth Amendment, these groups continued to pursue their separate agenda during the 1920s, demonstrating, as Nancy Cott has shown, far more continuity than discontinuity with the political role of women in the Progressive era. The community these women embodied remained largely intact, as manifested in the personal and professional network of reformers who surrounded Eleanor Roosevelt throughout the 1920s. When large segments of this network moved to Washington during the New Deal, it seemed that the goals of the separate community of women's organizations had finally been achieved. Their programs had become federal policy.

And there precisely was the problem. Estelle Freedman has suggested that women's strength as political actors depended on preserving a separatist base that would be woman-controlled and that would provide a means for defining the values and concerns of women's "separate sphere." Once women's programs, and women themselves, became assimilated into male-controlled structures, women would lose both their independence and their capacity for collective self-determination. They would, in other words, become *individuals*, standing alone, not part of a community with its own rationale and agenda. Thus, the very success of women reformers in finally securing action on their agenda resulted in the weakening of their home base. Assimilation into federal social-welfare bureaucracies could well signify the extinction of women's influence, not its triumph. Instead of retaining control over their own cultural and political worldview, women might lose their autonomy to a sex-neutral government bureaucracy whose ultimate agenda was still controlled by men.

----- III -----

The story of the Nineteenth Amendment's affect on women's political power thus turns out to be far more complicated and ambiguous than previously thought. Using the simple and mechanistic criterion of what difference women voters made to party politics and elections, it is relatively easy to conclude that enfranchisement for women meant very little. The vote itself had ceased to have the same importance that it once had, and even if it had retained that importance, women would have had to exercise the right to vote in a disciplined, cohesive manner for their influence to have been felt.

But, as we have seen, expectations that women voters would form a separate "bloc" were totally without foundation. The suffragists were correct in assuming that women shared some common experience based on their sex. But they failed to acknowledge all the differences of ethnicity, race, and class that made such a "common" experience impossible to translate into cohesive political behavior at the voting booth. Unlike some minority groups, women were distributed throughout the social structure, so they had little opportunity to develop a positive sense of collective self-consciousness. Moreover, one of the central experiences women *did* share was their relationship with men. Yet nothing did more to discourage the growth of an independent women's constituency. As long as women were expected to follow the lead of their husbands and fathers in activities outside the home, it was hardly likely that they could act as a separate and autonomous segment within the electorate. Occasionally, an issue like the suffrage focused overriding attention on the identity of women as women and generated a heightened sense of sex solidarity. But such issues emerged only rarely. If women did behave alike, the sameness of their actions represented conformity to the role of helpmate rather than an assertion of their independence as a sex. It could hardly be otherwise in an overall social structure whose patriarchal nature remained unchanged.

Thus, it seems clear that the Nineteenth Amendment, by itself, did little to alter either women's status or women's political power. Party politics remained primarily male-controlled, and the effort to make 1920 a key dividing line runs the risk both of using male standards as a measure for women's experience and of deflecting attention from the real story of women's political activity.

If Nancy Cott and others are correct in identifying that "real story" as one of continuous activity on the part of women's voluntary associations, however, the verdict on women's political power during the 1920s and 1930s must be more mixed. Clearly, the growth of such voluntary associations during the 1920s supports the argument that women persisted in developing their own institutions for political influence and change, to complement the existence of the right to vote. In other words, women retained control of their own instruments of social and political change regardless of the right that now existed for them to join as individuals with men in the electoral process.

Furthermore, the realization of many of these reform objectives in the governmental policies of the New Deal provides strong support to those who see a seamless web joining the women reformers of the Progressive era to the women activists of the New Deal. Just as a direct link existed between Eleanor Roosevelt's role as a reform activist in the New Deal and her experience in the Rivington Street Settlement, so, too, there is a connection between her many allies in the government during the 1930s, and the values they learned as settlement-house residents. The community of women constituted a tangible bridge between two eras, arguing both for continuity of personnel and for reliance by women in both eras on a home base of separate women's reform organizations. In some ways, then, the record of this community—with Eleanor Roosevelt at its center—speaks to the underlying political story of women during the first four decades of this century. Yet what happens to the story if it ends with the incorporation of women into government bureaucracies and the expropriation of "women's" issues by a faceless federal cabinet department?

Here we return to the issue of the primary goal of the suffrage movement. Was it to abolish all separate distinctions based on sex so that women could join as individuals in the activities of the body politic; or was it to enable women to put into political action the separate values and concerns they shared on the basis of their difference from men? As Nancy Cott has shown, the suffragists themselves had no answer. Rather, "the vote harmonized the two strands in . . . woman's rights advocacy: it was an equal-rights goal that enabled women to make special contributions; it sought to give women the *same* capacity as men so they could express their *differences;* it was a just end in itself, but it was also an expedient means to other ends."

By 1940, the only thing that was certain was that the choice between individualism and collectivism, assimilation and separatism, remained as unresolved as ever. Clearly, women were not going to vote as a bloc. But that did not necessarily mean they would not act politically as a separate force. The question was how they would do that and whether their choice of means would serve a collective or an individualist end. In the meantime, twenty years of experience had shown that the suffrage was no panacea. Discrimination against women remained deeply rooted in the structure of society—in the roles women and men played and how those roles were valued. Unfortunately, the Nineteenth Amendment had done little to alter that structure.

CHAPTER 3

Women's Rights and Ideology:
The ERA

IF THE SUFFRAGE MOVEMENT lacked a clear sense of how to proceed after ratification of the Nineteenth Amendment in 1920, it was in large part because no ideological consensus existed on the meaning of equality between the sexes. Suffragists themselves were torn between a natural-rights faith in individualism that would have abolished all distinctions based on sex and a belief that women should pursue a separate agenda, based on their sexual difference from men, that would create a more humane and nurturant social system. But that conflict simply reflected a larger ambivalence within the women's movement over what it meant to be a woman and what it meant to be equal. The suffrage, as an overarching symbol, had united women with disparate concerns and multiple objectives. Evangelical Protestants, freethinkers, Prohibitionists, intellectuals, immigrants, and union organizers could all find some common ground on the issue of securing the right to vote. Now, any prospect for moving forward on issues of sex equality required an ideological vision—shared by women leaders—on the goal eventually to be achieved.

Significantly, in the years around 1910, a new word entered the popular culture to describe at least one variant of such an ideological vision. The word was "feminism." Although historians have retroactively employed the term to describe nineteenth-century women thinkers, it came into popular usage only after the turn of the century, at least partly to denote a bolder and more free-wheeling kind of attitude about women's rights. The historian Nancy Cott has observed that feminism was both broader and narrower than suffrage: "broader in intent, proclaiming revolution in all the relations of the sexes, and narrower in the range of its willing adherents." It was a new concept because it sought emancipation for women from all the constraints previously imposed on females by virtue of their sex. It aimed both to end the notion that one biological sex was superior or inferior to the other and to create a new norm for what it meant to be a fully realized individual.

In some ways, it seemed, "feminism" harked back to the Seneca Falls declaration. The vote was only one means to a larger end: a transformation of women's social experience with elimination of the double standard, complete freedom to pursue a career of one's own choice, total educational and political independence—in short, emancipation from sexual stereotypes of any kind. As the Feminist Alliance led by Henrietta Rodman declared in 1913, feminists wanted "the removal of all social, political and economic and other discriminations which are based upon sex, and the award of all rights and duties in all fields on the basis of individual capacity alone." In short, women should be freed from *all* prior social expectations and enabled to become *their own individual person*. In the process, they could become bolder and more liberated than women had ever been before.

Clearly, there were similarities between the idea of natural-rights individualism that some suffragists talked about and the idea of women's emancipation celebrated by feminists. But feminists were talking about more than politics. Their vision encompassed economics, social roles, and sexuality as well as the franchise. Homosexuality, for example, was championed as one possible life-style. Many of these women reveled in their rebellion, the members of Heterodoxy—a New York feminist group—being specifically required to "not be orthodox" in their opinions. Indeed, Heterodoxy members referred to themselves as "the most unruly and individualistic females you ever fell among." Like their nineteenth-century forebears, these feminists envisioned emancipation as a multi-layered phenomenon, and though they derived strength from their existence as a community, their ultimate goal was complete individual freedom.

Like the suffragists, however, feminists were not clear on how their goal was to be achieved. Many of them believed in the need for women to unite, out of a collective sense of shared identity and consciousness, in order to work for the achievement of their ends. Others believed that women should simply pursue their own paths as individuals and forget about any common cause. In some ways, that split was parallel to the one between those who thought women in politics should join the mainstream political parties as individuals and those who believed that women should organize separately for a distinctive "women's" agenda.

Whatever the nature or parallelism of the splits, however, the fundamental fact was that no transcendent ideological vision existed after 1920 to give cohesion to the women's movement. Instead, there was profound conflict between different groups of women activists who saw themselves as carrying on—in diametrically opposite ways—the goals of the suffrage campaign. Fundamentally, the conflict went back to the primary question of what it meant to have equality between men and women; or, put another way, should women be treated the same as men, or differently?

That question, unfortunately, came more and more to narrow the focus of women's activities. Although feminism in the late 1910s and early 1920s had a rainbow of concerns, issues of women's rights soon devolved into a division over one particular proposal by the National Woman's Party (NWP)—a self-identified feminist group—for an Equal Rights Amendment to the Constitution (ERA). While many people with a variety of causes continued to call themselves feminists in the 1920s, the NWP was clearly in the forefront with its demand for an ERA. First submitted in 1923, the amendment read: "men and women shall have equal rights throughout the United States and every place subject to its jurisdiction." Deceptively simple on the surface, the ERA itself was obviously a political goal, but it symbolized divisions over class, culture, and issues of social philosophy that went to the very heart of what was meant by women's emancipation. Thus, the failure to arrive at a consensus on the ERA spoke to the more significant problem of women activists being unable to unite on a larger purpose or set of purposes. By the end of the 1930s, the women's movement had stalled, its various factions expending more energy in seeking to destroy each other than in forging ahead to overcome a common enemy.

—— I ——

In some ways, the conflict over the ERA represented an extension of the split between the National Woman's Party and NAWSA during the suffrage campaign. The Woman's Party (formerly the Congressional Union) constituted the more militant wing of the suffrage movement. Its adherents adopted radical tactics, chaining themselves to fences, picketing the White House, and engaging in hunger strikes in prison. NAWSA, on the other hand, sought to cooperate with the government and to work from within to achieve its goals. Alice Paul and Woman's Party members burned President Wilson in effigy, while Carrie Chapman Catt invited him to address the NAWSA convention. Although both organizations were seeking the same end, they frequently worked at cross purposes, and many women traced the subsequent conflict within the women's movement to the residual distrust of the earlier struggle.

More important though, the dispute reflected the different goals sought by various participants in the woman's movement. W. L. George noted in 1916 that women activists could be divided into two groups: suffragists who

wished to remove a specific inequality, and feminists who aimed to transform
the attitude of the entire society toward women. Subsequent historians have
followed a similar line, distinguishing between "social feminists" who viewed
suffrage as a lever for social welfare reforms and "hard-core feminists" who
perceived the vote as only a small part of the larger goal of full sexual equality.
That basic division—here described as between reformers and feminists—
emerged explicitly in the period after 1920 and dominated the relationships
between various women's organizations. One group sought coalition with
others for the larger purposes of social reform; the other pursued a single
cause only, now defined as the ERA. One had goals that, philosophically at
least, were collectivist in nature; the other, goals that were primarily individualistic. And to give the scenario an edge of irony, the group that embraced
individualism called itself the "Woman's Party" while the group that espoused collectivism sometimes even eschewed being identified with women.

The attitudes of the two principal antagonists toward the suffrage reflected
the extent of the conflict. The Woman's Party—headed by Alice Paul—minimized the value of the suffrage victory and declared in 1921 that "women
today . . . are still in every way subordinate to men before the law, in the
professions, in the church, in industry, and in the home." Rejecting the plea
of other women's groups to build a reform coalition on behalf of disarmament,
birth control, and social-welfare legislation, the NWP pledged itself to work
exclusively for the goal of total equality for women. Its members reasoned
that any expenditure of energy on issues extraneous to women's rights would
only impede progress toward their primary end. American women were still
enslaved, the NWP believed, and nothing less than complete dedication could
bring about their emancipation.

The narrowness of the Woman's Party approach was manifested in both
its membership and leadership. Although the party boasted of being able to
force through Congress any legislative measure it sponsored, it suffered from
a distinct lack of popular support. At the height of its strength in 1920, it
had only 8,000 members. Many party followers were "ingrown to the point
of fanaticism," one member later observed, and seemed "ignorant of the
methods of democracy." Alice Paul ran the organization with a tyrannical
hand, setting policy on her own authority and jealously guarding her own
position. Although she inspired total dedication from some, she alienated
others and her rigid, dogmatic personality represented at least one cause of
the hostility which the NWP provoked among other women leaders.

In contrast to the Woman's Party, the League of Women Voters—
NAWSA's successor—attempted to serve a broader constituency. Although
it too was composed primarily of middle- and upper-class women, it forged

alliances with other reform groups and addressed itself to a wide spectrum of issues. League members contended that with suffrage, women had secured most of their fundamental rights. Marguerite Wells, the league's president during the 1930s, urged that "the well-worn old 'equal rights' slogan [be] reverently and gratefully returned to the suffragists at Seneca Falls . . . Nearly all discriminations have been removed." While the league continued to work for such measures as equal pay and jury service for women, it concerned itself as much with child labor, wages and working hours, and disarmament as with legislation specifically focused on women's rights. Of the 304 legislative items on the agendas of state leagues in 1931, over half had to do with child welfare and only 25 dealt with women.

In fact, the league went out of its way to avoid being identified as a lobbying agency for one group only. Repeatedly, league representatives declared that their organization was devoted to the good of the whole nation and not to any special interest. "We of the League are very much for the rights of women," Dorothy Straus, a league leader, wrote, "but . . . we are not feminists primarily; we are citizens." When Congress passed a Depression measure that, in effect, prevented wives of government employees from working in the federal civil service, the league opposed the bill on the grounds that it infringed on the merit system, not because it discriminated against women. "I do hate to see the League support a position . . . on purely equalitarian grounds when the broad social justification is clear," the league's executive secretary remarked. In contrast to the narrow, authoritarian management of the National Woman's Party, the league sought the maximum possible consensus of its membership before proceeding with any program. Every measure endorsed by league leaders had to be approved by its biennial convention, and before an item could even be inscribed on the league's legislative calendar, it had to be studied for at least a year by the appropriate standing committee.

The gulf between the two groups was best illustrated by the divergent tactics they adopted in pursuit of their goals. The Woman's Party wished to eliminate in one blow all remaining laws which distinguished between men and women. To campaign in each state for piecemeal reform, the NWP reasoned, would take years of effort. Consequently, the NWP relied on a blanket amendment that would outlaw all discriminatory legislation throughout the country. The League of Women Voters, in contrast, endorsed a strategy of gradualism. "The LWV from the beginning has stood for step-by-step progress," its first president recalled in 1933. "It has been willing to go ahead slowly in order to go ahead steadily. It has not sought to lead a few women a long way quickly, but rather to lead many women a little way at a time." The league rejected the one-shot approach of the Woman's Party. "Panaceas work no better for the body politic than they do in the animal body," Dorothy Straus observed. "Radical changes cannot be effected except by gradual steps; sudden and violent advances have invariably been followed by repression."

Despite the hostility of the two groups, it appeared for a brief time that compromise might still be possible. After ratification of the Nineteenth Amendment, many women shared membership in both camps. Florence Kelley of the National Consumers' League had been a national officer of the Woman's Party. Maud Younger, treasurer of the NWP, had served as national vice president of the Consumers' League and was widely known as the "mother" of California's eight-hour law for women. Josephine Casey, a former union organizer for the International Ladies Garment Workers, was a prominent force in both the NWP and the Women's Trade Union League. And Alice Paul herself had once served in the WTUL and helped organize a milliner's union. Far from opposing social-welfare reforms, many Woman's Party members had been in the forefront of the Progressive movement.

Based on these associations and common participation in the suffrage fight, tentative efforts at cooperation were made in 1921. Alice Paul invited a speaker from the League of Women Voters to address the Woman's Party convention and requested the league to join the NWP in commemorating pioneers of the suffrage movement at the Capitol. Ethel Smith of the Women's Trade Union League appeared at the NWP convention and reported that the WTUL banner received more applause than any other in the formal procession. People on each side sought to compromise on legislative matters. In Massachusetts, supporters of the two groups worked out an agreement whereby they would endorse a common program to end certain discriminatory practices at the same time that they were introducing separate bills on issues where they disagreed. A similar attempt was made in New York. "It is immaterial whether the bills which are passed are those which we have drawn up or those which some other organization has drawn up," Alice Paul wrote a New York official. "The only important thing is to see that they are passed."

On the chief sticking point—protective legislation—the NWP seemed willing to make concessions in the beginning. Reformers prided themselves on having secured enactment of minimum-wage and maximum-hour laws for women; they now feared that the NWP's blanket equal-rights bill would abrogate such legislation by eliminating any statute which singled out women for special consideration. Alice Paul proposed that the problem be solved "by raising the standard of protective labor laws for men until they are equal to those now in existence . . . for women." Failing that, however, the NWP appeared ready to placate the concern of women reformers. In Massachusetts, the NWP agreed to drop its opposition to League of Women Voters bills designed to protect women in industry; Alice Paul wrote her lieutenants in

New York that they had leeway to frame a similar compromise; and the New York NWP announced that it was specifically opposed to legislation which discriminated *against* women, the word "against" to distinguish such laws from those which provided protection *for* women.

In the end, however, the accumulated grievances dividing the two groups proved fatal to the effort at compromise. Organizational jealousy, personal hostility, and ideological conflict were stronger than the will to unite. The League of Women Voters rejected the invitation of the Woman's Party to join in honoring the suffrage pioneers, fearing that the public might get the impression that the two organizations were connected. Carrie Chapman Catt complained about the "fake publicity" the Woman's Party was receiving and warned that local league members were being enticed by NWP recruitment efforts. On the other side, Alice Paul adamantly refused to give up her commitment to a national constitutional amendment. At a showdown meeting in December 1921, Florence Kelley and other reformers urged the Woman's Party to refrain from introducing the amendment until a solution to the protective legislation dilemma could be found, but Paul rejected the suggestion out of hand. Protective legislation was the concern of reformers, the NWP argued. Consequently, the burden for any legal solution to the conflict rested with Kelley and her friends, not with the Woman's Party. The meeting ended with the recognition by all concerned that hope for conciliation on a national level was shattered.

—— II ——

Although NWP supporters boasted relatively little strength compared to the reform coalition, they made up in energy and dedication what they lacked in numbers. The NWP kept a maximum amount of pressure on congressmen through intensive lobbying, legislative hearings, and imaginative uses of international conferences that raised the issue of equal rights. Their single-minded persistence guaranteed that the debate within the woman's movement would continue. Furthermore, the centrality of the debate over means and ends led to increasing polarization with each passing year, highlighting the extent to which disagreement over the definition of equality and freedom was preventing progress toward either goal.

One abiding point of conflict centered on the propriety of using a constitutional amendment to fight prejudicial laws. The NWP insisted that discrimination against women could be eliminated effectively only by writing the rule of equality into the basic law of the land. Despite the victory achieved in the Nineteenth Amendment, they pointed out, over one thousand state laws continued to discriminate against women. In 1940, eleven states provided that a wife could not hold her own earnings without her husband's consent; sixteen states denied a married woman the right to make contracts; seven gave the father superior guardianship rights; and over twenty prohibited women from serving on juries. Legislation regarding sexual mores was especially egregious. In Virginia, a father could not be required to contribute to the maintenance of his illegitimate child. In Maryland, a husband could divorce his wife if she had been unchaste before marriage. And in Minnesota, a man whose wife was guilty of adultery could collect damages from her lover—a recourse denied the wife in a similar situation.

Common law represented the worst villain of all. According to British precedent, a woman's legal existence merged with that of her husband upon marriage, so that in effect, she ceased to be a person in her own right. United States courts ruled that any interpretation of the Constitution had to take common law into account, and on numerous occasions, women had been denied legal standing as "persons" before state and federal judges. In 1872, the Supreme Court determined that Myra Bradwell, an aspiring lawyer, could not practice her profession in the state of Illinois because as a married woman, she was not covered by the "equal protection" clause of the Fourteenth Amendment. The harmony of the family institution, Justice Joseph Bradley declared, was repugnant to "the idea of a woman adopting a distinct and independent career from that of her husband." Fifty years later, the highest court in Massachusetts refused the right of jury service to women on the grounds that they were not "persons in the eyes of the law." And in Georgia, the Supreme Court ruled in 1945 that a wife must follow her husband from a five-room house to a log cabin because "the husband is the head of the family and as such has the right to fix the matrimonial residence without the consent of his wife."

In the face of such discrimination, the NWP contended that only a constitutional amendment could establish the principle of equality for the entire nation. "It is strangely unsympathetic," the educator M. Carey Thomas wrote, "for opponents of an Equal Rights Amendment to suggest removing the thousands of inequalities and injustices by slow and piecemeal work . . . while women are being born, living their lives and dying without the justice which they have been waiting for since the time of the caveman." The amendment promised to establish a uniform standard of sexual justice for the entire country and to nullify the pernicious heritage of common law. It was a one-step solution to "the ancestral tradition of sex inferiority and subjection," its supporters claimed, and a noble addition to the Bill of Rights.

Reformers responded by challenging both the content and approach of the NWP program. Most discrimination against women was rooted in custom, not law, they asserted. Consequently, the Equal Rights Amendment was a "quack nostrum" which would have little constructive effect. In addition, they pointed out, the amendment would not even eliminate laws which did discriminate against women since additional legislative action would be required to implement the amendment's principle. "It is not practical," Mary Anderson charged. "It deals with abstract rights, not real rights." The amendment established a standard but did nothing to make it a reality. "I want equality, yes," wrote Cornelia Bryce Pinchot, "but I want equality that is a fact, not an empty phrase."

But what bothered reformers most was the potentially destructive effect of the amendment on protective legislation for women. Equal rights, declared one opponent, was "one of those weasel-like phrases like 'fraternity,' 'equality,' and 'democracy' "; it meant nothing until the Supreme Court interpreted it. On the basis of the Court's decisions on minimum wages for women and on child labor, however, the reformers had good reason to believe that judges would invalidate the protective legislation which the reformers had worked so hard to gain. The Woman's Party cavalierly argued that however the courts decided, "we can rest serene in our reliance on the righteousness of the principle of equal rights for men and women and not worry as to the details of how it will work out"; yet the details are what perturbed women reformers. The amendment, they feared, would endanger wage and hour laws for women, undermine support laws for wives and children, and terminate special penalties in the law for rape and sexual offenses against women. "The Equal Rights Amendment would operate like a blind man with a shot gun," one legal expert warned. "No lawyer can confidently predict what it would hit."

As a result of their apprehension, reformers sought to discredit the entire equal-rights drive. "The Constitution is not the place to theorize on the relations between the sexes," one reform lawyer told a congressional hearing. "Law is law. It is not a place for emotions or hopes." Reformers contended that the simplistic formulation of the Woman's Party bore no relation to the complexity of women's actual situation. "Only those who are ignorant of the law . . . or indifferent to the exacting aspects of women's life," Felix Frankfurter wrote in 1923, "can have the naïveté, or the recklessness, to sum up women's whole position in a meaningless and mischievous phrase about 'equal rights.' " Legal equality between the sexes could not be achieved, Mary Anderson asserted; indeed, the whole concept of equality was a myth.

More than a question of legal propriety was involved in the dispute, however. At the root of the conflict was the issue of whether protective legislation helped or hindered the quest for equality. From the NWP's point of view, laws which singled out women for special treatment represented a conspiracy to deny them their economic rights. "Whatever the effects on women of sex legislation aimed to protect them," Alma Lutz declared, "it has been a real

protection to men by slowing down the competition of women for their jobs."
As early as 1836, the New England Association of Farmers, Mechanics and
Other Workingmen had advocated special labor legislation for women in order
to control the size of the work force; in 1923, the American Federation of
Labor (AF of L) offered a similar rationale for its renewed interest in protective
statutes. If women were prohibited from lifting certain weights or from working long hours, male workers could feel safe in their jobs. NWP supporters
were convinced that under the guise of concern for women's health and safety,
unions actually sought special wage and hour legislation for women as a way
of preventing them from taking work away from men. The only purpose of
protective legislation in the age of the new woman, Maud Younger wrote,
was "to lower women's economic status, keep them in the ranks with little
chance for advancement . . . and perpetuate the psychology that they are cheap
labor and inferior to other adult workers."

To support their contention that special labor laws discriminated against
women, the NWP marshaled an impressive array of evidence. In New York
City, over 700 women employees of the Brooklyn Rapid Transit System lost
their jobs when a statute prohibiting split shifts for women prevented them
from working the morning and evening rush hours. Waitresses, clerks in
drug stores, women printers, and reporters all suffered when New York declared that women could not work after ten p.m. One study concluded that
if it were not for protective legislation, 2 to 5 percent more women would be
gainfully employed, many of them in jobs which represented "frontiers" in
women's work. The case of Mollie Maloney, a bookbinder who earned $46.50
working the night shift in 1919, illustrated the NWP's argument. After passage of New York's night-work statute, she was forced to move from her
former job to the less-remunerative day shift. When another law limiting
women's hours of overtime prevented her from filling rush orders, she lost
her job entirely. From Maloney's point of view, protective legislation was
manifestly unfair. "We working women can protect ourselves if we have
equality of opportunity under the law," she declared.

NWP advocates singled out minimum-wage laws for special condemnation. Establishing a set rate for women's services, they argued, placed an
unfair value on women's work and invited men to undercut them by accepting
lower pay. In Ohio, women's employment declined by over 14 percent after
a minimum-wage law was passed. At Harvard University, twenty scrub-
women were fired when the state ordered their pay to be increased by two
cents an hour. And in California, the director of finance reported in 1932 that
thousands of women were out of work because men were willing to accept
less pay than the legal base set for women. "In not a single state having
minimum-wage legislation . . . do women receive a living wage," Jane Nor-

man Smith declared. "On the other hand, whenever this legislation has been enforced . . . women have lost their jobs and been replaced by men."

Ultimately, the NWP objected to special labor legislation because it symbolized the evil of a social system which set women apart as a separate class and assigned them a place less equal than that of men. The phrase "protective legislation" carried the distinct connotation that women lacked the ability to care for themselves and were second-class citizens. "Under the common law, women were 'protected' from themselves in being placed under the guardianship of father and husband," a New York equal-rights pamphlet declared, "[but] modern women do not wish 'protection' as inferior beings." Special labor laws, the NWP argued, categorized the whole sex as weak and dependent—the equivalent of classifying all men as disabled because a few were wounded veterans. Only when women ceased to be grouped with children as helpless creatures could they enjoy the full status of mature persons that was their birthright.

Within such a context, the real purpose of the Equal Rights Amendment was to obliterate sex as a functional classification within the law. Feminists argued that women could not achieve real freedom until they were treated as individuals, not members of a sexual group. "It is time sex be forgotten and men and women become co-workers in all that concerns the destiny of the human race," Mary Woolley of Mount Holyoke wrote. Not every member of the Woman's Party agreed with Alice Paul that equality was incompatible with acknowledging difference, but most joined in the conviction that women should be accorded the same legal status as men. "We are not asking for any special rights," Anita Pollitzer told a Senate hearing. "We are not asking for anything but the same opportunity [as men] to be human beings in this land of ours."

As they had on other issues, the reformers rejected both the specific claims and underlying premise of the NWP argument. Legislation regulating women's hours, wages, and working conditions, they contended, had ameliorated the horrors of sweatshop labor and given workers protection against unprincipled employers. Far from undermining female equality, such laws were responsible for "bringing the women's standard up a little toward the standards of men." Passage of the Equal Rights Amendment might correct a few instances of discrimination, but it would also wipe out years of progress and restore the intolerable factory conditions of the late nineteenth century. For the sake of giving an individual woman the right to drive a taxi in Ohio, the NWP was willing to junk the rights of almost all female industrial workers to decent working conditions. The historian Mary Beard summed up many of the reformers' arguments when she declared that supporters of the Equal Rights Amendment "ran the risk of positively strengthening anachronistic competitive industrial processes; of supporting . . . ruthless laissez-faire; [and] of forsaking humanism in the quest for feminism." In service to an abstract theory, the well-being of millions would be endangered.

Indeed, reformers believed that the entire feminist drive was motivated by the selfish desire of a few business and professional women to advance their own interests at the expense of the rest of the sex, especially of working-class women. In a brilliant article analyzing the class bias of feminism, Mary Van Kleeck pointed out that the Woman's Party and its allies were concerned primarily with liberating the individual woman. The feminists placed special emphasis on personal freedom and accomplishment—values which appealed to career women who aspired to success in positions which were competitive with men. The nature of industrial labor, on the other hand, barred individualistic competition. The factory was a collective institution, and the women working in it cared more about economic security than personal liberty. The two classes thus had distinctly opposite economic interests, but feminists refused to acknowledge the difference and instead attempted to impose their own point of view on all women. The result, Van Kleeck declared, was that in the name of freedom, a small number of career women were undercutting the only protection that female factory workers had.

Subsequent events seemed to confirm the accuracy of Van Kleeck's analysis. The Woman's Party filed a legal brief in the 1923 *Adkins* case urging the Supreme Court to invalidate Washington, D.C.,'s minimum-wage law for women. Thirteen years later, it repeated its performance in the celebrated New York State minimum-wage case. In both instances, the Court appeared to endorse the NWP's contention that placing a floor beneath the wages of women amounted to a denial of their freedom of contract. To some feminists, such decisions represented a bold advance toward equal rights, but to social reformers, the opposite was true. Mary Anderson asserted that the Court's ruling in the New York case had about as much to do with freedom for women as the right-wing Liberty League had to do with liberty. The NWP position on equality, the *Nation* commented, "is as always logically sound and theoretically progressive. Humanly, however, it is impractical and reactionary."

Whatever the merits of the specific arguments, however, the conflict ultimately centered on the reformers' assumption that women *did* differ fundamentally from men and *should* be treated as a separate class. Summarizing the reform point of view, the National Consumers' League declared that while women had the same rights as men, they were "not identical in economic or social function or in physical capacity" and, hence, could not be dealt with in the same way. The contention that women possessed distinctive attributes requiring special attention constituted the principal rationale for protective legislation. In his landmark brief before the Supreme Court in 1908 in the case of *Muller v. Oregon*, Louis Brandeis stated that the "two sexes differ in structure of body, in the function to be performed by each, in the amount of physical strength [and] in the capacity for long-continued labor." The difference, Brandeis asserted, justified special legislation regulating women's hours of work. In its decision, the Court adopted the reformers' position and articulated a theory of women's nature hardly designed to please feminists. "Woman has always been dependent upon man," the Court declared. "Even though . . . she stood as far as statutes are concerned, upon an absolutely equal plane with him, it would still be true that she . . . will rest upon and look to him for protection."

Although some may have been less than happy with the more invidious aspects of the Court's opinion, most reformers accepted such a definition of women's identity as a necessary prerequisite for achieving social-welfare legislation. Rose Schneiderman of the Women's Trade Union League observed that most women could not do the same work as men and needed safeguards to protect their health. In particular, Schneiderman rejected the idea that women should be employed as absolute equals with men. Those who "want to work at the same hours of the day or night and receive the same pay," she declared, "might be putting their own brothers or sweethearts, or husbands out of a job." Full-time work, by implication, remained the exclusive prerogative of men. The Court's interpretation in the *Muller* case coincided with the reformers' own conviction that the two sexes had separate roles to play in life. "Nature made men and women different," Felix Frankfurter asserted; "the law must accommodate itself to the immutable differences of Nature."

Consistent with Frankfurter's reasoning, the reformers placed special emphasis on woman's role within the family in their campaign against the Equal Rights Amendment. "No law . . . can change physical structures that make women the child-bearers of mankind," a group of reformers asserted. Nature had decreed that women should devote their lives to caring for children. A man could not nurse a baby, Al Smith observed. Consequently, the two sexes could not be treated identically. The clear inference of the reformers' argument was that any effort to obliterate sexual differences in the law was a direct assault on God's creation. "To deny that women require care and protection," one writer charged, "is equal to a denial of their physical mission of motherhood."

Reformers and feminists thus held diametrically opposite conceptions of female equality. The Woman's Party and its allies were convinced that protective legislation discriminated against women and that women could not be free until they achieved absolute identity with men in all areas of public policy regulated by the law. Reformers, in turn, believed that differences of physical and psychological makeup prevented women from ever competing on a basis of total equality with men and that special labor laws were required if women were to be protected against exploitation and given just treatment in their economic activities. One side was committed to the philosophy that women were exactly the same as men in all attributes relevant to law and public policy; the other, to the position that women were so different that their rights would be destroyed unless safeguarded by special legislation. The division of opinion could hardly have been greater.

Ironically, both sides presented arguments which were legitimate if not carried to an extreme. The number of discriminatory state laws still in existence made the NWP call for a new constitutional amendment seem a sensible and expedient way of carrying on the fight for equality. On the other hand, reformers correctly pointed out that women differed from men in some ways and that laws which took such differences into account were not necessarily prejudicial to women's best interests.

By the 1930s, however, the woman's movement had become so embroiled in emotional antagonism over the Equal Rights Amendment that the justice that existed on each side was ignored by the other. Instead of moving ahead together to attack the practical problems of discrimination, women's groups were polarized over doctrinaire questions of ideology. The conflict had degenerated into a "holy war," with each side resorting to polemics and adopting a position as far from the other as possible. Reformers denounced the Woman's Party as a "small but militant group of leisure-class women" who resented "not having been born men," and the NWP responded by calling the reformers "Tories" whose hearts bled "for the poor working girl but who would oppose for themselves the restrictions as to pay and hours imposed on these same working girls."

—— III ——

Such inflammatory rhetoric suggested just how basic the issues were that occupied the attention of the opposing sides. When the Fair Labor Standards Act of 1938 established the precedent of providing protective wage and hour legislation for both men and women, one of the key problems allegedly dividing women activists appeared to be removed—even more so when the Supreme Court upheld the new statute in *U.S. v. Darby* three years later. Yet the conflict did not abate, and if anything became worse, signifying just how far beyond "practical" politics the underlying issues went.

One deleterious consequence of the conflict could be seen in its impact on the women reformers who had persisted in their quest for social-welfare programs during the 1920s and who now occupied crucial roles in the New

Deal. Although their energies had been devoted to the positive goal of collective reform ever since the Progressive era, they now became increasingly fixated on the *negative* goal of stopping the ERA. Reformers created a "Committee of Five Hundred Against the Equal Rights Amendment" and then devised a much ballyhooed initiative called the "Women's Charter" to steal the thunder from the NWP by rallying support for the principle of women's equality. Enormous amounts of correspondence went back and forth between government officials and women's voluntary associations focused specifically and exclusively on the task of *defeating* other women who had a different conception of what sex equality meant. Thus, these reformers not only lost their separate base and agenda during the 1930s by having their program taken over by sex-neutral federal bureaucracies but also found themselves relying to an increasing extent for their unity and *raison d'être* on being *against* rather than *for* something.

On the other hand, feminists suffered a similar narrowing of vision. Growing out of a new boldness and imagination among women during the 1910s and 1920s, the word "feminism" initially conveyed a sense of openness and possibility about subjects as diverse as art and sexuality. By the 1930s, however, "feminism" had become almost exclusively associated with the NWP and its single-minded agenda of action on the ERA. Led by the authoritarian Alice Paul, the NWP all too often engaged in mean-spirited, tendentious activities that were reactionary, not progressive. Instead of being associated with openness, feminism became identified with a closed worldview; rather than connoting daring and imaginativeness, the word came to imply rigidity and orthodoxy. Neither NWP feminists nor social-welfare reformers recruited effectively among the young, with the result that by 1940, both seemed cut off from the vitality and concerns of a new generation.

Obviously, the issues that divided the women's movement were important, both tactically and strategically. Paradoxically, the group that championed individualism and argued for women being treated the same as men was also the group that organized, theoretically at least, as the "Woman's" Party. By contrast, those who believed that women were different from men and should act on the basis of their separate values and concerns also sought to work in coalition with men and other reformers, de-emphasized their identification with women *per se*, and frequently employed the rhetoric of "citizenship." If nothing else, the tortuous path that women activists traveled in the 1920s and 1930s testified to the complexity and difficulty of defining a shared vision for women's equality.

By 1940, it seemed clear that such a vision would not emerge from that generation of women activists. These women had literally "made" history for nearly half a century, leaving behind a legacy of social-welfare programs and the triumph of important gains for women's citizenship rights. If, in the end, they could not resolve the fundamental questions of women's identity that bedeviled them, they were in good company. Their nineteenth-century predecessors had experienced no better luck. Not surprisingly, the issues that they did not resolve continued to frame the debate over freedom and equality during subsequent decades. For the moment, however, the energy that had infused the drive for women's equality for nearly half a century seemed stalled, the woman's movement paralyzed by its own involvement in the politics of mutual recrimination. It would take another generation and a dramatically altered set of social and economic conditions before the active pursuit of gender equality would resume.

PART TWO

WOMEN AND
THE ECONOMY,
1900–1940

CHAPTER 4

Women and Economic Equality

ALTHOUGH THE POLITICAL activities of women naturally attracted the most attention after enactment of the suffrage amendment, many observers—especially feminists—viewed women's economic progress as a more important barometer of what had been gained or lost in the fight for equality. The ballot provided a potential opportunity to influence public policy, but by itself, it did little to transform woman's "place" in the home or to alter her life chances as a worker in the labor force. If one source of systemic inequality between the sexes was the extent to which women's roles—in and out of the home— were totally prescribed by their sex, a clear sign of ending that inequality would be women being able to participate in all areas of life. Within that context, the economic experience of women became a crucial index of how much had been gained in the fight for the vote.

Not surprisingly, many observers predicted that passage of the Nineteenth Amendment would help to establish women's independence in the economic as well as in the political arena. "Emancipation in the industrial field," the dean of Boston University Business School declared, "will follow as a natural sequence the equalization of men and women politically"; nor did such assessments seem off base. In the years preceding final victory in the battle for the franchise, economic progress appeared to be a realistic possibility. State legislatures enacted minimum-wage and factory safety laws to protect women workers (largely, as we have seen, at the behest of women reformers). World War I created new job opportunities for women. And Progressive reformers promised to build a world of greater social and economic justice. In the flush of optimism generated by wartime enthusiasm, leaders of the woman's movement were convinced that a new era of sex equality was dawning. "Wonderful as this hour is for democracy and labor," Margaret Dreier Robins told the Women's Trade Union League in 1917, "it is the first hour in history for the women of the world. . . . At last, after centuries of disabilities and discrimination, women are coming into the labor and festival of life on equal terms with men."

The economic ventures of women in the years surrounding passage of the suffrage appeared to lend credibility to Robins's observation. The census of 1920 revealed that over 8 million women were employed in 437 different job classifications. Women plastered walls, climbed steeples, preached in churches, trapped furs, managed offices, and hauled freight. Before the new decade was a year old, a woman lawyer had defended a man accused of murder, and a group of women entrepreneurs had formed their own bank. News stories told of society matrons starting tearooms, of universities graduating women engineers, and of female suburbanites volunteering as motorcycle police. "Even the girls who knew that they were going to be married pretended to be considering important business positions," Sinclair Lewis wrote in his 1920 novel *Main Street*.

Social commentators seized on women's new economic independence as one explanation for the "revolution in manners and morals" that was sweeping the country. Although observers differed on the overall significance of the 1920s, almost all agreed that the age was one of unprecedented personal liberation. Magazines and novels portrayed the decade as a nonstop revel featuring jazz bands, risqué dances, and uninhibited sex. As much as anyone else, the "new woman" seemed to symbolize the era. Cigarette in mouth and cocktail in hand, she appeared to be both shocking and unshockable. In the eyes of many, economic freedom was directly responsible for her liberation. Frederick Lewis Allen noted in 1931 that, after passage of the suffrage amendment, middle-class girls "poured out of schools and colleges into all manner of occupations." Their economic activity, he concluded, provided an indispensable condition for the "slackening of husbandly and parental authority."

According to this view, an inextricable connection existed between economic freedom and women's liberation. Once young women escaped the tight moral control of the home and found an apartment and job of their own, they could be in charge of their own destinies—politically, sexually, economically, and socially. A job constituted a critical stepping stone in woman's "headlong pursuit of freedom" and comprised an integral part of the flapper's life. The female labor force had grown 26 percent during the 1920s, with over 500,000 of the new women workers in clerical or kindred positions and another 450,000 in the professions. By 1930, almost 2 million women were employed as secretaries, typists, and file clerks, with another 700,000 working as saleswomen in department stores. These were the young women who provided the model for Frederick Lewis Allen's "new woman." White, middle class (or aspiring to that status), and newly liberated in their outlook, they seemed truly able to seize the "new freedom" and maximize it in both their personal and occupational lives.

In retrospect, however, it appears that Allen and others overstated the amount of economic change that occurred during the 1920s. There is little evidence that a revolution took place in women's economic roles after World War I, nor can it be said that the 1920s represented a time of significant improvement in the history of women at work. In fact, the period from 1920 to 1940 witnessed very little progress toward the goal of economic equality. If the word "emancipation" is taken to mean the ability of women to function in the world outside the home on a basis of autonomy and equal access to job opportunities, then women workers remained almost as unemancipated in 1940 as in 1920. Aspiring career women were still limited to positions specifically set aside for women; the overwhelming majority of American working women continued to toil at menial occupations for inadequate pay, and the drive to abolish economic discrimination enlisted little popular support. Although important changes did occur in the composition of the labor force and the distribution of jobs women performed, most women workers functioned as they always had—as second-class citizens, powerless to alter their inferior position.

—— I ——

Popular misconceptions about the 1920s can be traced in part to the belief that World War I dramatically transformed the the status of the woman worker. At the height of the fighting in France, thousands of women in Bridgeport, Connecticut, and Springfield, Massachusetts, and other cities across the country swarmed into factories to take up the work of men at the front. The number of women employed in iron and steel trebled. Over 100,000 women entered munitions factories. Countless others served as streetcar conductors, elevator operators, furnace stokers, and bricklayer helpers. Women lawyers were appointed to the government's legal advisory committees, and women doctors for the first time gained access to the U.S. Public Health Service. The Women's Bureau—established in large part as a result of the war—required four pages to list all the jobs in which women substituted for men during the fighting.

The wartime experience generated widespread enthusiasm among women leaders and led many observers to declare that women had reached a new plateau of economic equality. Alice Hamilton, a pioneer in industrial medicine and a prominent social reformer, recalled the "exaltation" of women workers and their sense of "joyful release" at the chance to serve their country in time of need. As a result of women's contribution, the writer Mary Austin asserted, female economic emancipation had moved ahead a hundred years. The progress made during the war reinforced the conviction of many women's rights advocates that victory in the suffrage fight would be accompanied by a lowering of barriers against women in all spheres of life. "[S]ervice to their country in this crisis," feminist Harriet Stanton Blatch observed, "may lead women to that economic freedom which will change a political possession into a political power."

The facts did not support such an optimistic interpretation, however. Contrary to popular opinion, only 5 percent of the women war workers joined the labor force for the first time in the war years. The rest had transferred from lower-paying jobs and were expected to return to them when the emergency passed. Only 10 of 173 women operators on the Cleveland Street Railway, for example, had never worked before. Despite the critical need for women in war industries, the Federal Board for Vocational Education provided training only for such traditional female occupations as dressmaking and embroidery, and it actively discouraged women from registering at its local schools. The Women-In-Industry Service promulgated strict regulations designed to protect women doing war work, but the government did little to enforce the new rules. Less than 20 percent of the firms sampled by the Women's Bureau instituted a forty-eight-hour work week and daily rest periods, while only 9 percent of the women replacing male workers in New York received the equal pay to which the War Labor Board said they were entitled.

More important, whatever positive impact the war did have was short-lived. "The brief interlude . . . which some enthusiasts heralded as launching a new era for women in industry," Constance Green later observed, "came and went with astonishingly little permanent effect upon women's opportunities." In 1919, the Central Federated Union of New York declared that "the same patriotism which induced women to enter industry during the war should induce them to vacate their positions after the war." Male workers went on strike in Cleveland in order to force women streetcar conductors out of work, and in Detroit, female conductors were dismissed despite a National War Labor Board decision in their favor. Twenty women judges in New York were forced to resign immediately after the Armistice on the grounds that their appointments were for the duration of the emergency only.

The federal government itself continued to discriminate against women employees, despite its formal commitment to fair hiring practices and equal pay. A Women's Bureau study in 1919 showed that women were excluded from 60 percent of all civil-service examinations, including 64 percent of those for scientific and professional positions. Women biologists might analyze potatoes, the government said, but not tobacco. They could study plant diseases, but not animal parasites. (The latter area dealt with breeding.) The assumption that women constituted a separate category, inferior to men, pervaded both the assignment of women personnel and the salaries they were paid. Fourteen female lawyers who passed the civil-service examinations for law clerk were appointed instead to clerical posts at half the salary. A Treasury official decreed that no woman in his department could earn more than $1,200 yearly; and Congress, when it established the Women's Bureau as a permanent agency, limited the salaries of its professional experts to $1,800 in contrast to the $3,000 received by individuals doing similar work in the Bureau of Labor Statistics.

Contrary to the hopes of some women activists, World War I produced no substantial change in what one observer called women's "nebulous, will-o'-the-wisp" status. In 1920, women's participation in the total labor force remained similar to that in 1910, and their employment in the war-related areas of manufacturing and mechanical industries had actually dropped from 17.1 to 15.3 percent. Whatever gains had been made during the nineteen months of American involvement were cut short by the signing of the Armistice. Neither the labor movement nor the government was ready to accept a permanent shift in women's economic role. Called forth in crisis to fill an urgent need, women were relegated to their former position as soon as peace pace returned. "When the immediate dangers . . . were passed," reformer Mary Van Kleeck wrote, "the prejudices came to life once more."

In the twenty years after the passage of the Nineteenth Amendment, few changes occurred to alter women's basic economic position. Alice Hamilton noted in 1930 that the public had vastly overestimated the economic advances made by women in the war and afterward, and the evidence supported her judgment. Although slightly more than two million additional women joined the labor force during the 1920s, the proportion of women over fourteen who held jobs increased by only 1 percent. The latter figure represented a more accurate index of economic change than the former, because it took into account the growth of the population and measured with greater precision the actual number of women at work relative to those eligible for employment. If the economic role of women had expanded significantly during the 1920s, evidence of the shift should have appeared in the proportion of women employed. The percentage remained almost constant, however, suggesting that the numerical increase in the female labor force reflected the growth rate of the population and economy rather than a radical change in women's economic activity.

Throughout this period as well, the primary determinants of women's labor-force participation remained age, marital status, and race. Each proved pivotal, but as the historian Lois Helmboldt has observed, "the absence of an employed husband [was] the single most important factor in understanding women's employment." More than 70 percent of single white women aged twenty to forty-four were working in 1930, but fewer than 12 percent of married white women were. When we consider the fact that 83 percent of white women were married by age thirty, it is possible to get some sense of how much being young and single dictated the likelihood of work, at least for *white women*. Race, on the other hand, proved decisive for whether or not a married woman worked. More than three times the proportion of black married women were employed as white married women. When the variable of class is added as well, it becomes clear how age, class, race, and marital status determined the likelihood of a woman seeking gainful employment. In short, if a woman were young and single, she would likely be employed, but only until she married (usually in her twenties). Married women did not work as a rule unless they were black or poor.

Nevertheless, some important shifts did occur during these years, especially in the type of work women performed, who occupied those positions, and—eventually—in the age and marital status of women workers. Few changes were more important than the rapid growth of white-collar and clerical positions. At the turn of the century, almost all gainfully employed women worked as domestics, farm laborers, unskilled factory operatives, and teachers. By 1940, in contrast, white-collar work had become a dominant category of employment for white women. In absolute numbers, female clerical jobs increased 1,400 percent between 1900 and 1930, with stenography and typing moving from the eighth largest occupational category in 1910 to the third largest in 1930. Overall, the proportion of women workers engaged in nonmanual occupations grew from 28.2 percent in 1910 to 45 percent in 1940. Although much of this change occurred before 1920 (the proportion of women holding clerical and sales jobs, for example, jumped from 17 percent in 1910 to 30 percent in 1920, changing little in the twenty years after that), there could be no gainsaying the significance of this redistribution of jobs, especially in the opportunities it opened for white, middle-class single women—and some married women as well.

Some important changes also took place in the age and marital status of women workers. In the 1890s, the average woman worker was single and under twenty-five; she worked for a few years, then married and left her job. By 1940, however, the median age of women workers had risen to over thirty. At the same time, the percentage of married women seeking employment also increased, moving from 10.7 percent in 1910 to 11.7 percent in 1930 and then climbing dramatically to 15.2 percent in 1940. Married women joined the labor force at a rate five times faster than that of other women and comprised 35 percent of all female employees in 1940—though again, the change was far more dramatic for white married women then for their black counterparts who had long lived with the double day.

Both the upsurge in clerical jobs and the shift in age and marital status of women workers affected women's long-range economic situation. White-collar work provided an important employment possibility for middle- and upper-class women who previously had been unable to find positions commensurate with their social status. Historian Lois Helmboldt has noted that "compared to the drudgery of the factory and the demeaning personal relationships of domestic work, typing, filing, running office machines, and completing other clerical duties appeared to be a glamorous opportunity to take part in the world of business." Many of these jobs, in turn, required the kinds of stylish clothes and appearance that went hand in hand with middle-class status. Thus, the shift toward white-collar positions created a variety of vocational options for middle-class young women that had simply not been available for their mothers and grandmothers. In addition, the increase in the number of working wives established a precedent for women's employment outside the home during and after World War II. The Depression years, in particular, provided a significant acceleration in the long-term growth of married women's participation in the labor force.

Neither of these changes, however, signified the emancipation of women workers. The increase in married women's employment, for example, had little if anything to do with women's freedom to pursue a life outside the home on a basis of equality with men. The greatest jump in employment among wives occurred during the 1930s when half the nation's families earned less than $1,200 annually. Married women worked, not because they sought liberation from the burdens of domesticity or enjoyed a new equality with men in the job market, but so that their families could survive economically. Moreover, the jobs they filled were of the most menial sort, with the greatest increases taking place among white married women displacing black married women from jobs as domestics. Thirty-six percent of married women in the labor force were employed in domestic and personal service, and another 20 percent worked in apparel and canning factories. "None of these occupations . . . is notable for its high wages," Mary Anderson wrote Eleanor Roosevelt, "so it is correct to deduce that the married woman must be at work because her husband's wages are not enough." The poorest states—South Carolina, Mississippi, Louisiana, Georgia, and Alabama—had the highest proportion of married women working. All were concentrated in the area of the country least likely to encourage a revolution in women's status. In 1940, only 5.6 percent of married women held jobs if their husbands earned over $3,000 a year, but 24.2 percent were employed if their husbands received less than $400. In short, rather than illustrating female emancipation, work by wives more often testified to family poverty.

Assertions of a new era of economic independence also overlooked the makeup of the female labor force and the type of positions held by the majority of women workers. As late as 1930, nearly 60 percent of all employed women were either blacks or foreign-born whites. Both groups worked primarily as domestic servants or operatives in apparel industries. Despite the large number of women who took clerical positions during the 1920s, by far the largest bloc of new workers—almost 700,000—served as domestics in the nation's homes, a numerical increase during the decade of more than 60 percent. Such women toiled for ten or twelve hours a day for wages that in many cities did not rise above a dollar a day and that during the depths of the Depression fell to as little as ten cents an hour. Some black domestics, as Elizabeth Clarke-Lewis has shown, were able to win greater autonomy by moving from "live-in" jobs to "day" service, but these victories—however important to the individuals and their families—were only relative. For the most part, these women enjoyed neither the freedom nor independence associated with the "new woman," yet their story describes the economic situation of women in the years after World War I just as much as the emergence of the typist or stenographer.

Significantly, even business and professional women did not benefit that much from the "new freedom." It was the career woman whom many feminists had in mind during their campaign to topple the barriers to female employment. Yet the status of such women improved only slightly in the period from 1920 to 1940. The absolute number of women professionals increased at approximately the same rate as men during the 1920s, and the proportion of women workers engaged in professional life climbed from 11.9 percent to 14.2 percent. But the numerical gains did not signify any expansion of opportunities or represent inroads into fields previously dominated by men. Although more women college graduates now planned to enter business or social-service positions, most graduates still concentrated in careers customarily set aside for women or in occupations newly opened but already dominated by women, such as social work. Three out of four new professional women went into teaching, nursing, or other fields that were "women's" work—jobs that, in most cases, offered little chance for advancement. Grace Abbott observed, "A boy can come home from college, begin the practice of his profession, and advance rapidly in his hometown. But when a girl comes back, what can she do? She can teach, but after she's done that she finds that she has reached the top, that there is nothing more for her." Very few women entered those fields denoted as the "higher professions" dominated by men.

The proportion of architects and lawyers who were women remained almost constant between 1910 and 1930 (less than 3 percent); female enrollment in professional schools increased by only a small amount; and the number of women doctors actually declined from 9,015 to 6,825. On the basis of such facts, one economic historian concluded that the "feminist approach to careers as the main hope for fulfillment faded into obscurity [during the 1920s]."

The coming of the Depression compounded the already tenuous status of women workers. The percentage of women seeking employment reached a new high as a result of the need for women to supplement meager family incomes, but most of the jobs they took were part-time, seasonal, and marginal. The unemployment rate among women was below that of men in 1930, but by the end of the 1930s, the percentage of women out of work exceeded that of men. Women experienced special difficulty in finding work that paid a living wage. One black woman had started to do domestic work in Philadelphia in 1926 for fourteen dollars a week. Seven years later, she took home only five dollars and was making ten cents an hour. Part of the reason was that there were three times as many applicants as jobs in Philadelphia in 1934, and two-thirds of the openings were for domestic servants. The same thing was true in New York, with many black women journeying each morning to "slave markets" near major subway or bus stops where prospective employers would come to hire them—sometimes for only two or three hours at a time— for wages of less than fifteen cents an hour. The woman wage-earner, Senator Robert Wagner concluded, was the "first orphan in the storm."

The deepening economic crisis proved equally damaging to college women interested in entering business or the professions. Teaching jobs almost disappeared from the market because of an oversupply of applicants (many of them male), and the number of teachers who were women fell from 85 percent in 1920 to 78 percent in 1940. The Barnard placement office reported that only one-third of the class of 1932 desiring jobs secured paid work, most of it part-time, and Smith College officials told students that there were no positions open for women with a bachelor's degree only. A graduate education became essential for a woman student desiring a decent position, but even then, most fields of advanced study were excluded. The Institute of Women's Professional Relations advised women students to specialize in home economics and interior decoration in order to avoid competition with men. Only by concentrating in "feminine" occupations, the institute's director declared, could women achieve success. During the Depression, the proportion of all woman workers engaged in professional occupations fell from 14.2 to 12.3 percent, reflecting the extent to which the economic decline had curtailed the opportunities available to prospective career women.

Far from stimulating a revolution in women's work, then, enactment of the Fourteenth Amendment seemed to bring little tangible progress toward the goal of economic equality. Popular articles on the flapper conveyed the impression that women had entered a new era of economic emancipation, yet the overall percentage of women at work remained relatively stable, and despite some numerical gains, aspiring career women failed to break down the barriers to professions traditionally dominated by men. The major statistical shifts in the female labor force occurred before 1920 and although the continued growth of clerical positions offered middle-class young women a greater opportunity to work, there was little basis, on balance, for concluding that women had substantially expanded their economic role or risen to a new level of equality with men.

—— II ——

What remains most striking in retrospect is the persistence of two patterns that highlight the ongoing paradox of women's experience in the workplace. The first is the extraordinary difference in women's work opportunities and treatment based on the variables of class, race, and ethnicity. Clearly, a woman doctor, a white female textile operative, and a black woman domestic had very little in common, either in the circumstances of their work or the life chances they could envision. Yet the second pattern is the prevalence of certain systems of institutionalized discrimination and structural inequality that, despite these differences, created a common fate for all women employees, regardless of their job, their race, or their class. Only when both of these realities are appreciated does the full complexity of women's dilemma in the work force become evident.

Class and race differences were most obvious in the case of domestic work. In most instances, the employer was a relatively well off white woman, not employed herself, who sought to hire help at the lowest wage possible. If carfare and a meal were included in the pay package, the food was often limited to bread and butter, with a prohibition on consumption of any meat or dairy products. During the Depression, Lois Helmboldt notes, employers often took advantage of the crisis both to exploit their workers further and to display their racism, hiring black workers to do the heavy labor and then firing them and employing white women as substitutes. The scenario provided little evidence of sisterhood between either the white woman employer and her hired help or between the workers thrown into bitter competition for the crumbs that were available.

Similar race and class differences operated at the other end of the employment scale. Poor women of whatever background could not afford to apply for clerical jobs because they lacked the financial wherewithal to buy the cosmetics or dresses that were a *sine qua non* for employment. And all such jobs came with the unspoken yet universally understood condition that no blacks, Hispanics, or Asians need apply. Historian Susan Porter Benson writes in her description of the new salesclerks in department stores that employers tried "to match their selling staffs to their desired clientele; this meant always excluding black women and weeding out as much as possible those with a too-obvious immigrant or working-class demeanor."

Cultural differences among various ethnic groups also led to conflicting expectations of the work experience. Mexican-American families, for example, emphasized traditional values, with close-knit kin networks and close surveillance of younger women workers to make sure they were not enticed by the life-styles of the "flapper" or "new woman." In textile mills as well, white rural women worked for mill owners who emphasized the "family" nature of the work experience, with children toiling in one area of the mill, fathers in another, and mothers in still another. In Afro-American families, a younger relative might provide child care and household help while an older woman worked as a "live-in" servant six days a week for a white employer. Needless to say, all these experiences were different from that of a working-class salesclerk or middle-class clerical worker who were more independent of traditional family supervision and "freer" to pursue their own life-styles. In many ways, then, the spectrum of women's employment circumstances reflected the diversity of their class, ethnic, and racial backgrounds, with differences based on race and class far more striking than similarities.

Yet commonalities based on gender also suggest how much a larger structure of sex inequality created shared instrumentalities of discrimination and forms of control. Despite differences of class, education, and ethnicity, for example, both career women and female industrial workers experienced the common fate of being concentrated overwhelmingly in occupations defined as "women's work." Over 40 percent of all women in manufacturing were employed in textile mills or as apparel operatives, and more than 75 percent of female professionals were either teachers or nurses. As a general rule, men worked with men and women with women.

Not surprisingly, sex segregation severely circumscribed opportunities for women in the labor force, once again without regard to their class. Women laborers were discouraged from taking positions as streetcar conductors or steamfitters, just as potential career women were discouraged from becoming doctors and lawyers. The 1920 American Medical Association Directory listed only 40 of 482 general hospitals that accepted women interns, and from 1925 to 1945, American medical schools placed a quota of 5 percent on female admissions. During the 1920s, both Columbia and Harvard Law schools refused to consider women applicants, and as late as 1937, the New York City Bar Association excluded prospective female members.

Women could also share in common the dilemma of being treated as sex objects. Sexual harassment was a frequent occurrence, both in white-collar and blue-collar jobs. One white woman applicant for a secretarial position during the Depression was asked whether she would pose in the nude. Another was told that she should be willing to be a private companion as well as a public worker. Black families were most sensitive to sexual exploitation, since so often their daughters and wives had been assaulted sexually by employers. As a result, one Chicago black woman told an interviewer, "[our] family didn't allow the girls to work because they didn't know who you were going to work with and you couldn't mix and mingle with anybody and everybody." Yet few families could afford to safeguard their daughters when their employment as domestics provided the only margin between starvation and survival.

For most groups of women also, discrimination placed a ceiling on possible job advancement. Women industrial workers rarely became supervisors, and women in the professions only infrequently received promotions or executive responsibility. Despite the fact that women constituted over 80 percent of the nation's teachers, they served as superintendents of schools in only 45 of 2,853 cities. Women teachers were concentrated in the elementary grades, and their numbers declined substantially in the better-paying, more prestigious high-school and college positions. Although women received approximately one-third of all graduate degrees, they comprised only 7.9 percent of the professors in the country's colleges. The disparity prompted widespread despair among female doctoral candidates and led women students at the University of Chicago to protest against the inequitable number of fellowships and teaching positions they received relative to men.

Inadequate pay constituted the most blatant example of women's inferior economic position and plagued women workers in every job category. A survey of 9,000 professional women in 1934 revealed that 50 percent of all teachers, librarians, and social workers had never received a salary of $2,000 and that half the elementary school teachers were paid under $1,500. Women clerical workers in 1931 earned a median wage of $99 a month. The jobs employing the largest number of women, moreover, paid the lowest amounts. Women working in Southern mill towns in 1929 received $9.35 a week, while the average annual, income of household workers in 1940—predominantly black—was $312.60. Throughout industry, women earned at best only 50 to 65 percent of what men were paid, and the Social Security Administration disclosed in 1937 that women workers took home an average of $525 a year in contrast to an annual income of $1,027 for men.

The most dramatic proof of gender discrimination was that women regularly received less pay than men, even when they performed exactly the same work. In 1939, male teachers earned an average salary of $1,953, while females were paid $1,394. Men social workers took home $1,718; women, $1,442. Eighty percent of the women college graduates surveyed by the American Association of University Women reported that they received less pay than men for comparable work. The same pattern of discrimination pervaded the lower occupational categories. A male finisher in the paper-box industry in New York earned $35.50 a week, but a female doing exactly the same work was paid only $17.83.

The plight of women workers was further exacerbated by the public's general unwillingness to think of them as equal participants in the labor force. To a large extent, women's economic involvement in the years after 1900 reflected far-reaching social changes which affected the entire nation. Domestic functions such as clothesmaking and baking had been transferred out of the home and into the factory. The rise of the city meant that fewer and fewer women spent their days tending gardens or helping with farm chores. And the inadequate wages paid most male industrial workers made it necessary for many wives and daughters to take jobs in order to make ends meet.

A few public officials recognized the significance of such developments for women's economic role. During the debate over the creation of the Women's Bureau, one congressional supporter observed that "women, by virtue of the change in the economic conditions of this country, are no longer able to remain in the home. They must go out in the field of actual activity and earn a living." Most people, however, rejected the notion that women should depart from their traditional responsibility in the home. In large part, older definitions of family roles persisted, especially the "patriarchal-employer" conception of the husband. "[T]he tradition lingers," Alice Hamilton wrote in 1930, "that woman's place is in the home, and the social philosophy regarding her status has not changed as rapidly as have the various social and economic organizations." If a few public leaders understood the need to recognize women as economic equals, most shared the opinion of Congressman Joe Eagle of Texas who declared that "woman's work should be making one good man a good wife and properly rearing a family of children."

Perhaps the most pernicious example of public misunderstanding was the widely held belief that women joined the labor force solely to earn extra pocket money. Even experts who should have known better gave credence to the impression. Ralph G. Hurlin, writing the authoritative report on employment for President Hoover's Committee on Recent Social Trends, asserted that many women looked for jobs "as only semi-casuals, seeking pin-money, commonly receiving subsidies" from home. The pin-money hypothesis assumed that women workers were already well-supported and sought a paying job only as a means of securing extra cash to indulge frivolous feminine desires. The theory followed women workers wherever they went and, by implication, justified the inequality from which they suffered. If women were subsidized by their families, there was no compelling reason to treat them as well as men. Employers could rationalize paying women low wages on the grounds that they did not need their earnings to live on, and public officials could dismiss women workers as casual members of the labor force who had no serious grievances.

In fact, the pin-money argument rested on an almost total misapprehension of the reasons for women's employment. Repeated studies by social workers and economists demonstrated that women sought work primarily to help their families and support themselves. As early as 1907, sociologists investigating industrial conditions in Pittsburgh discovered that many women were forced to take jobs because their husbands in the steel mills and railroad yards received wages which were inadequate for family support. A multi-volume study by the government's Bureau of Labor arrived at essentially the same conclusion. As many as one-half of all industrial workers did not earn enough for a decent standard of living, and the family budget could be maintained only if wives and daughters also took jobs. Employers frequently claimed that women did not need high wages because they had no economic responsibilities, but the facts indicated otherwise.

The most convincing refutation of the pin-money theory came from a series of investigations conducted by the Women's Bureau in the 1920s and 1930s. Approximately 90 percent of employed women, the Bureau found, went to work because of economic need and used their income for support of themselves and their dependents. The average family required approximately $1,500 as a minimum for a decent living in the late 1920s, yet most families had an annual income of less than that. Hardest hit by poverty were the immigrant and black families from which the majority of female workers came. Far from seeking extra money for luxuries, then, the primary role of women workers was to provide supplemental income so that their families could buy the food and clothing necessary for survival. "What [married women] are working at such great cost to obtain," a Women's Bureau official wrote, "is a chance for their children to have health and education, for their families to have a satisfactory home life."

One out of every four employed women was the principal wage earner for her family, and as many as 95 percent of working wives contributed all their earnings to family support. Among single women living at home, two out of three gave all their income to the household. On the basis of such facts, Mary Anderson acidly commented that "a woman's so-called pin money is often the family coupling pin, the only means of holding the family together and making ends meet."

Nevertheless, government spokesmen, employers, and public opinion leaders continued to insist that women belonged in the home and that female employment could be tolerated only as a casual dalliance before marriage. Wives who worked came in for special attack. The employment of married women, Mrs. Samuel Gompers declared, took jobs and bread away from men and obstructed the proper fulfillment of women's natural role. "A home, no matter how small," she observed, "is large enough to occupy [a wife's] mind and time." Echoing the same sentiment, the secretary of labor warned in 1923 that the employment of mothers in industry would sooner or later result in the nation's economic system "crashing down about our heads." Women might work for a few years after high school, but they were discouraged from contemplating a full-time career. Women participating in the American Institute of Banking convention in 1923 were told that they were "merely temporary employees" in the nation's banks and businesses and that their ultimate goal should be a return to the home. Even the Women's Bureau—established to protect female workers and educate the public on women's economic role—voiced the opinion that married women's employment represented a dangerous aberration. "The welfare of the home and family is a woman-sized job in itself," the bureau declared, and wives who worked menaced the health and happiness of the home.

Thus, even as women from different social and economic groups experienced a variety of circumstances that separated them and prevented the development of shared concerns, they also suffered from *forms* of institutionalized discrimination that were common to all women and operated uniformly to perpetuate inequality. A white woman textile operative and a black woman laundry worker certainly held different worldviews, and both of them were separated by the barrier of class from a female pediatrician, or even a woman bank clerk; but all of these women, whatever their differences, were "kept in their place" by occupational segregation, a double standard of pay, social attitudes, and outright exclusion from most occupations that conferred wealth and power. Race and class served as instruments of oppression and hierarchy *between* women, but gender itself overlapped these categories to operate independently as an additional source of inequality shared, to some extent, by all women.

—— III ——

In the end, therefore, the experience of women in the economy after 1920 provided little encouragement to those who hoped that political rights would bring economic rights as well. Indeed, a profound gap separated the reality of women's economic situation from public discourse about "the new woman" or the "liberated flapper." Almost all women who sought employment were motivated by pressing economic need; most were poor and black; yet business and political leaders persisted in dismissing these workers as casual seekers after pin money. Although women had supposedly achieved a new degree of freedom from conventional definitions of their "place," most employers continued to treat them as marginal employees and to insist that their real responsibility was in the home. While popular journals were full of commentary on sexual equality, women job seekers were assigned primarily to segregated positions that provided little challenge and even less possibility of advancement—and this experience prevailed notwithstanding the profound differences of circumstance that divided women of varied social and economic backgrounds.

Despite popular impressions, then, the years after 1920 did not represent a time of economic emancipation for women. Partial shifts had taken place, and some women of 1928 undoubtedly felt more freedom than their counterparts of a generation earlier—especially white women for whom there were new horizons of opportunity in white-collar work. But these changes, for the most part, were of degree rather than kind. Most women workers were poorly paid; most were denied the opportunity to participate in occupations not already defined as "women's work"; and most were treated as "temporary" employees, even in business and the professions. In the idealistic years surrounding World War I, it had seemed possible that women might substantially enlarge their economic sphere and achieve a new level of equality in the labor force. A decade later, such hopes had become illusory. Some might emphasize the changes that had occurred, but more accurate was the observation of Alice Rogers Hagar, a labor expert. "The woman," she wrote in 1929, "is nearly always the cheap or marginal worker, and she is expected by the public and employer to remain one."

CHAPTER 5

Women in Industry

ON THE NIGHT of November 23, 1909, thousands of shirtwaist makers gathered at New York's Cooper Union to protest the wages and working conditions in the city's garment industry. Some of the women earned as little as $3.50 a week. Others were forced to buy the needles and thread they used on the job and to pay for their own electricity. In the preceding months, tensions between workers and employers had worsened, and now the women had been called together by the International Ladies Garment Workers Union (ILGWU) to voice their grievances. The meeting progressed in orderly fashion until, suddenly, a young Russian woman stood up and announced that she had heard enough speeches. "I am one who thinks and feels from the things they describe," she declared. "I too have worked and suffered. I am tired of talking. I move that we go on general strike." The young woman's plea electrified the crowd, and within minutes, her motion to strike received thunderous applause. By the next night, over 25,000 garment workers had walked off their jobs.

The "Uprising of the Twenty Thousand," as the strike came to be called, attracted immediate public sympathy. Most of the strikers were women, and their struggle against sweatshop working conditions had an appeal which crossed class and economic lines. When newspapers headlined stories of police brutality on the picket lines, people from a variety of backgrounds rushed to the workers' defense. In a rare and exceptional display of cross-class solidarity, prominent socialites joined in demonstrations outside garment factories; Alva Belmont rented the Hippodrome for a giant rally addressed by leading suffragists; and women's clubs and college students contributed substantial sums to the strike fund. Most important, the garment workers themselves displayed total dedication to the fight. "Thousands of them have come to worship the union," the *New York Times* reported, in a somewhat patronizing tone. "They are not clear about what the union is, what it can do for them, and what they want it to do . . . but the idea of this vague and powerful protector . . . draws them into it."

The garment strike demonstrated the potential of labor organization among women. Although the employers refused to recognize the closed shop, most of them instituted a fifty-two-hour week, limited the use of overtime, and took steps to spread work out over the slack season. The ILGWU grew from a small union of a few hundred before the strike to a mass organization of over 100,000 afterward. A few years later, the Amalgamated Clothing Workers (ACW) scored a similar success in the men's apparel industry. Like the ILGWU, the ACW championed the principle of organizing workers on an industrial rather than a craft basis, and it quickly gained dominance over its rival the United Garment Workers, which had consistently ignored the interests of the rank and file. As a result of the success of both unions, almost half the women workers in the clothing trades had been organized by 1920. The ILGWU represented 65,000; the ACW, 66,000. For the first time, industrial unionism had been successful, and women were in the forefront of the struggle.

—— I ——

If the precedent set by the garment unions had extended to other industries, much of the poor treatment experienced by workers might have been alleviated. The labor movement held the key to the condition of women in industry as much as to that of men. Both male and female workers were underpaid, overworked, and exploited, but in addition to the problems which beset men, women suffered from the heavy burden of discrimination based on sex. They were assigned to the least skilled jobs, given the fewest possibilities for advancement, and treated as the most expendable members of the work force. Even more than men, they lacked the collective strength to combat the methods of unscrupulous employers and needed a labor organization to guarantee their rights.

As it was, however, almost all women outside the garment industry lacked union representation. In 1924, the Women's Bureau surveyed eighty-two unions with jurisdiction over 3 million women workers and found that barely 140,000 women had been organized. Five years later, the Women's Trade Union League (WTUL) upped the estimate to 250,000 out of 4 million, but the change did not signify any radical improvement. Of 471,000 female textile workers, only 20,000 belonged to unions in 1927. Seventy-two thousand women were employed in iron and steel, but only 105 were organized. Overall the labor movement had reached one of every nine male workers but only one of every thirty-four women. Half of all women union members came from the garment industry, indicating the extent to which those in other industries were unorganized and unprotected. It was this overall failure of organized labor to incorporate women that had led many women workers—and the organizations of which they were a part—to turn to the suffrage crusade in the 1910s as a possible avenue to improved working conditions through legislation.

To some extent, the low degree of female participation in the labor movement reflected the type of work women performed. Most women in industry were clustered in low-paying, unskilled jobs in candy factories, textile mills, canneries, apparel centers, and commercial laundries. By virtue of their seasonal nature, many of these jobs entailed substantial turnover, obstructing the development of a permanent, cohesive work force that a union activist could organize effectively. Employers could also use racial and ethnic schisms to segregate workers into different occupations and discourage interracial solidarity. Tobacco factories in North Carolina, for example, fomented racial divisions, hiring black women for the dirtiest jobs and then segregating those women from the white women hired to run the cigarette-making machines. In addition, the labor movement itself had historically proven indifferent to any but the most skilled workers. The majority of its members came from the mining, construction, and transportation industries—areas with few female employees. Since women workers were grouped in occupations that fell outside the mainstream of organized labor's concern, they were largely ignored.

These factors, together with stereotypes about women as "pin-money" workers, persuaded many observers—including friends of women laborers—that women were mere transients in the labor force, with no serious commitment to collective organization. Theresa Wolfson, a labor economist, observed in 1929 that there was a "mental attitude of impermanency among women workers." Rapid job turnover in seasonal industries reinforced the theory that women had no sense of lasting group consciousness. Women industrial workers could be divided into two categories, the social activist Alice Hamilton noted in 1924: the young who were "reckless of health . . . and individualistic," and the old who were tired from carrying a double burden of housework and factory work. Neither group, Hamilton observed, had the interest or the time for union activity.

Fundamentally, however, women failed to join the trade-union movement in greater numbers because they were not welcome before the late 1930s. Although labor claimed with some justification that women were in jobs that made organizing difficult, the example of the garment workers suggested that where an opportunity for collective action presented itself, many women responded with enthusiasm. As we shall see later, there were similar examples in Southern textile mills and California canneries. If unions had tried seriously to organize women workers, their protestations about female indifference might have carried more credibility. With the exception of the garment industry, however, there was little evidence that such an effort had been made. The American Federation of Labor treated women workers with open hostility. And the Women's Trade Union League (WTUL)—the group to which others looked for leadership—proved inadequate for the task.

—— II ——

The WTUL was established in 1903 by a coalition of settlement-house workers and labor officials "to assist in the organization of women workers into Trade Unions." Its seriousness of purpose was attested to by the background of its founders. Mary Kenney, a former bindery worker, had organized the women of Boston into a "Ladies Federal Union." Leonora O'Reilly, a shirt-collar worker from New York, had gone back to school to finish her education so that she could devote her life to the labor movement. The women from the settlement houses had an equally distinguished history of affiliation with trade unions. At Hull House, Alice Hamilton recalled, "one got into the labor movement as a matter of course." Mary McDowell of the University of Chicago Settlement helped to form the first women's union in the meatpacking industry, and settlement houses in other cities provided meeting space and moral encouragement for budding labor groups. It was natural, therefore, for social reformers to join trade-union women in spearheading a drive to help women "secure conditions necessary for healthful and efficient work and to obtain a just return for such work."

In the first few years of its existence, the league gave some evidence of fulfilling its purpose as a labor organization. Although many of its members were involved with middle-class reform groups such as the National Consumers League, the WTUL consciously sought to follow the lead of working women themselves and explicitly stated in its constitution that trade unionists should compose a majority of the executive board. Mary Dreier of the New York league observed in 1909 that while passing laws was necessary, organizing women into unions was more important, "for we know that the greatest power to enforce labor laws is trade unions, and a strong trade union can demand better conditions and shorter hours than the law will allow." Pursuing such a philosophy, the league played a major role in the shirtwaist makers' strikes of 1909 and 1910. League leaders recruited women for the union, organized a parade of ten thousand workers to protest the arrest of peaceful picketers, and mobilized hundreds of volunteers to demonstrate outside the garment factories. Almost singlehandedly, Mary Dreier coordinated strike activities, and the WTUL's assistance was as important as any other factor in the ILGWU's victory.

By 1913, however, the league had shifted its emphasis away from organization and toward education and legislation. To some extent, the change in strategy represented a pragmatic response to events. The Triangle Shirtwaist fire of 1911 had demonstrated the need for a radical improvement in factory conditions, and it became increasingly obvious that only statewide legislation could mandate the sweeping reforms that were essential. Consequently, the league devoted more and more of its energies to building public support for stringent new health and safety laws. In addition, local league chapters encountered growing difficulty in their relations with established unions. The New York WTUL expected to exercise a dominant voice in the internal affairs of the labor movement as a result of its contribution to the garment workers' victory, but many unions interpreted the league's intentions as interference and an attempt to impose direction from outside. The issue came to a head when the White Goods Workers of New York called a strike without consulting the WTUL's leadership. The walk-out caused consternation among league members, and although it ended successfully, league leaders began to reassess the value of working directly with unions and to place more emphasis on legislative reform. Class differences, it seemed, were creating a clash of perspectives and priorities between unions and the league.

Basically, however, the shift in emphasis reflected a redistribution of power within the WTUL itself. From the very beginning, the league had tried to serve two constituencies—reformers and unionists—each of which had its own conception of how the league should pursue its goals. Reformers viewed the WTUL's primary function as educational and believed that the interests of the workers could best be served by investigating industrial conditions, securing legislative action, and building public support for the principle of trade unionism. Women unionists, on the other hand, insisted that organizing women and strengthening existing unions represented the league's principal purpose. One group perceived the WTUL as primarily an instrument of social uplift, the other as an agency for labor organization.

The division of opinion was demonstrated most clearly over the issue of who should belong to the league. Reformers encouraged rich "allies" or "sympathizers" to become members and provide financial support for league activities. The "allies" were urged to exhibit "great patience, lofty faith, and unalterable humility" and to remember that "the girls . . . must ever be the movement." Yet their participation inevitably created tension. Unionists looked with distaste on the presence of so many prominent socialites and feared that their influence would compromise the WTUL's integrity. Leonora O'Reilly temporarily resigned in 1905 because she doubted the league's commitment to organize women workers; four years later, her fellow unionist Josephine Casey left for the same reason. Although the league provided courageous leadership during the garment strikes, its members were not required to subscribe to the principle of a union shop, and many chapters were dominated by "allies" who at times seemed more interested in sponsoring "Union Balls" and teas than in organizing women factory workers.

The conflict between unionists and reformers was held in check in the years before the garment strikes, but in the years afterward, the reformers gradually gained the upper hand, at least in part because the suffrage fight—and their involvement in it—seemed to provide a more promising means to improve women's working conditions through legislation. Because of their wealth and influence, "allies" exercised considerable control over the league's fate, and many of them preferred the process of legislative change—a much more typical middle-class approach—to worker organization. The New York league set the trend for the national WTUL when it established a legislative committee in 1913; thereafter, other chapters as well began to focus primarily on publicity and lobbying activities. The change in emphasis was not without controversy, and a strong minority continued to insist that unionization of women represented the league's primary responsibility. But a shift in philosophical orientation had occurred, and with the passage of time, the WTUL became more and more a group dedicated to legislature change rather than labor organization. It retained its basic goal of improving the economic condition of women workers, but its methods increasingly reflected the attitude of reformers rather than trade unionists.

The league's national president, Margaret Dreier Robins, personified the reform approach. Endowed with a warm personality and a considerable fortune, she actively espoused Progressive causes. After marrying the popular lecturer Raymond Robins, she went to live in a Chicago tenement to share the life of those she sought to help. Passionately concerned with social justice, Robins protested against the persecution of radicals and anarchists and lent her name and prestige to innumerable reform crusades. During the Chicago garment strikes, she organized a commissary for hungry workers, appointed a platoon of distinguished women to oversee the conduct of city police, and formed a respected citizens committee which condemned sweatshop conditions and urged unionization of the workers. She financed a large share of the league's activities and more than any other person shaped its policies in the years after 1910.

Robins's social philosophy centered on uplift of the workers. The primary value of the trade-union movement, she believed, was that it called forth "personality." "The social gains of the union shop are not generally better wages and shorter hours," she declared. "Beyond these is the incentive for initiative and social leadership. . . . The union shop calls up the moral and reasoning faculties, the sense of fellowship." Robins's primary concern was to impart the vision of a better life to the young working woman. In that task, education in the arts and humanities played an important part. Poetry reading, concerts, and classes in literature filled the extracurricular programs sponsored by local chapters. "The League believed that the first need of these girls was the awakening of their imagination and sense of beauty," Robins noted in 1920. "The dullness and monotony of factory life had starved them of the very essentials of a young girl's life." Clearly, these were concerns that said as much about Robins's upper-class socialization as about the priorities of working-class women.

In her own way, Robins made a distinct contribution to the league's growth and prestige. Her connections gave the organization access to the highest levels of government and some of the wealthiest individuals in the country. Moreover, her capacity for leadership made the WTUL one of the most influential members of the Progressive coalition. During the garment strikes in Chicago, she brilliantly used her social position to build a broad base of support for the workers, and her contacts with other liberal reformers ensured that the league's voice would be listened to with respect on most social-welfare issues. Nevertheless, her basic approach was that of a missionary rather than an organizer. She dedicated herself to helping the downtrodden, but she lacked the background and temperament which would have enabled her to treat the workers as equals and mobilize them into an effective industrial force. Ironically, the very qualities that made her a successful reform leader prevented her from transforming the league into a true labor organization. Her frame of reference remained that of an upper-class "do-gooder," creating inevitable differences of perception and priorities with workers themselves.

Trade unionists continued to protest the League's sense of priorities, and one troubled member commented with dismay on the absence of a clear commitment to work directly with women in industry. "The purpose of the League as I understand it is to organize workers into trade union groups," she reported in 1921, "and yet at the convention little time was given to this question." Such observations caused league leaders to engage in frequent self-examination. Their crisis of identity reached a peak in 1925 when the treasurer, concerned with falling revenues, insisted that the league define once and for all its reason for existence. Contributions from friendly unions, she pointed out, had declined from 10 percent of the total budget in 1920 to 3 percent in 1925. Over 90 percent of total revenues came from "allies," many of whom "would not find favor in trade union ranks." Furthermore, the greater the league's dependence on "sympathizers," the less time it spent on organizing unions. Executive Secretary Elizabeth Christman agreed that the time had come for the league to reassess its status. She pointed out to board members that only two chapters out of twelve employed organizers, that only three had budgets, and that league membership had fallen to an appallingly low figure. "It would be illuminating to know," Christman concluded, "how great a contribution to the labor movement is represented in the above summary."

As it had done so often in the past, the executive board responded by reaffirming that organization constituted "the heart" of its work. To implement its resolve, the league mounted an ambitious campaign to help unionize Southern textile workers, dispatching its only organizer, Matilda Lindsay, to Richmond to set up a regional office. Although a significant degree of union insurgency was already taking place in the South, the league had taken on a difficult task, and Lindsay did surprisingly well, especially in the textile uprisings that took place in Marion, North Carolina, and Danville, Virginia, in 1929 and 1930. Jacquelyn Hall has shown in her work on Elizabethton, Tennessee, and Janet Irons has found in her study of the general textile strike of 1934 that women workers were already playing a decisive role in banding together against employers, albeit through the use of their own locally based and regionally rooted forms of organization.

Once again, however, the league could not escape the inevitable proclivity of its leadership for education. The principal thrust of the Southern drive was devoted to "interpreting . . . the aims of the League," and to securing the "cooperation of understanding people who themselves are not in the tobacco or textile mills." In short, the league was seeking to reach out to "opinion" leaders of the middle and upper classes. Yet the workers themselves, in places like Elizabethton, were using tactics—including some that flaunted working-class attitudes toward sexuality—that expressed contempt for bourgeois sensibilities and a clear preference for expression of class conflict and pride rather than accommodation. The league's efforts may have been helpful in developing a sympathetic climate of opinion among a minority of community leaders, but "finding friends among the thinkers of the South" was not the same thing as organizing workers within the mills.

Despite a divided conscience, therefore, the league remained most concerned with converting the world outside the factory to its point of view. Although it performed distinguished service as an agent of unionism during the garment strikes of 1909 and 1910, its primary focus was on educating the public about the condition of women workers and developing support for legislative reform. In the latter task, it was frequently an effective force for social-welfare innovations, as witnessed by the critical role many of its members played in Eleanor Roosevelt's network of women reformers, and it would be a mistake to underestimate its importance as part of the Progressive coalition of the 1910s and 1920s. But given the criterion of its original purpose, the WTUL's record was one of disappointment. By the 1930s, the league's annual budget had fallen below $10,000, and its last full-time field representative had resigned. A skeletal staff continued in Washington until 1950, but in substance, the league was dead. The one national group dedicated in theory to unionizing women workers, it expired without ever having approached its goal. Part of the problem was the obvious difficulty of organizing unskilled workers in seasonal jobs where employers could use ethnic and racial tensions as a barrier to unionization. But in a deeper sense, the league also contributed to its own failure. Despite its profession of cross-class unity and solidarity, it could not overcome the profound conflict of worldviews and priorities that grew out of the difference between working-class and middle- or upper-class backgrounds. Torn between these two conflicting points of view, it never made the lasting commitment to unionism which was a prerequisite for even the chance of success. Perhaps, given the power of class as well as race to divide women from each other, the choice for unionism was never even a possibility.

—— III ——

Yet in our overall assessment, the primary blame for the failure to organize women must rest with the American Federation of Labor (AF of L) itself. Always committed more to the recruitment of skilled crafts workers than industrial labor, the AF of L was even more retrograde when organizing blacks or women. Participating in the dominant culture's stereotypical prejudice toward minorities, union leaders actively discouraged any effort to make the ranks of membership more inclusive.

In large part because of the WTUL's ambivalence toward organization, the AF of L treated it with distrust from the beginning. Samuel Gompers, president of the AF of L, told a 1905 league convention that the unionization of women "is not a work of charity. . . . It is instituted so that the girls and the women may be placed in a position where they may be helped to help themselves." Gompers had little use for intellectual reformers who were primarily concerned with uplifting the poor and examining workers "under the lenses of a microscope." Although he provided verbal support and financial aid to the WTUL, he clearly had reservations about its credentials as a full-fledged labor organization. WTUL representatives were barred from the AF of L's 1905 convention because Gompers claimed that the fate of the entire working class was involved and that his members would resent the presence of outsiders. Reflecting the same suspicion of the league's motivation, the Carpenter's Union insisted that its 1915 contribution of $500 be spent only on work approved by the AF of L. When league leaders protested, the Carpenter's chief charged them with disloyalty to the labor movement and indifference toward the organization of women workers.

Yet the AF of L itself did almost nothing to unionize women. Despite repeated requests, Gompers failed to hire a full-time woman organizer until 1918. The federation leadership, in the eyes of one observer, "was guided solely by St. Paul in its policy toward even skilled women." Like the author of the letters to the early church, AF of L leaders seemed to believe that women should be obedient and silent. Both Gompers and his successor William Green attacked the presence of married women in the work force and asserted that women should direct their energies toward getting married and raising a family. The AF of L refused to support a strike by female telephone operators in Boston, and the International Moulder's Union resolved at its twenty-fifth convention to restrict the employment of women in all foundries, with the ultimate goal of ending work by women in any job "recognized as men's employment." The problem with most union leaders, Katherine Fisher observed in 1921, was that too many of them believed in "men's right to dictatorship over women."

To some extent, the AF of L's indifference to women workers represented a calculated decision that the benefits to be gained from an organizing campaign did not justify the expense and effort involved. Even during the garment strikes, Gompers had questioned whether "poor undernourished, stunted, weak girls could maintain sufficient cohesiveness and force and determination" to form a permanent union. If women were transients in the labor force, as Gompers evidently believed, there was little sense in organizing them one day, only to see them replaced by new workers the next. Furthermore, the labor movement had only limited resources, and male union leaders reasoned that the strengthening of existing craft unions constituted the best investment they could make, especially given their conviction that women could be helped most if their husbands earned enough to support the entire family. The decade of the 1920s witnessed a concerted campaign by employers to roll back the gains of organized labor. The ILGWU's membership fell from 120,000 to 40,000, and other unions suffered similar reverses. In a time of peril for labor, some AF of L leaders argued that it was better to safeguard unions already in existence than to embark on an expensive and risky new campaign to organize women.

Too often, however, the AF of L's actions seemed to be motivated by hidebound conservatism and, on occasion, outright bias and stupidity. Even when women workers organized themselves, they were denied recognition. In New York, when women printers who worked side by side with men applied for membership in the International Typographical Union, they were turned down on the ground that they were unskilled. Candy workers in Philadelphia, hairdressers in Seattle, and streetcar conductors in Cleveland all received a similar response. Women could not stay together, the unions said; consequently, they could not be admitted to membership. The result, Philadelphia candy workers charged, was that the AF of L was responsible for "allowing an organization already formed to go to pieces by refusing to give the guidance . . . necessary."

The AF of L's attitude toward women was disclosed most revealingly in 1921 when the WTUL petitioned the AF of L executive council to issue federal charters permitting women to organize in sexually segregated unions. The same device had partially mitigated the problem of discrimination against blacks, and the WTUL proposed it as an acceptable, if not desirable, alternative to membership in the established internationals. Once again, however, the AF of L refused to cooperate, arguing that it could not issue charters unless authorized to do so by its constituent craft unions. Responding to the WTUL's request, the vice president of the Street Railway Union declared that "the rear end of a street car is [no] place for a woman." On the basis of such reasoning, the AF of L rejected the WTUL's petition. When the women accused the executive council of prejudice, Gompers replied that the AF of L discriminated against "any non-assimilable race," leaving the unmistakable impression that women might never be fully integrated into the labor movement. A vicious circle was thus created. Most of the internationals that asserted jurisdiction over women in male-dominated industries refused to admit women. The AF of L executive council, in turn, rebuffed women's attempt to establish sexually segregated locals. The result was that even in those areas of industry where women had contact with organized labor, they were denied the support necessary to protect themselves through union representation.

In such a situation, cooperation between the AF of L and the WTUL represented the only opportunity for progress. For a brief period after the Supreme Court invalidated minimum wages for women in the 1923 *Adkins* case, the AF of L revived interest in unionizing female workers. The Court's action raised the specter of women undercutting men in competition for jobs, and the AF of L convention recommended in 1924 that "especial attention be devoted during the coming year to the complete organization of women wage earners . . . not only for their own protection but for the protection of men."

Gompers spoke of creating a special women's bureau within the AF of L and corresponded with Mary Anderson and Elizabeth Christman about the possibility of a joint venture.

Organizational jealously doomed the effort before it got started, however. Margaret Dreier Robins viewed the Gompers proposal as a direct threat to the continued existence of the WTUL and refused to contemplate the demise of her own group until the AF of L proved that it was really committed to helping women workers. The AF of L, on the other hand, charged that the WTUL was a largely academic group that had repeatedly shown itself inadequate to the task of unionization. The only course which might have resolved the conflict—choosing a WTUL person to head the new AF of L bureau—was rejected out of hand by leading elements within the AF of L, who alternately protested the employment of a WTUL staff member and claimed that they could not find another woman capable of handling the job. Thus, the tentative effort to build a new coalition collapsed. The AF of L campaign to unionize women was so "puny and half-hearted," one observer noted, "that practically nothing was accomplished."

In the absence of labor interest in recruiting women, government action offered the only hope for safeguarding women industrial workers. Many middle-class reformers felt more at home with legislative protection than with trade unionism in any event, and during the years after 1890, they pressed vigorously for state regulation of wages and hours as a solution for women's economic plight. The movement to limit hours received official sanction when the Supreme Court ruled in 1908 that preservation of a woman's health fell within the proper police powers of the state. Using the Court's decision in the *Muller* case as a springboard, reform groups such as the National Consumers League embarked on a nationwide crusade to place a floor under women's wages as well as a ceiling over their hours. A pay scale sufficient for the necessities of life, the Consumers League argued, was just as essential to a woman's health and morals as reasonable hours of labor. Responding to the league's appeal, Massachusetts enacted the first minimum-wage law in 1912 and was followed in the next eleven years by fourteen other states.

The Supreme Court, however, dashed reform hopes that protective legislation might sweep the nation. In the 1923 *Adkins* case, a conservative majority led by Justice George Sutherland declared that Washington, D.C.'s minimum-wage law was unconstitutional because it violated a woman's freedom to bargain directly with her employer for the value of her services. Although women had previously been exempted from the freedom-of-contract doctrine on the grounds that they deserved special protection, Justice Sutherland ruled that the Nineteenth Amendment obviated the need for such statutes by establishing the equality of the sexes. The judge's reasoning seemed specious at best, given the de facto inequality from which women suffered, but it placed an effective constitutional barrier in the way of enacting additional laws that singled out women for special consideration. In addition, it seemed to uphold the National Woman's Party contention that women should be treated the same as men and not as a separate group.

The *Adkins* decision thoroughly demoralized reform groups because it removed the principal grounds on which they had sought legislative help. In the wake of the judicial action, minimum-wage statutes were struck down in Arizona, Arkansas, Kansas, and Wisconsin, while in other states similar laws fell into disuse due to fear of legal challenge by employers. The Court, Florence Kelley declared, had taken "progress backward," and written a "new *Dred Scott* decision" which guaranteed the "inalienable right of women to starve." Without judicial sanction, there seemed little chance that women could secure the protection they needed through labor laws. "Under the present Constitution, interpreted by the present Court," Kelley concluded, "all effort to improve industrial conditions . . . is purely academic." Only a new philosophy on the Court, and a substantial shift in circumstances could improve the legislative prospects for women workers.

—— IV ——

The New Deal and the Depression helped to bring about both conditions. In an effort to mitigate the suffering caused by unemployment and hard times, the government was forced to take ameliorative action, regardless of the Supreme Court's attitude toward social-welfare legislation. Prompted by reports of women receiving starvation wages and sleeping on subways, public officials started a new campaign to safeguard female workers from exploitation. Seven state legislatures enacted minimum-wage laws in the early 1930s; governors throughout the Northeast banded together to regulate women's working conditions; and the Roosevelt administration established the National Recovery Administration (NRA) with authority to institute industry-wide codes regulating wages and hours. Perhaps the most important step forward was the enactment of the federal Fair Labor Standards Act (FLSA) of 1938. The statute established the unprecedented principle that the federal government had the right to control the wages and hours of both men and women engaged in occupations related to interstate commerce. Although the act contained excessive compromises—permitting a differential in wages between the North and South and setting an initial minimum wage of only twenty-five cents an hour for a forty-four-hour week—it inaugurated a potentially far-reaching course of government intervention in the economy.

For a brief period, the Supreme Court continued to block the implementation of such laws. Within one eighteen-month span in 1935–36, it struck down the NRA, a federal law regulating the pay of miners, and New York's statute setting a minimum wage for women. The Court abruptly reversed itself, however, when public outrage and the decisive reelection of President Roosevelt indicated that popular opinion was running in a different direction. A few weeks after the chief executive announced his plan to enlarge the Supreme Court, the judges overruled their own decision in the *Adkins* case and upheld a minimum-wage law that duplicated in almost every respect the New York measure they had invalidated nine months earlier. The Court followed its action in the *West Coast Hotel v. Parrish* case with a series of positive rulings on other New Deal measures and in 1941 upheld the constitutionality of the Fair Labor Standards Act in the case of *U.S. v. Darby*. Although Florence Kelley did not live to see the day, her hope for a judicial and constitutional revolution had been partially realized.

The minimum-wage laws passed during the 1930s substantially improved the situation of women workers on the lowest rung of the economic ladder. In May 1933, about 84 percent of the female laundry workers in New York City earned less than thirty-one cents an hour. Eighteen months later, after passage of the New York minimum-wage statute, the figure had dropped to 1.4 percent. The National Industrial Recovery Act (NIRA) had a similar effect. In the textile industry, where women comprised 39 percent of the work force, average weekly earnings increased from $10.85 in 1932 to $13.06 in 1935. Forty percent of the women laundry workers in Connecticut were paid less than twenty-five cents an hour in 1932, but two years later, the proportion had declined to 1.3 percent. The Fair Labor Standards Act resulted in an increase of wages for one out of every four workers in the needle trades (166,000) and for 120,000 textile workers. In addition, New Deal legislation helped to eradicate some of the worst abuses of the sweatshop system. The NRA prohibited homework in most industries—employment which paid as little as five to eight cents an hour—and the FLSA decreed that persons who did perform such work must receive the same minimum wage as those employed in the factory.

The most important contribution of the New Deal, however, was its support of legislation protecting the right of unions to organize free of employer interference. Section 7(a) of the NIRA asserted that the workers of any industry had the right to choose their own collective bargaining agent, and when 7(a) was invalidated by the Supreme Court—along with the NIRA— the Wagner Act took its place, providing additional administrative machinery to ensure that unionists would not be discriminated against. Both laws offered a much needed incentive to organized labor, and unions which had been on the defensive throughout the 1920s embarked on vigorous organizing campaigns. The ILGWU—down to 40,000 members in 1933—used 7(a) as a basis for reasserting its control over the ladies' garment industry. The union sent out organizers immediately after passage of the NIRA to consolidate its strength before industry codes were adopted, and a timely strike by dressmakers resulted in a growth in membership of the New York Joint Dress Board from 10,000 to 70,000 in two weeks. Under the NIRA, 95 percent of the workers in the cloak and silk-dress industry were unionized, and the ILGWU's rank and file grew to 200,000 in two years—an increase of 500 percent.

The formation of the Congress of Industrial Organizations (CIO) marked the most dramatic advance for women in trade unionism. Even under the protective aegis of the New Deal, the AF of L had refused to commit itself to organize unskilled workers on an industrial basis and had defended the right of craft unions to restrict their memberships. The CIO, however, set out to recruit workers without regard to skill, or sex, and in the years after 1935 engaged in a massive effort to organize the rank and file of the automobile, electrical, and textile industries, all of which contained a substantial proportion of women employees. Not all the campaigns met with immediate success, but the CIO's commitment to a policy of industrial unionism meant that for the first time women workers interested in collective representation had a powerful ally within the labor movement.

The history of the textile workers—almost 40 percent of whom were women—illustrated the transformation accomplished by the creation of the CIO. The United Textile Workers (UTW) had built a union of 110,000 members by 1920, largely as a result of gains made during World War I. In the next decade, however, the UTW crumbled. A series of disastrous strikes decimated its ranks, and the number of workers in the cotton mills who were organized fell from 80,000 in 1920 to 13,000 in 1930. In part, the collapse reflected the absence of AF of L financial assistance at critical junctures. More important, however, were the union's own reactionary policies. Repeatedly, the UTW used unskilled and foreign-born workers to march on its picket lines, only to refuse them membership in the union lest the skilled craftsmen be outnumbered. Like the garment workers, the women showed themselves willing to risk their jobs for the labor movement, but their devotion was not reciprocated. The UTW's leadership settled disputes without consulting the rank and file and even went so far as to break strikes called by other labor organizations seeking to help the unskilled workers. Although the UTW enjoyed a brief revival under the NIRA, it suffered a grievous setback in the 1934 textile strike, and by 1935, its membership had fallen from a high of over 200,000 in 1933 to 20,000. Overall, the UTW represented the worst of the AF of L's approach to mass-production employees.

The UTW leadership also reflected the persistent refusal of the AF of L to be attentive to the distinctive quality of women workers and the need to orient organizing activities toward women's special concerns and values. All too often, Alice Kessler-Harris has pointed out, male leaders insisted on imposing their own values and style on women, completely insensitive to the fact that women might have their own insights into organizational strategy. Thus, one union refused to organize married or Gentile women because they allegedly cared less about union ideology or job security. Yet as Jacquelyn Hall has shown, in many Southern communities these women were the backbone of the union effort and deserved support. Being married, wrote one union vice president in protest, made women "independent and full of fighting spirit," not mild-mannered and indifferent. Still, the AF of L seemed almost congenitally incapable of recognizing women's own needs and interests.

The CIO immediately reversed this policy of ignoring women and unskilled workers. Through what amounted to a *coup d'état*, CIO leaders forced the UTW to accept the direction of an ad hoc Textile Worker's Organizing Committee (TWOC), analagous to a similar committee formed to mobilize the steelworkers. The TWOC spearheaded a comprehensive drive to organize unskilled workers in textile mills throughout the country. Led by people like Sidney Hillman and funded by a substantial war chest, the TWOC developed strong, entrenched locals throughout the South. Women who once walked picket lines only to be ignored by union chieftains now proudly wore the button of the Textile Worker's Union of America (TWUA). Because the union demonstrated its staying power and represented the collective commitment of a nationwide organization, the TWUA earned the trust of the workers and succeeded in multiplying the number of union members in the cotton mills from 20,000 in 1936 to 120,000 in 1943.

CIO unions also proved more attentive to the ethnic and cultural priorities of different groups of women workers. Historian Vicki Ruiz has demonstrated how effectively the United Cannery, Agriculture, Packing and Allied Workers of America (UCAPAWA) worked with Mexican-American women to improve their lot and build a union. Coming out of a traditional, family-oriented culture, the Mexican-American women in the canneries sought primarily to enhance the status and living standards of their families of origin. By recognizing the priority of such values, UCAPAWA was able to mobilize the women so that they became leaders of the union. Dedicated activists, the Mexican-American women held the highest percentage of shop stewardships and committee positions in the union, helping to make its 1939 organizing effort a great success.

As a result of such CIO victories and the revival of protective legislation for both men and women at the end of the New Deal, prospects for easing the plight of women in industry had clearly been enhanced. Any woman in a job that was related to interstate commerce could look to the federal government for help in the fight against exploitation, and persons employed in mass-production industries could anticipate the possibility of additional empowerment through union representation. The courts no longer posed an obstacle to social-welfare measures, and the Roosevelt administration was more committed than any of its predecessors to providing some help for those least able to help themselves.

But even with such progress, women continued to experience a substantial amount of discrimination based on sex. Under the NIRA, for example, one out of every four industry codes permitted women to receive a lower minimum wage than men; moreover, the businesses affected were precisely those which employed the largest percentage of women workers. In the cloak and suit industry, women were assigned a basic wage ten cents an hour lower than men. The same discrepancy appeared in the electrical industry, where 40 percent of all workers were females. Women who were employed in laundries were permitted to earn as little as fourteen cents an hour, while waitresses in some areas received only twelve cents. Despite the benefits of government protection, female workers gained at a lesser rate than males and suffered from a persistent pattern of discrimination.

Furthermore, protective legislation by itself did not necessarily ensure an across-the-board improvement in women's economic condition. In both California and New York—the nation's leading industrial states—poor enforcement weakened the positive impact of minimum-wage orders. Observing that the New York law covered only 80,000 of the 1,080,000 women it was designed to affect, Elinore Herrick of the National Consumers League suggested that the government might better devote its energies to implementing statutes already on the books rather than enact additional protective laws. Even where minimum-wage laws were enforced, moreover, they frequently mandated pay scales which fell below the level needed to purchase basic necessities. In 1933, New York ruled that a laundry worker must receive $12.41 a week, yet the city's Welfare Council set $16 as the minimum essential for a decent standard of living. The FLSA established a minimum wage of 25 cents an hour for a forty-four-hour week as its original standard, but an $11 weekly paycheck was not enough to survive on in many areas of the country. Thus while wage and hour statutes helped to eliminate the worst instances of industrial exploitation, they did not provide a solution to the problem of low wages or lead to an end of economic deprivation.

Most important, inequality continued to pervade the ranks of organized labor, even in those unions which were most progressive. Although the membership of the Amalgamated Clothing Workers was divided almost equally between men and women, the union sanctioned lower wages for females than for males and granted women only token recognition in its hierarchy of officers. In the ILGWU, where three out of every four members were women, only one woman served on the twenty-four-person executive board as late as 1940. A total of 800,000 women had been organized by the end of the 1930s— a 300 percent increase over ten years earlier—but in many industries women union members were grouped in sexually segregated locals. Labor contracts frequently included provisions for unequal pay between men and women, and women were assigned to separate seniority lists so that they could not interfere with the accumulated privileges of male workers. Inside as well as outside the union movement, women were still thought of primarily as transients in the labor force. They might be given protection, but they did not receive the same treatment or consideration as men.

Moreover, despite the attentiveness of some CIO unions like UCAPAWA to ethnic differences and the distinctive values of women, class and racial circumstances continued to dictate the condition of those workers who were worst off. In each part of the country, domestic workers suffered a continuing decline in wages, with no protection from either government or unions. Whether they were blacks in the South, Italians or Slavs in the Northeast, Mexican-Americans in the Southwest, or Asians in the West, whichever ethnic group occupied the bottom rank among minority groups in a given area also filled the most menial jobs. In addition, the ability of employers to use intergroup ethnic tensions to divide and conquer workers continued to frustrate efforts at unionization in many industries.

—— V ——

The condition of women workers in 1940 thus contained elements which justified both pessimism and optimism. On the one hand, the legislative innovations of the New Deal provided minimum standards of wages and hours for those engaged in interstate commerce. If a cotton garment worker still received only $11 a week under the Fair Labor Standards Act, she at least knew that her wage would not fall below that level and that the federal government was her ally in fighting the abuses of sweatshop labor. Equally important, the philosophy of trade unionism had changed, and for the first time, a national labor organization was committed to providing collective protection for people performing unskilled work in mass-production industries. The number of women actually enrolled in unions had increased, and the dynamic effectiveness of the CIO had only just begun to make itself felt.

On balance, however, persistent economic deprivation remained the most striking characteristic of women workers. As late as 1939, twenty-one states still had no minimum-wage laws for women, twenty-nine failed to regulate industrial homework, and thirty were without eight-hour statutes. Even where protective legislation did exist, it affected primarily those who were at the bottom of the economic ladder and did not signify an improvement for all women workers. Despite some inroads, a relatively small percentage of women were unionized, and the CIO registered its greatest impact after 1940, not before. At the close of the decade, women workers, for the most part, remained an oppressed group. The overwhelming majority still earned barely a living wage, and most were concentrated in "marginal" areas of the economy where turnover was frequent. Though there were some signs that the future might be better than the past, it was still too early to be optimistic.

To some extent, the absence of greater progress could be attributed to historical conditions which made difficult any transformation of the labor force. The type of work women performed, for example, loomed large as a barrier to labor organization. Similarly, attempts to enact protective legislation were frustrated for a long period by the reactionary rulings of the Supreme Court. The judicial philosophy that prevailed from 1923 to 1937 had roots not directly related to the issue of women's economic condition, but women workers were among the foremost victims of the Court's *laissez-faire* policy. At least in part, then, the ill-treatment accorded women in industry was a by-product of circumstances beyond the control of workers or unions.

Yet such an explanation fails to answer the deeper problems posed by the experience of women industrial workers. The garment strikes and repeated walkouts of textile workers had amply demonstrated that many women *wanted* to be organized and were willing to do their part. Similarly, the WTUL's success in unionizing activities before 1913 suggested that under different policies and leadership, an approach more conducive to the organization of women workers *might* have been followed. Finally, the AF of L had exhibited during the entire period an unnecessarily hostile approach toward the unionization of women. Even given the problems that existed, AF of L leaders displayed an attitude toward women workers that was myopic at best.

In all of this, of course, problems of class conflict between reformers and workers and of ethnic divisions between different groups of women posed a structural barrier to women's solidarity and progress. But it is at least conceivable that a different set of responses by trade-union leaders and others might have substantially altered the fate of women workers. The objective impediments to progress were substantial, and it would be wrong to view discrimination based on sex as the *only* reason for the condition of women in industry. In assessing the experience of women in these years though, it is difficult not to conclude that their condition was rooted in an unspoken but powerful assumption—that women, as women, did not deserve good jobs, decent pay, or fair union representation. Until that reality changed, there was little likelihood that the basic status of women workers would improve.

CHAPTER 6

From Feminists to Flappers:
College and Career Women

ALTHOUGH THE EXPERIENCE of women in industry was pivotal to long-range prospects for equality, many feminists placed their immediate hopes for progress on the young college women who came of age during the early twentieth century. For reasons of economic necessity, the daughters of the poor had always worked outside the home; but most middle- and upper-class women had refrained from taking jobs, conforming instead to the convention that a woman's proper place was to be a housewife and mother. Now, many women's rights leaders hoped for a reversal of that pattern, with women college graduates seizing the opportunity to assert their equality with men in business and the professions, breaking down, in Carrie Chapman Catt's words, "all artificial barriers which laws and customs interpose between women and human freedom. . . ."

As if to reinforce such hopes, the number of women pursuing higher degrees skyrocketed during the early years of the century. Ten percent of all graduate students in 1890 were women, but this figure rose to 41 percent in 1918, a 2,000 percent increase in absolute numbers. Women's college enrollments increased as well, leaping 1,000 percent in public colleges and 482 percent in private schools from 1900 to 1920. According to a 1915 survey of alumnae of nine women's colleges, 70 percent of women graduates worked. Many of the more recent students had participated as well in the suffrage movement and other Progressive crusades. Since educated women had traditionally formed the vanguard of the women's rights struggle, women activists looked to the new generation to carry forward the fight for equality.

On the surface, developments during the 1920s appeared to fulfill feminist expectations. The number of women employed in the professions increased by over 450,000 and in business by over 100,000. The proportion of all women workers who were professionals grew from 11.9 percent in 1920 to 14.2 percent in 1930. Women became editors in publishing houses, sold real estate, practiced pharmacology, and took up important positions in banks and department stores. They formed their own business and professional associations and published national journals focusing on their collective advancement. Only in the area of domestic service did the female labor force expand more rapidly.

Yet the statistical gains inflated the degree of progress actually achieved. As we have seen, most prospective career women were restricted to "female" occupations and did not enter male- dominated fields. The number of women in medical schools actually diminished from 1,280 in 1902–1903 to 992 in 1926. Despite a great deal of talk about new jobs open to women, there were only 60 female certified public accountants and only 151 dentists at the end of the 1920s. Instead of breaking down barriers to positions from which they had previously been excluded, career women of the 1920s clustered in occupations traditionally marked out as women's preserve. Among professional women in New York, there were 63,637 teachers and 21,915 nurses but only 11 engineers and 7 inventors. The distribution accurately reflected the absence of any startling advances by women into new professions.

Significantly, those women who did enter careers rarely received the same treatment accorded men. A woman might sell bonds on Wall Street, but she was listed on company personal forms as a technician rather than as an account executive. Banks frequently employed women specialists to handle female clients, but those who were hired almost never rose above the position of assistant cashier—an office which quickly became woman's place in the banking community. In addition, businessmen exhibited little confidence in the staying power of potential career women and consciously discouraged them from pursuing their ambitions. Roger Babson, a prominent business spokesman, declared that women represented a poor economic investment because of their brief tenure at work. Another executive wrote that the "highest profession a woman can engage in is that of charming wife and wise mother." And an editorial in the *Commercial and Financial Chronicle* warned that banking held no future for "bright, capable educated young women" because "propagation among the higher groups" constituted the chief call on the women college graduate's energies.

Such stereotyping created a vicious cycle from which it was almost impossible to escape. The very wifely qualities that some male business executives looked for in their private secretaries and female assistants fit into patterns designed to deny women other jobs. As one career secretary wrote, "the more efficient [a secretary] became and the more indispensable she is to him in a secretarial capacity, the less likely will he be to run the risk of crippling or inconveniencing himself by recommending her promotion to an independent position in business." In short, the qualities deemed essential for women employees in the first place often represented impediments to their moving into more independent business or professional positions.

Even in occupations they dominated, women were frequently denied top positions. Although women constituted eight out of every ten teachers, women were only one out of every sixty-three superintendents of schools. Women chaired less than one in six of the departments of education in the nation's universities and headed less than one in three of the country's women's colleges. While women earned approximately one-third of the graduate degrees awarded in the country, they occupied only 4 percent of the full professorships. To some extent, the low percentage reflected women's preference for teaching over publishing and for small colleges over large universities. Nevertheless, a survey of woman academicians in 1929 found widespread discontent over the apparent lack of correlation between training and rank. No matter how much a woman studied or taught, she was likely to remain an instructor, burdened with the greatest teaching load and recompensed with the smallest salary. "The rank and file [of women teachers]," the survey concluded, "seem to have developed a defensive attitude bordering on martyrdom."

Black women, of course, experienced even fewer opportunities. Black women's colleges like Spelman and Bennett trained teachers for segregated school systems, and nurses who were black helped make an enormous impact on public-health programs for minority communities. But as Darlene Clark Hine and others have shown, these victories took place against a backdrop of systematic prejudice from white professionals and occurred only within an already segregated environment.

As the new decade of the 1930s began, prospects for all career women grew worse rather than better. When Julia Lathrop died in 1932, the New York *Herald Tribune* described her as one of "the vanishing race of pioneer women," and the obituary had a ring of truth to it. During the 1930s, the percentage of women who received doctorates declined relative to men, and those who earned advanced degrees put them to less use. Even in women's colleges, the number of female faculty members declined. As the Depression swept the country, it became less likely that women would enter male-dominated careers, and the proportion of women workers in the professions fell from 14.2 percent in 1930 to 12.3 percent in 1940. The 1940 figure was only 0.4 percent more than the comparable figure for 1920, highlighting the extent to which women's basic economic status remained unchanged.

—— I ——

At least in part, the absence of greater progress reflected ambiguities in the feminist message about just what equality should entail. As we have seen, in the political arena this ambiguity focused on whether women should retain a separate identity and operational base or join mainstream parties as fully integrated individual members. But there was also a larger ambiguity. The young women who embraced the label "feminism" and joined such groups as Heterodoxy in New York shared in common a celebration of freedom, a rebelliousness against social convention, and a devotion to self-realization. "We intend simply to be ourselves," the founder of Heterodoxy said, "not just our little female selves, but our whole big human selves." "Self-development," "free will," "individualism," "spontaneity"—all of these were umbrella words that most young feminists embraced.

Yet beneath such vague signs of unity were multiple interests, some of them contradictory. Women like Crystal Eastman wanted to forge new patterns that harmonized political activism and marriage; others, like Elizabeth Gurley Flynn, focused both on working class solidarity and on sexual independence; still others were primarily concerned with revolting against convention in the arts and literature or creating alternative child-care and family-support institutions. Some seemed to care exclusively about issues of sexuality, whether that meant free love, bisexuality, homosexuality, or simply independence from conventional marriage. And there were also the members of the National Woman's Party with their fixation on the Equal Rights Amendment. The problem was that feminists who cared about sexual freedom or artistic independence did not necessarily give a second thought to legal reforms, a constitutional amendment, or career independence. Feminism, in short, lacked coherence and definition, with a resultant loss of momentum and direction.

But more important was the absence of enthusiasm for feminism of the new generation, especially as time passed. Women's rights leaders had looked to the young to fulfill their goals, but as the suffragist Mildred Adams observed, "the first of the future generations seemed little interested" in carrying on the fight for equality. Ironically, the lack of enthusiasm coincided with, and in some ways reflected, the burgeoning growth of the female college population. At an earlier time when higher education was a rarity, women students had been infused with a conscious sense of mission and obligation. The very act of going to college set them apart as a select group with a special responsibility. Between 1890 and 1910, a Vassar professor recalled, women students "proudly... marched in militant processions and joyfully... accepted arrest and imprisonment for the sake of 'Votes for Women,' free speech and to help a strike." By the 1920s, however, going to college had become an act of conformity rather than deviance, and the atmosphere of special purpose began to evaporate. " 'Feminism' has become a term of opprobrium [for the young]," Dorothy Dunbar Bromley noted in 1927. "The word suggests either the old school ... who wore flat heels and had very little feminine charm, or the current species who antagonize men with their constant clamor about maiden names." Neither type had any appeal for the college woman. She enjoyed the benefits which the feminists had won but refused to consider their cause as her own. "We're not out to benefit society ... or to make industry safe," one student commented. "We're not going to suffer over how the other half lives." As a League of Women Voters official lamented, the woman's movement had ceased to hold any attraction for the "juniors."

Youthful apathy toward the cause of women's rights inevitably affected the prospects for achieving economic equality. A woman did not have to be a feminist to pursue a career, but she did have to display dedication to an overriding goal. Those women considering a life in business or the professions, a journalist noted in 1921, had to "spurn delight ... love laborious days," and be prepared to recognize that everything else took second place to her job.

Yet it was precisely such a commitment that many young women appeared to lack. They may have been individualists—or thought themselves so—but their interest in self-expression seemed to be more hedonistic than career-oriented. The discipline, seriousness, and intensity of serving a higher goal, political or economic, was missing. Instead, Virginia Gildersleeve of Barnard remarked, the female college student of the 1920s was characterized by "blase indifference, self-indulgence, and irresponsibility." Business and professional women were outraged by the absence of seriousness among the young and commented that the new generation showed little willingness to "pay the price" of success.

The story of women in academic life illustrated the impact of the shift in attitude. The founders of women's education, a Wellesley historian observed in 1915, had been motivated by "heady enthusiasm" and "fiery persistence." On trial before the world, they were dedicated to proving that women had the brains, as well as the endurance, to develop their own institutions of higher learning. Only those who took part in the experience, she wrote, could know "how exciting and romantic it was to be a professor in a woman's college during the last half century." A spirit of independence and commitment reigned. "I can't stand being dependent on anybody," M. Carey Thomas, the president of Bryn Mawr, wrote as a young woman, "and I want to do something besides eating, reading, and dressing." Thomas and the women like her created professional lives that sustained their independence and private lives—usually with other women—that offered reinforcement and support. Most often, these stories of professional success were tied to separate, women-dominated institutions.

With the passage of time, however, the ardor of the pioneers faded. "By the 1920s," Jessie Bernard has noted, "the éclat of the earlier years had spent itself, and all of a sudden, . . . the increase in the percentage of academic personnel who were women slowed down. The excitement which had characterized the first generation of academic women ebbed." Vida Scudder, a prominent reformer and Wellesley professor, described the 1920s as a period of "surging . . . disillusion" and declared that she had never before felt so discouraged. The crusading spirit had disintegrated, and with it the warmth of old comradeships held together by devotion to a transcendent goal. Most observers traced the change in mood to the war, but whatever the reason, all agreed that the new generation of college women lacked the single-minded purpose which had sustained those who led the battle for women's education. During the 1930s, the proportion of college teachers who were women fell from 32.5 percent to 26.5 percent, and the figure continued to decline until the late 1950s.

—— II ——

If anyone symbolized the new age, it was the carefree flapper rather than the dedicated career woman. In fact, the difference between the two said a great deal about the nature of women's "emancipation." Popularized in the novels of F. Scott Fitzgerald and worried over in magazines as diverse as the *American Mercury* and the *Ladies' Home Journal*, the flapper seized the public imagination in the years from 1910 to 1930 and dominated conversation about manners and morals. Portrayed as checking her corset in the cloakroom, partying without a chaperon, and dancing to hot jazz with skirts hiked above her knees, she personified a life-style totally alien to the older generation. "I mean to do what I like . . . undeterred by convention," one short-story heroine remarked. "Freedom—that is the modern essential. To live one's life in one's own way." With her bobbed hair and rolled hose, the stereotypical flapper moved from adventure to adventure, celebrating experience for its own sake. From New York City to Muncie, Indiana, her antics bemused, outraged, and frustrated those who had been raised to believe in an ideal of "dainty femininity." There was no way of knowing how many young women actually behaved in the manner described in magazine articles, and some degree of skepticism was probably warranted. But in Muncie's high school, over half the junior and senior girls agreed that "petting" was nearly universal at teenage parties—a fact which provided at least partial confirmation that a "new woman" had arrived on the national scene.

Indeed, there was a substantial amount of evidence that a revolution in morals and manners had occurred in America, although for the most part it occurred prior to 1920. Popular discussion of sex reached an unprecedented level during the years from 1910 to 1930. The number of articles on birth control, prostitution, divorce, and sexual morality soared, and an analysis of short stories revealed that "between 1915 and 1925, taboos associated with sex in general and marital infidelity in particular were lifted from the middle-class mind in America." More important, it appeared that talk about the new morality was translated into action as well. When Lewis Terman surveyed 777 middle-class women in 1938, he found that among those born between 1890 and 1900, 74 percent remained virgin until marriage, while among those born after 1910, the figure plummeted to 31.7 percent. Alfred Kinsey's more elaborate sample corroborated Terman's conclusions. Women born after the turn of the century were twice as likely to have experienced premarital sex as those born before 1900, and the critical change occurred in the generation which came to maturity in the late 1910s and early 1920s. Extramarital sex increased in the same decades, disproving the notion that the new morality was a youthful fad which would end with the assumption of family responsibilities.

The sexual habits of the flapper generation indicated that many women had been emancipated from conventional patterns of behavior. If the Lynds' survey of Muncie was any measure, a growing number of middle-class women were using artificial contraceptive devices, introducing a new degree of freedom into their personal lives. Family size could be controlled, women could express their sexual desires with less fear of becoming pregnant, and the double standard ceased to exert the same restrictive influence over women's behavior that it once had. There could be little question that the "revolution in manners and morals" had substantially increased the amount of equality which women enjoyed in at least one area of male-female relationships.

If the flapper symbolized a particular kind of "emancipation," however, the nature of her freedom had only the most tenuous connection to most of the concerns of feminism. Many of the older veterans of the women's rights struggle strongly disapproved of the new morality and condemned what appeared to them as irresponsible and frivolous behavior. Charlotte Perkins Gilman, for example, avowed that sex was intended for procreation, not recreation, and denounced the phallic worship of Freud's disciples. Other suffragists railed against the manners of the young—especially their lack of seriousness—and attacked the flappers as a disgrace to their sex.

But even the more ardent advocates of sexual liberation among feminists endorsed a different view of sexuality than that symbolized by the flapper. In their commitment to elevate women's sexual passions to the same level of legitimacy as men's, feminists like Olive Schreiner, Ellen Key, and Louise Bryant had in mind a serious alternative structure of relationships between the sexes that would depose the conventionality of bourgeois marriage, not just co-exist with it. Female eroticism was perceived both as an end in itself and as pivotal to fulfillment in other areas of life. It would lead to a transformation of all social relationships.

Thus, even if feminists disagreed among themselves about the importance of sexuality, they understood the issue to be one of substantive importance, requiring a major commitment. As Gilman put it in a long-standing debate with Ellen Key, there were two kinds of feminists, "human" ones, like herself, and "female" ones like Key. The latter "considers sex as paramount, . . . underlying . . . all phases of life," while the former considers "that the main lines of human development have nothing to do with sex. . . . " In either case, however, one's position on the issue shaped an entire worldview.

Flappers, by contrast, saw sexual costuming and manners as casual indulgences that added spice to a generational life-style. They did not seek to transform a whole way of living. The flapper might be seen by some as reflecting a "feminist" rebellion against convention, but the revolt was for the most part superficial, not structural. It focused on style, not substance—on the appearance of sexual liberation, not on the radical restructuring of all relationships that people such as Ellen Key had in mind. Nothing did more to eviscerate feminism of the radical potential than this popular tendency to equate "freedom" with the life-style of the flapper.

Perhaps most important, the increase in sexual freedom did not necessarily alter the basic distribution of roles between men and women. A woman could smoke, drink, swear, and even have extramarital affairs while still remaining a wife and mother. Shifts in manners and morals did not interfere with the perpetuation of a sexual division of labor where middle-class women assumed responsibility for the home and middle-class men went out into the world to earn a livelihood. The nuances of a relationship might change, but the structure remained the same. For less well-to-do women, the new sexual freedoms were even less likely to signify progress toward equality. In their lives, dating, "treating," and the exchange of sex for food, clothes, and entertainment simply reflected the realities of trying to survive on a less-than-subsistence wage. Thus, neither the sexually liberated housewife nor the barely independent working woman was in a position to challenge the underlying inequities that persisted in male-female relations.

A career, on the other hand, involved a drastic modification of woman's status and challenged the basic institutions of society. The family would lose its central personality—the mother who soothed a distraught child, the wife who provided solace to a discouraged husband, and the housekeeper who performed the chores of cooking and cleaning. In effect, women could achieve economic equality only if one of two things happened: the family as then constituted ceased to exist, or someone else helped care for the children, prepare the meals, and preserve the integrity of the home. In either case, the changes threatened traditional definitions of woman's place and required a social revolution which most Americans appeared unwilling to accept.

The greatest obstacle to economic equality, then, remained the existing distribution of sexual roles, especially in middle-class families. Society operated on the assumption that women would carry out certain indispensable functions such as child rearing and household care, and the entire process of living reinforced the assumption. From earliest childhood, women were trained to assume domestic responsibilities. "One becomes what one plays at," the sociologist Peter Berger has observed, and girls played at keeping house, dressing dolls, and cooking food. Although the Lynds noted that parental authority was declining somewhat in Muncie during the mid-1920s, they also underlined the extent to which children were taught to conform to established group norms. Girls were urged to sew and cook, boys to build club houses and tinker with automobiles. The identity which society bestowed on a woman was that of wife and mother, not an economic competitor with men. Marriage and childbearing constituted the socially sanctioned goals of female existence, just as material success in the outside world represented the goal of men.

Within such a system, middle-class men and women continued to occupy sharply separate spheres of responsibility. In their study of Muncie, the Lynds discovered that husbands and wives shared little in common and gravitated into separate groups even on social occasions "to talk men's talk and women's talk." Marriage was often characterized by a lack of frankness between mates, and one local minister went so far as to warn prospective bridegrooms against feeling that they "must tell everything they know to their wives." Moreover, members of both sexes seemed to accept conventional definitions of each other's place. Men were expected to be providers, women homemakers; husbands made the decisions, women were helpmates. The motto of the local women's club declared that "Men are God's trees; women are his flowers," and the Lynds found little evidence to suggest that wives disagreed with such a sentiment. Indeed, the pattern of male-female relationships constituted one of the most stable features of the community. When the Lynds returned to Muncie in 1935, they found that the worlds of men and women still constituted "something akin to separate subcultures" with each sex emphasizing those attributes most different from the other.

The existence of clearly defined gender roles provided comfort and security for many, but it also discouraged deviancy and placed a formidable obstacle in the path of those who wished a life of greater independence. The Lynds noted that a woman who consciously endeavored to share more of her husband's world succeeded only at the price of isolation from the rest of the female community. The same point was made with even more cogency in Sinclair Lewis's novel *Main Street*. Carol Kennecott, married to the town's doctor, had come to Gopher Prairie inspired by a missionary's impulse to transform the town. College-educated, and very much her own person, she aggressively set out to mobilize the support of community leaders for her projects of social and cultural renewal. Instead of being welcomed, however, she was greeted with suspicion and antagonism. The women of the town disliked her because she disparaged traditional patterns of female behavior, and the men viewed her as a meddlesome interloper trying to intervene in matters which were men's.

Although Carol invited hostility by her condescension and arrogance, the principal problem was not her personality but her refusal to accept prevailing definitions of "woman's place." "She was a woman with a working brain and no work," Lewis observed. When she tried to engage men in conversation about burning social issues and when she spurred women to take leadership roles in the community, she violated entrenched social customs and appeared to be a troublemaker. Her husband and others were convinced that the presence of children would ease her discontent, and the antagonism between Carol and the town did diminish after a son was born and she more closely conformed to the ideal of what was expected of women. But motherhood was only a temporary palliative; it quickly gave way to a new round of bitterness and despair. Carol yearned for a "conscious life" of individuality and freedom, not just the housewife's routine of "drudging and sleeping and dying." Yet a woman could not easily find her life's work, or build a "room of [her] own" when all around her was pressure to abandon ideas of independence and settle down. For a brief period, Carol worked in Washington as a government clerk, but in the end, she returned to Gopher Prairie, resigned to accepting the community's values.

The case studies of Muncie and Gopher Prairie illustrated the social barriers to greater participation by middle-class women in business and the professions. Despite the pioneering achievements of an Elizabeth Blackwell in medicine or an Antoinette Brown in the ministry, there were few successful models in male-dominated professions for the potential career woman to emulate. A young girl met an abundance of female nurses and teachers—one reason for the popularity of these professions among women—but their jobs represented an extension rather than a repudiation of the traditional female role. Magazines generally viewed women's work as a threat to the family, and in novels and short stories, the happy ending usually consisted of the single woman rejecting a job for a life of marital bliss. *This Freedom* —one of the most popular novels of 1922—attacked career women as traitors to their sex and announced that "the peace of the home . . . rests ultimately on the kitchen." Other novels of the period adopted the same theme, portraying most flatteringly those women who deviated least from the role of supportive wife.

The woman who did pursue a career in a male-dominated field traveled a largely uncharted course and violated the most deeply held conceptions of her proper role. Instead of serving a man at home, she competed against him at work. That fact by itself created difficulty, since it challenged the powerful forces of tradition. Anne Fullerton, a medical doctor, reflected on the unhappiness that she and other women physicians had to face daily because of their unconventional role. "[B]eing a woman . . . she has had to face the fact that many people still feel that *skilled* medical advice must be masculine, and she is subjected to the mortification of seeing her own advice often set aside for that of some man whom she knows to be her inferior professionally."

Equally important, the career woman lacked signposts to direct her in her endeavor. If she acted demurely and accepted a subservient role, she missed opportunities for advancement. On the other hand, if she anticipated prejudice and compensated by being aggressive, she alienated those around her and highlighted the extent to which she departed from conventional norms. In either case, she was bound to experience the ambivalence of being a stranger in foreign territory, confronting repeatedly the conflict between the passivity expected of women and the assertiveness demanded of men.

The greatest dilemma of all involved the choice between marriage and a career. Many college women had been encouraged to compete with men as students and to achieve the best grades possible. On the other hand, they were brought up to act and think of themselves as future wives and mothers. If a woman could both marry and have a career, the conflict might have been mitigated. In fact, an increasing number of women attempted that combination, seeking, in historian Joyce Antler's words, to "work out that balance of interests between the private and the public that would allow them to achieve the self-determination and autonomy that they posited as their highest goal." Yet as late as 1920, only 12.2 percent of all professional women were married, and 75 percent of the women who earned Ph.D.'s between 1877 and 1924 remained single. "A woman cannot undertake the duties of a wife and mother," commented one woman doctor, "and at the same time give herself as she should to the demands of a life so strenuous both mentally and physically as that of the physician and surgeon." Reflecting such attitudes, many employers refused even to consider hiring married women because of their supposed preoccupation with the home.

Just as important, the traits seen as most conducive to winning a husband were seen as least conducive to securing success in a career. A woman had two choices, the anthropologist Margaret Mead observed in 1935. Either she proclaimed herself "a *woman* and therefore less an achieving individual, or an *achieving individual* and therefore less a woman [italics added]." If she chose the first option, she enhanced her opportunity of being "a loved object, the kind of girl whom men will woo and boast of, toast and marry." If she selected the second alternative, however, she lost "as a woman, her chance for the kind of love she wants." Before 1920, women like M. Carey Thomas possessed the sense of self-conscious mission that made such a choice both possible and even desirable. But by the 1920s and 1930s, that sense of mission had faded, and fewer women seemed prepared for such a commitment.

For a brief period beginning in 1925, Smith College sought to find ways to combine home and career through its Institute to Coordinate Women's Interests. Headed by Ethel Puffer Howe, a former Wellesley College professor, the institute tried to end the dichotomy between "the queen bee and the sexless worker" and to make it possible for college-educated wives to enter professional occupations. Experimenting with cooperative nurseries, communal laundries, shopping groups, and central kitchens, it set out to release women from the "inexorable routine of housework." Howe attempted to plan and then to initiate a "revolution in the organization of the home" and to establish a pattern of education and professional life geared to the problems of middle-class women. Acting from the same motivation, Virginia Gildersleeve at Barnard College granted maternity leaves with pay to women faculty members. Women had just as much right to a full life as men, she believed, and ought not to be condemned to celibacy in order to pursue a career.

The experiments at Barnard and Smith proved exceptions to the rule, however. Despite its efforts, the Smith Institute to Coordinate Women's Interests expired after only six years. More typical than either Howe or Gildersleeve were the authorities of a Midwestern land-grant college who dismissed a woman dean when she married. Upon appealing the ruling, the woman was told that "marriage itself is for a woman an adequate career." The vast majority of Americans agreed. Suzanne La Follette noted in 1924 that while being a husband represented only one of the many roles assigned to a man, being a wife constituted the only role assigned to a woman. She was expected to devote full time to her family, and if she worked outside the home, her action reflected negatively both on her own womanhood and on the ability of her husband to support her. A married woman who was poor might seek work for reasons of economic necessity, but employment was fundamentally inconsistent with the status of a middle-class wife. Carol Kennecott repeatedly talked about embarking on a career of her own, yet she knew that a job for herself was impossible in the conservative community of Gopher Prairie and would thoroughly undermine her husband's social standing. "To the village doctor's wife," Sinclair Lewis observed, "[outside employment] was taboo."

—— III ——

In the end, therefore, the real question confronting potential career women was whether they wished to marry and forsake their professional ambitions or enter a lifetime job and renounce marriage. The distribution of sexual roles made it difficult, if not impossible, to do both, because in order to achieve success in a man's world, they had to accept failure in a woman's world. In a different type of family, where "independence [was] equal, dependence mutual, and obligations reciprocal," women might have been able to combine a career with a life in the home. As it was, however, most Americans rejected such a radical change. Even those women who entered careers wondered about their ability to sustain a commitment to work. "We have not the motive to prepare ourselves for a 'life-work' of teaching, of social work," Ruth Benedict confided in her diary. "We know that we would lay it down with hallelujah in the height of our success, to make a home for the right man."

Significantly, during the 1920s an increasing number of women college students expressed a preference for marriage. At the end of the nineteenth century, half of the graduates of the best women's colleges remained single, and they constituted the core of female professional workers. Among Vassar women who graduated prior to 1912, the desire for a career represented one of the most frequently cited reasons for having chosen a Vassar education. Alumnae of the post-World War I period, in contrast, stated over and over again that they had selected Vassar because of its popularity or because their friends were going there. As the student population broadened and became more representative of middle-class values, a larger percentage of graduates chose to become wives and mothers rather than career women. A survey of alumnae from Hollins, Bryn Mawr, Barnard, Vassar, and Smith illustrated the change that had occurred since the turn of the century. In one school, 80 percent of those graduating in the years from 1919 to 1923 got married, while in another school, the figure was 90 percent. A newspaper poll of Vassar women in 1923 revealed that 90 percent wanted to be married, with only 11 of 152 preferring a business or professional position. Most believed that marriage was "the biggest of all careers." Seven years later, almost 70 percent of the graduates of New Jersey's College for Women agreed that winning a husband and starting a family took precedence over pursuing a career. Thus, the female students who attended the schools most likely to produce a new crop of business and professional women chose to marry rather than stay single. Moreover, the critical shift occurred precisely in those years when feminists expected a boom in the number of career women as a result of suffrage and the war.

The curriculum of women's education underwent a striking change at the same time, reflecting a growing concern with preparing women for marriage and the home. The founders of most women's colleges had sought as much as possible to make them carbon copies of Harvard and Yale. Four of the eight original professors at Vassar taught science, and Mount Holyoke, Smith, Barnard, and Bryn Mawr all insisted on offering the same courses as the best men's colleges. By the early twentieth century, however, the older view of women's colleges came under increasing attack. Ethel Puffer Howe, a Radcliffe graduate and later head of the Smith Institute to Coordinate Women's Interests, urged women's colleges in 1913 to develop courses in domestic science, eugenics, hygiene, and the aesthetics of the home in order to train women for the domestic tasks which lay ahead. In a similar vein, an insurgent group at the 1923 convention of the American Collegiate Association condemned women's colleges for not preparing women for the occupation of homemaking and child rearing.

The leaders of at least one feminist institution heeded the call for reform. In the spring of 1924, the Vassar board of trustees unanimously endorsed the creation of an interdisciplinary School of Euthenics that would focus on the development and care of the family. The purpose of the institute, its first director declared, was to re-route "education for women along the lines of their chief interests and responsibilities, motherhood and the home." Supporters of the program believed that women's colleges had treated women for too long as if they were celibate, while ignoring their chief vocations—wifehood, maternity, and homemaking. To correct the imbalance, Vassar offered a series of courses. ("Husband and Wife," "Motherhood," and "The Family as an Economic Unit") designed to train students to be "gracious and intelligent wives and mothers." As the chief financial backer of the institute said in 1929, "our purpose . . . is to raise motherhood to a profession worthy of [woman's] finest talents and greatest intellectual gifts."

Although feminists viewed such innovations as a direct threat to the dignity and usefulness of higher education for women, similar endeavors appeared throughout the country. At the University of Chicago, Marion Talbot proposed a graduate program of home economics. Cornell quickly gained prominence as a center for domestic science, and state universities adopted such programs as a mainstay for female students. The field of family care or home economics boomed in the first quarter of the twentieth century, in part as a result of federal financing under the Smith-Lever Act, and in part as a result of a vocational demand for teachers of cooking and hygiene in the public schools. At a time when an unequal sexual division of labor posed the primary obstacle to the advancement of economic equality, it appeared that the nation's colleges and universities were reinforcing the image of woman as wife and mother. Dr. Charles Richmond, head of Union College, articulated the new focus of women's education in his address at the inauguration of Skidmore's president in 1925. "One of the chief ends of a college for women is to fit them to become the makers of homes," he declared; "whatever else a woman may be, the highest purpose of her life always has been . . . to strengthen and beautify and sanctify the home."

With increasing stridency, women's magazines voiced the same theme, insisting that the roles of mother and housewife represented the only path to feminine fulfillment. In the years immediately after passage of the Nineteenth Amendment, occasional articles justified female independence and defended the right of women to work. By the late 1920s, however, the attitude of tolerant permissiveness had changed to one of outright condemnation. The switch in tone was announced officially in a 1930 *Ladies' Home Journal* editorial. "[A] new keynote is creeping into the lives of American women," the editorial observed. "Yesterday, and for a decade past, the great desideratum was Smartness. Today, and for the years that lie immediately before us, it is Charm." Women's magazines, geared to the middle class, urged their readers to return to femininity and constructed an elaborate ideology in support of the home and marriage to facilitate the process.

As a first step, the magazines defined the role of the housewife as exciting, rewarding, and creative. Homemaking, the *Ladies' Home Journal* declared in 1929, "is today an adventure—an education in color, in mechanics, in chemistry." *McCall's* magazine asserted that no other task possessed such universal appeal: "it exercises an even more profound influence on human destiny than the heroism of war or the prosperity of peace." Both magazines urged a woman to conceive of her job as a profession—home engineering, one called it—and to utilize "current labor saving devices" to ease her burden. The perfection of modern conveniences, the magazine argued, had increased rather than diminished the housewife's role by elevating her position in the world and giving her more time to develop socially and to train her children. With fewer routine chores to perform, a wife could devote herself to the more important job of creating happiness for her family. No task was more important, no profession more demanding. "The creation and fulfillment of a successful home," a *Ladies' Home Journal* article declared, "is a bit of craftsmanship that compares favorably with building a beautiful cathedral." Only as a wife and mother, *McCall's* observed, could the American woman "arrive at her true eminence." The "feminine mystique," as Ruth Schwartz Cowan has pointed out, was as strong between World Wars I and II as it was after 1945, with advertisers and editors alike dedicated to the proposition that "housework was . . . an expression of the housewife's personality and of her affection for her family."

The magazines coupled their glorification of domesticity with a bitter attack on feminism. "Liberated women," they claimed, had thrown away the essence of femininity without putting anything better in its place. One article declared that "the office woman, no matter how successful, is a transplanted posey." Another argued that women who pushed for equality had destroyed the "deep-rooted, nourishing, and fruitful man-and-woman relationship." A woman's career was to make a good marriage, to be "deeply, fundamentally, wholly feminine." Laura Cornell, dean of Temple University, told her readers that women who demanded recognition for themselves were violating their own true nature. Women required protection, she wrote, and men needed to give it.

Career women were singled out for special condemnation by the proponents of homemaking. Dorothy Thompson, herself a prime example of a successful professional woman, observed that "men demand and need in marriage the full emotional power of the women they love. . . . If that power is dissipated in demanding intellectual or creative work, or shared with some boss, the husband and children will feel they are being cheated." In Thompson's opinion, society had more need of good mothers than of additional private secretaries or laboratory technicians. Claire Callahan, another veteran of work outside the home, publicly repented her career and declared that, if she had to do it again, she would remain a homemaker. "I know now without any hesitation," she wrote, "that [my husband's job] must come first. . . . I am like the invaluable secretary to a big executive. He produces but I make it possible for him to produce efficiently. And once I had the right slant on my work . . . I would begin to see my job as a real job. . . . I would work toward an executive position in my home." According to women's magazines, a woman could achieve a "real" career only by renouncing an outside job and devoting herself to full-time service in the home.

Occasionally, an element of uncertainty crept into the defense of domesticity. Some writers admitted that housework was monotonous, and others acknowledged that a business career might appear more daring and glamorous. The same writers, however, insisted that if a woman approached homemaking with the proper attitude, she would find it the most rewarding occupation of all. "Just as a rose comes to its fullest beauty in its own appropriate soil," one article declared, "so does a home woman come to her fairest blooming when her roots are stuck deep in the daily and hourly affairs of her own most dearly beloved." A woman might resent at times "the thoughtlessness and omissions" of her husband, but once she accepted "that big biologic fact that man was intended to be selfish" and woman self-sacrificing, the way to fulfillment was clear. Only if a woman rejected her natural identity would she have cause to experience dissatisfaction and despair.

The editorial policy of women's magazines added one more voice of support for traditional sexual values. For the most part, periodicals like *McCall's* and the *Ladies' Home Journal* catered to readers who were already housewives; they did not need to be persuaded to renounce careers or devote full time to the home. But the ideology presented in such journals helped to bolster prevailing opinion. Over 7,000 of the 9,200 families in Muncie read either the large women's magazines or *Pictorial Review* and *Delineator*, while fewer than 40 families subscribed to *Harper's* or *Atlantic Monthly* —journals more receptive to a feminist point of view. It may have been coincidental that Muncie's citizens espoused the same values articulated in the periodicals they read, but it seems more likely that the magazines provided reinforcement for existing attitudes and helped to justify their perpetuation.

The advent of the Depression provided the final blow to feminist hopes for economic equality. During a time of massive unemployment, many people believed that women should sacrifice personal ambitions and accept a life of economic inactivity. As we have seen, women may have worked in increasing numbers during the Depression, but the barriers to fair and equal treatment remained. Black and Latina women were discriminated against in New Deal work-relief programs, as were all married women. Julia Kirk Blackwelder has shown in her study of San Antonio during the Depression that women from different ethnic groups followed different cultural patterns, but all had an equally difficult time holding families together under the stress of massive unemployment.

Career women came under special attack during these years. Congresswoman Florence Kahn spoke for most of her colleagues when she declared that "woman's place is not out in the business world competing with men who have families to support," but in the home. Dean Eugenia Leonard of Syracuse University urged women college graduates to enter volunteer work rather than accept a salary. And George Mullins, acting dean of Barnard told his students that the greatest service they could render would be to "refuse to work for gain and to prolong [their] study." Liberal women reformers voiced similar sentiments. Frances Perkins denounced the rich "pin-money worker" as a "menace to society, [and] a selfish, short-sighted creature, who ought to be ashamed of herself." Any woman capable of supporting herself without a job, the future secretary of labor declared, should devote herself to motherhood and the home.

The Depression especially sharpened public disapproval of work by married women. Employed wives were "thieving parasites of the business world," a Kansas woman wrote to President Roosevelt. A Chicago-based civic organization urged that married women workers be forced back to the home because "they are holding jobs that rightfully belong to the God-intended providers of the household," and the executive council of the AF of L resolved that "married women whose husbands have permanent positions . . . should be discriminated against in the hiring of employees." Almost all Americans agreed. When the pollster George Gallup asked in 1936 whether wives should work if their husbands were employed also, a resounding 82 percent of the respondents said no. Gallup reported that he had "discovered an issue on which voters are about as solidly united as on any subject imaginable—including sin and hay fever."

Consistent with such opinion, employers increasingly denied married women the right to work. A National Education Association study in 1930–31 showed that of 1,500 school systems surveyed, 77 percent refused to hire wives, and 63 percent dismissed women teachers if they subsequently married. A San Francisco married woman was told when applying for a teaching job that she would have to get a divorce first. From 1932 to 1937, federal legislation prohibited more than one member of the same family from working in the civil service. Designed to combat nepotism, the law, in fact, discriminated almost exclusively against wives. In nearly every state, bills were introduced to restrict the employment of married women, and at times whole cities embarked on crusades to fire working wives. The Federation of Labor in Cedar Rapids, Iowa, called on every merchant to dismiss any married woman whose husband could support her, and the City Council of Akron, Ohio, resolved that the school board, the Goodyear Tire Company, and all local department stores should deny employment to wives.

The campaign against women working in large part reflected the dire circumstances of the Depression. At a time when many families were without any breadwinner, there was understandable resentment against those which had two. Although most working women were not taking jobs away from men (women were concentrated in occupations where few men were employed), most Americans believed that in a period of economic distress husbands and fathers should be given the first opportunity for employment. Implicit in such a belief, however, was the assumption that women did not deserve the same treatment as men. The Depression did not *create* antagonism toward female employment, but it raised that antagonism to a new level of intensity and by so doing placed one more barrier in the way of economic equality.

—— IV ——

From a women's rights point of view, the experience of the years after 1920 raised profound questions about how much freedom women had actually won in America. If some suffragists had been satisfied with gaining the right to vote, other activists—however they defined feminism—desired more far-reaching change that would alter dramatically the social and economic order as it related to women. For many of these activists, economic equality was a basic part of that alteration. "No matter what other equality might be obtained," Charlotte Perkins Gilman wrote in 1923, "so long as one sex [is] dependent on the other for its food, clothing, and shelter, it [is] not free." For Gilman and many others, sexual equality required economic equality— the right of women to pursue whatever vocation they desired on a basis of equality with men and equal sharing of tasks previously allocated to women alone. By those standards, women in 1940 were far from being either equal or free.

Most women activists viewed the developments since 1920 with anger and disillusionment. "In giving woman the vote," one Michigan woman wrote, "men never had any intention of giving her anything more and never has. The really interested woman . . . has had to fight for a place, and in fighting, man has . . . pushed her aside like a sticky fly, and gone serenely on his way managing the universe." Others were equally bitter. Women's influence was "almost totally lacking in the centers of American national life," Pearl Buck declared in 1940. "Men and children have proceeded with the times, but woman has not, and today the home is too peculiarly hers." Women's rights leaders charged that the United States was fundamentally hostile to the cause of female advancement and unwilling to grant women the basic rights given to men as a matter of course. "Profound as race prejudice is against the Negro American," Buck concluded, "it is not practically as far reaching as the prejudice against women. The truth is that women suffer all the effects of a minority."

Although such statements greatly underestimated the oppression from which blacks suffered and reflected once again the racial blinders that many white leaders wore, women activists were clearly correct in their charge that prejudice was at least partly responsible for women's status. Professional schools placed strict quotas on the number of women they would admit. Hospitals, law firms, and business establishments frequently denied women the opportunity to compete for positions held by men. And when women did enter male-dominated fields, unequal pay and inadequate promotion opportunities discouraged them from staying. In general, women were treated as a class apart, with separate qualifications that severely restricted the type of jobs they could fill. Even sympathizers perceived career women as a special breed. The Institute of Women's Professional Relations declared that "women must be directed into occupations for which they are [peculiarly] adapted," and Frances Perkins told a conference on women that the greatest need of government was for women "who can be humble . . . and who are willing to begin at the bottom." Character and conscience, she asserted, were more important requirements than brilliance. Such statements reflected a subtle but pervasive attitude that women were less than first-class citizens and had their own place in the worlds of business and government.

In a deeper sense, however, women's inequality was embedded in the social structure, part of a process of living which provided its own best defense against change. In most families, boys and girls were trained to assume substantially different responsibilities. Social, political, and economic institutions were all characterized by a sharp division of sexual roles. And the qualities essential to success in a woman's world were directly opposite those necessary to success in a man's world. In a society which functioned on the premise that men and women occupied completely different spheres, it was not surprising that most women had little choice but to accept the roles of wife and mother. Indeed, woman's place in the home seemed to have been strengthened rather than weakened in the years after 1920. More and more college women married. Over 75 percent of the women responding to George Gallup's 1936 poll disapproved of wives working. And no massive outcry greeted the passage of legislation restricting women's right to gainful employment during the 1930s. If women were enslaved, as feminists claimed, the evidence suggested that their servitude was part and parcel of the entire socialization process, reinforced by institutions and structures that could only be called patriarchal.

The road to economic equality thus proved much longer and more difficult than some women's rights activists had anticipated. The issue of careers for women potentially challenged nearly every entrenched assumption about the roles and responsibilities of the two sexes. For economic equality to become a reality, a fundamental change was required in how men and women thought of each other and in how responsibilities within marriage and the family were distributed. Yet throughout the 1920s and 1930s there was little indication that such a change was either possible or desired. As the nation prepared to enter a new decade, it seemed unlikely that women activists, by themselves, would be able to achieve such fundamental changes. Perhaps only when events created circumstances more conducive to a modification of sex roles would it be possible to seek a redefinition of men's and women's appropriate "place" in American society.

PART THREE

THE WAR DECADE

CHAPTER 7

A Study in Change

AT THE END of the 1930s, the prospects for improvement in women's economic status appeared bleak. Despite important statistical changes in the number of women seeking work, the Depression had fostered a wave of reaction against any change in woman's traditional role. Legislatures enacted laws restricting the employment of married women; labor, government, and the mass media joined in a campaign urging women to refrain from taking jobs; and the overwhelming majority of average citizens—including women—showed little interest in altering existing gender roles. Although shifts of long-term significance had occurred in the two decades after suffrage, the overall stability of women's economic and social status was remarkable. In 1940, the percentage of women at work was almost exactly what it had been in 1910, and there seemed little reason to expect any change in the future.

Over the next five years, World War II dramatically altered that situation. The eruption of hostilities generated an unprecedented demand for new workers, and in response, over six million women took jobs, increasing the size of the female labor force by 50 percent. Wages leaped upward, the number of married women holding jobs doubled, and the unionization of women grew fourfold. Even public attitudes appeared to change. Instead of frowning on women who worked, government and the mass media embarked on an all-out effort to encourage them to enter the labor force. In fact, the war experience for women was mixed, bringing a combination of improvements in some areas and persistent discrimination in others. But temporarily at least, the war caused a greater change in women's economic status and outlook than a prior half century of reform and rhetoric had been able to achieve.

—— I ——

During the first months of the defense crisis, the attitudes of the 1930s pre-vailed, and employers resisted hiring women to fill jobs historically performed by men. A survey of 12,000 factories in early 1942 showed that war industries were willing to employ women in only one-third of the jobs available. Plant managers feared that use of women would require the construction of expen-sive new sanitary facilities and would entail a substantial modification of the production process. Equally important, they hesitated to violate traditional ideas of woman's place by enlisting women to do men's jobs. A woman might be permitted to sew fabric for bomber wings in an aircraft factory, but she was not allowed to learn welding or do metal work. Public opinion would not "countenance the use of women as long as men could be found to do the emergency work," a Women's Bureau official remarked, and for the first few months, there were enough men available to fill the need.

The reluctance of employers to hire women seriously retarded female participation in government training programs for defense work. After sur-veying several key war industries in 1940, the Women's Bureau had urged that women be given equal opportunity with men to learn the skills required for production of war matériel. The government's vocational education pro-gram, however, was geared to the policies of employers, and public officials were unwilling to enroll women students until industry expressed a desire to use them. When Mary Anderson requested equal training for women, John Studebaker, head of the Office of Education, replied that training would be provided only when employers changed their policy and started to hire women. As a result, women comprised only 1 percent of the 1,775,000 work-ers who had received special training as of December 1, 1941. Three hundred thousand persons attended the first series of courses which ended in February 1941, but only 595 were women.

The Japanese attack on Pearl Harbor swiftly erased opposition to hiring women workers and cleared the way for a massive expansion of the female labor force. Within a few months after the United States declared war, mil-lions of men had left their positions in factories and offices to take up arms. Male workers who were ineligible for the draft filled the gap momentarily, but as their ranks dwindled, women became the only available labor reserve. Although acting more slowly than they might have, both industry and gov-ernment abandoned their reluctance to use women in war industries. The government declared that the only answer to the manpower crisis was to "employ women on a scale hitherto unknown," and after a brief survey of two hundred war jobs, the United States Employment Service concluded that women could fill 80 percent of the positions with only brief training. Em-

ployers experienced a similar change of heart. "Almost overnight," Mary
Anderson observed, "women were reclassified by industrialists from a marginal to a basic labor supply for munitions making." A week after Pearl
Harbor, the American Management Association asked the Women's Bureau
to help it set up new policies on the employment of women. By April 1942,
the proportion of women receiving government-sponsored vocational training
had leaped from 1 percent to 13 percent. And within seven months, the
number of jobs for which employers were willing to consider female applicants
had climbed from 29 percent to 55 percent.

Women responded to the manpower crisis with an unprecedented display
of skill and ingenuity. The beautician who overnight became a switchwoman
for 600 Long Island Railroad trains represented but one example of women's
readiness to assume new responsibilities. Josephine von Miklos, an Austrian
aristocrat and designer of perfume bottles, took a job as a precision toolmaker
in Hoboken's shipyards. A former cosmetics saleswoman from Philadelphia
operated a 1,700-ton keel binder. In Gary, Indiana, women maneuvered giant
overhead traveling cranes and cleaned out blast furnaces. Elsewhere, women
ran lathes, cut dies, read blueprints, and serviced airplanes. They maintained
roadbeds, greased locomotives, and took the place of lumberjacks in toppling
giant redwoods. As stevedores, blacksmiths, foundry helpers, and drill-press
operators, women demonstrated that they could fill almost any job, no matter
how difficult or arduous.

Those who did not go directly into war industry found other ways of
helping to meet the manpower shortage. When a scarcity of taxi drivers
developed in New York, women hackies took the wheel. A group of grandmothers operated the police radio in Montgomery County, Maryland, and
women drove the public buses of Washington, Detroit, and New Orleans.
Two thousand female volunteers saved a million-gallon strawberry crop in
Tennessee, while 29,000 others answered the government's plea to "Take a
Fruit Furlough" by joining the Women's Land Army. Women's colleges did
their part by training students for wartime work and by encouraging students
to enlist in civil-defense activities. Barnard offered courses in auto repair, map
reading, and airplane spotting; Smith set up an Officers' Training School for
women; and Rockford and Mount Holyoke gave credit to students who devoted part of their week to working in munitions factories.

Volunteer organizations absorbed the energies of those women who did
not wish to take full-time jobs but wanted to demonstrate their patriotic
fervor. Over three million women flocked to local Red Cross headquarters,
helping to prepare bandages, run motor pools, and start community centers.
The Cleveland Federation of Women's Clubs inaugurated its own Civilian
Service Bureau with lists of members who could step in at a moment's notice

as teachers, waitresses, and secretaries. Countless civilian defense groups boasted of women airplane spotters and ambulance drivers. Even sports became feminized. Ball fans across the country were entertained by a thirty-four-team women's softball league, called by the *Saturday Evening Post* a "baffling mixture of Dead End Kids and Sweet Alice."

The use of conventional gender stereotypes to rationalize these shifts served to highlight both the limits and possibilities of war induced changes. On the one hand, employers resorted to traditional imagery to explain women's success, claiming that an overhead crane operated "just like a gigantic clothes wringer" and that the winding of wire spools in electrical factories was very much like crocheting. One government propaganda film waxed lyrical about the easy transfer of women's skills from the home to the factory. "Instead of cutting a cake," the newsreel said, "this woman [factory worker] cuts the pattern of aircraft parts. Instead of baking a cake, this woman is cooking gears to reduce the tension in the gears after use. . . . [Women] are taking to welding as if the rod were a needle and the metal a length of cloth to be sewn." If a woman worked in a secretarial position, she was described as nurturant and "wifely" in the way she took care of her boss; if she toiled on an assembly line, she was praised for her manual dexterity and her attention to detail. But whether the stereotype invoked was physical or emotional, reliance on such traditional images said a great deal about the difficulty of changing fundamental assumptions about sex roles.

On the other hand, the same stereotypes created a framework within which women could begin to do work that would ultimately shatter traditional images. The fact that women were adept at using acetylene torches as well as sewing machines called into question some of the more rigid distinctions that had been established between the type of labor performed by males and that by females. Women had demonstrated that they could do any work well, and as the war progressed, at least some men in the factories started treating their women co-workers as equals. A Women's Bureau official noted after an extensive tour of a California shipyard that men barked orders at women, refused to pick up their tools when dropped, and withheld the deference associated with traditional male-female relationships. Thus, while sex stereotyping continued on one level to constrain and limit women's opportunities, the actual conditions of the workplace caused sex labels to lose some of their past power, both in the type of jobs assigned and in the attitude of workers toward each other. After witnessing the extent to which women had been integrated into the formerly all-male industries of the Connecticut Valley, Constance Green observed that "presenting a tool chest to a little girl need no longer be dubbed absurdly inappropriate."

The greatest changes in female employment occurred in those areas of the country where defense industries were most concentrated. In eight of ten war-impacted cities surveyed by the Women's Bureau, the number of women workers doubled from 1940 to 1945. In Detroit the female labor force soared from 182,000 to 387,000, while in San Francisco it grew from 138,000 to 275,000. Most of the increase came in manufacturing industries. During one fourteen-month period, women comprised 80 percent of all new workers added to factory payrolls. The number of female industrial workers multiplied five times in Detroit and three times in Baltimore. In many cities, there were more women employed in factories by 1944 than had been in the entire labor force in 1940.

A substantial portion of the new workers had migrated from their former place of residence during the war. As husbands and boy friends left home for duty in distant cities, wives and girl friends followed. Over seven million women changed their county of residence during the first three and a half years of the war, and a third of them joined the labor force. The migration caused some social problems. Delinquency increased substantially, especially among young girls, and the number of teenage runaways soared. As newcomers poured into cities like San Diego and Portland, social welfare agencies were frequently unable to cope with the difficulties experienced by people trying to adjust to a new environment. But the women migrants also contributed mightily to the war effort, comprising approximately 50 percent of the female labor force in such war centers as Mobile, San Francisco, and Wichita.

Industries directly related to the war understandably attracted the largest bloc of new female workers. Defense plants had the most critical need for additional workers and the fewest traditions of prejudice to overcome. In addition, these were the best jobs with the highest wages. The production of airplanes, parachutes, and artillery also held a special appeal for women whose primary motivation in working was to help their sons and husbands fighting in the field. Thus while the female manufacturing force as a whole grew 110 percent during the war, the number of women in war industries shot up 460 percent. A few months after Germany invaded Poland, a total of 36 women were involved in the construction of ships. By December 1942, over 160,000 were employed welding hatches, riveting gun emplacements, and binding keels. The number of women automobile workers grew from 29,000 to 200,000, electrical workers from 100,000 to 374,000. At the beginning of the conflict, 340,000 women had been engaged as operatives in heavy industry. Four years later, the figure had skyrocketed to over two million. In California alone, the increase amounted to 1,697 percent.

Employment patterns in the aircraft industry highlighted the impact of the war on women workers who were able to move into the defense jobs.

When the Women's Bureau visited seven airplane factories in April 1941, it found 143 female employees. Eighteen months later, the same seven plants employed over 65,000 women. Nationwide, women's participation in the air industry soared from 1 percent, or 4,000 women, in December 1941 to 39 percent, or 310,000, by December 1943. More important, female aircraft workers had graduated from sewing fabric for the wings of planes to assembling navigation systems and welding fuselages. So urgent was the demand for women workers in the air industry that almost 500,000 enrolled in the government's Vocational and College War Training Program to learn about aircraft production alone. Although the full-scale recruitment effort was late and did not take complete effect until early 1943, the results were impressive.

Not all the new women workers entered manufacturing or war industries, of course. A tremendous number—over two million—went to work in offices. The war seemed to produce as much tonnage of paperwork as of bombs, and women provided almost all the help in reducing it to manageable proportions. As might have been expected, the federal government accounted for the largest increment. From 1940 to 1945, nearly one million women went to work for Uncle Sam. Female employees multiplied four times faster than male employees (they increased 260.5 percent from 1941 to 1943 alone) and by the end of the war constituted 38 percent of all federal workers, more than twice the percentage of the last prewar year. Nationwide, the clerical force almost doubled, outpaced in the speed of its growth only by the categories of craftsmen, foremen, operatives, and laborers.

The war also made a dent in some of the barriers blocking women's employment in business and the professions. Rensselaer Polytechnic Institute enrolled its first woman student; the Curtiss-Wright Company sent eight hundred women engineering trainees to college; and giant corporations like Montsanto, Du Pont and Standard Oil began to hire women chemists. In Washington, the government sought to fill its depleted legal staffs with women lawyers, and on Wall Street, brokerage houses embarked on a concerted campaign to recruit female analysts and statisticians. Even the close-knit Washington press corps opened its ranks. Male reporters still excluded thirty-seven women from the annual White House correspondents dinner—a fact which May Craig protested vigorously—but on Capitol Hill, the number of women journalists tripled from thirty to ninety-eight. Mary Anderson declared in 1943 that doors were opening to professional women "in an unprecedented way. Women doctors, dentists, chemists, personnel directors and lawyers are in demand as never before." Although Anderson considerably overstated the case, some progress had been made.

Perhaps the most important unanticipated consequence of the war was that thousands of women already at work enjoyed an opportunity for occupational mobility. In addition to hiring 1.3 of the 2.5 million women who joined the manufacturing force for the first time, war industries also attracted hundreds of thousands of women from other industries and occupations. The labor crisis placed a premium on employing the largest number of women in the shortest period of time, and women who had previously been forced to take menial or low-paying jobs rushed to war plants to take advantage of the opportunity. One woman who had worked as a waitress for twenty cents an hour (with no tips allowed) increased her wages by more than 500 percent when she took her position on the bomber assembly line at Willow Run for $1.15 an hour.

The assembly line of one such airplane factory represented a cross-section of most of the female population. Former saleswomen worked alongside filing clerks, stenographers beside seamstresses. A Women's Bureau survey showed that two-thirds of the women who held jobs in eating and drinking establishments at the beginning of the war had transferred to other work by the end of it. Over six hundred laundries were forced to shut down in 1942 because they could not find women willing to shake clothes and run hot steam irons. In war-affected areas like Mobile and San Francisco, nearly half of all women employed before Pearl Harbor shifted from their old jobs into military production. Even those who remained in their former positions benefited. Beauticians' wages increased 28 percent as a result of the competition for women workers, and the pay of domestics nearly doubled.

The experience of black women underlined the extent to which the war brought significant change, yet also demonstrated the continuation of prejudice. In the years preceding the war, black women were twice as likely to be employed as white, but their economic horizons were severely limited. Over 70 percent worked as domestic servants in private homes, and another 20 percent toiled in the fields, picking crops and hoeing gardens on small farms. For many of them, the war represented a moment of substantial opportunity. The labor shortage helped break down rigid employment barriers and created an unparalleled possibility for job change. In response to the call for new workers, over 400,000 domestics left their former jobs. The number of black women who held positions as servants fell from 72 percent to 48 percent, and the number of black women farm workers declined from 20 percent to 7 percent. At the same time, the proportion of black women who were employed as operatives in factories grew from 7.3 percent to 18.6 percent.

On the other hand, whatever gains were made occurred within a context of continuing racism and oppression. Frequently black job mobility simply meant shifting from domestic service jobs in someone's home to jobs in commercial laundries and restaurants. Factories in states with liberal laws, such as New York, were willing to hire black women operatives, but most states did not have such laws and the federal government did little to enforce its own anti-discrimination edicts. In 1942, as many as 1,000 black women had been through the vocational training to prepare them for war jobs, yet none were hired. While nearly 30,000 black women were available for war jobs in Detroit, most factories would hire them only as janitors or matrons. And in many cities—Evansville, Indiana, and Baltimore, Maryland, to name just two—"hate" strikes occurred when an effort was made to create racial integration in the work force. White women objected to sharing rest-room facilities with black women in Baltimore, and a majority of the union voted to go out on strike rather than change customs. The strike was eventually successful, and the rest rooms remained segregated, testifying both to the absence of sisterhood across racial barriers and to the inability of government officials to root out discrimination in the workplace. Thus, while some breakthroughs occurred, it was within a framework of deeply imbedded structural discrimination—perhaps a sign of what would occur with other nonwhite women workers as well. The experience of Japanese-American women, of course, represented the worst case scenario. Though most worked, many did so under the supervision of internment-camp authorities who held them captive through most of the war.

Although much was made of the patriotic fervor that motivated women to take war jobs, many of those who shifted workplaces were attracted primarily by improved conditions in war industries. Early in the manpower crisis, the Women's Bureau insisted that factories provide rest rooms, adequate toilets, cafeterias, good lighting, and comfortable chairs for their female workers. To a surprising extent, management complied, and conditions in war factories excelled those in other industries. A Women's Bureau study of Bridgeport, Connecticut, for example, reported that women war workers "experienced a marked change in their surroundings. Ventilation, lighting, seating and service facilities . . . usually were much better than on their old jobs." Another survey of upstate New York indicated that half the war plants had established a rest period, and Constance Green's study of the Connecticut Valley showed that twenty-four of twenty-seven factories had instituted improved health and accident facilities. The presence of so many female workers hastened the simplification of jobs and the installation of long-needed safety regulations. Machines were protected; coveralls, slacks, and goggles were made mandatory equipment; and light tools were substituted for heavy ones. One industry official commented, "These are machines we always knew we ought to guard, and now we are guarding them." For the first time in their lives, many women worked in a safe, clean, and pleasant environment.

Higher pay provided the greatest incentive for moving into war industries, however. Wages in munitions plants and aircraft factories averaged 40 percent higher than in consumer factories. In the Connecticut Valley, an operative in a war plant earned $34.85 weekly in contrast to $24.65 for an operative in a regular factory. The starting pay for a woman in an aircraft plant was twice that offered by a commercial laundry. The advantages of war work were especially noticeable in low-wage areas like the South. A female shipbuilder in Mobile took home $37 a week, while a saleswoman received $21 and a waitress $14. Not surprisingly, over half the women employed in Mobile in 1940 had changed jobs by 1944. Although recent studies have shown that women's wages did not rise as fast as men's, the war did bring substantial gains.

In addition, the women who entered war plants usually enjoyed the benefits of union representation. Until the late 1930s, with the exception of the garment industry, organized labor had largely neglected the unionization of women employees. The CIO was committed to redressing that imbalance, however, and under the protective aegis of the National War Labor Board, it set out to ensure that all workers in mass-production industries would be organized. During the war years, the CIO became an entrenched power in many of the areas in which a large number of women were employed. The auto, steel, and electrical unions all boasted significant female memberships, and the number of women enrolled in labor organizations jumped from 800,000 in 1939 to over 3,000,000 in 1945. Here, too, there was still substantial discrimination, with women suffering from inadequate representation, separate seniority lists, and indifference from male leaders. But in wages and working conditions, women still benefited substantially from union membership.

Thus, wartime opportunities broadened significantly the life chances of most women who were already employed, while offering a whole series of new possibilities to those who had never worked before. Race and class differences among women remained substantial, and even where gains occurred, they often took place without altering the fundamental structure of inequality from which women suffered both in attitudes and behavior. But for the woman who had waited on tables for $2.00 a day in a Mobile coffee shop in 1939, there could be no gainsaying the positive immediate results of new jobs with better working conditions in shipyards and munitions factories.

—— II ——

The most lasting and significant change wrought by the war, however, involved the age and marital status of the new recruits to the labor force. It was important that Rosie riveted, but far more critical in the long run was the fact that she was married and over thirty-five years old. From the time women first joined the ranks of the gainfully employed, the young and single had predominated; now the pendulum swung to the married and middle-aged. To some extent, this represented simply a continuation of long-term trends. As Winifred Wandersee, Louis Scharf, and Lois Helmboldt have shown, more and more married women were seeking jobs throughout the 1930s, so that in part, this wartime explosion of married women's employment reflected women taking advantage of opportunities that had simply not been there before. Still, the role of the war in providing a pivotal push to that long-term trend should not be underestimated. By the end of the war, it was just as likely that a wife over forty would be employed as a single woman under twenty-five. The proportion of all married women who were employed jumped from 15.2 percent in 1940 to more than 24 percent by the end of 1945, and as the fighting drew to a close, wives for the first time composed almost a majority of women workers.

Margaret Hickey, head of the Women's Advisory Committee to the War Manpower Commission, remarked in 1943 that "employers, like other individuals, are finding it necessary to weigh old values, old institutions, in terms of a world at war." Her observation accurately described the contemporary transformation of public and private policy toward the hiring of married women as war workers. In the past, employment of wives had been frowned upon. A woman's place was in the home, and popular convention assumed that if she left its confines, the family and all that was related to it would disintegrate. In the midst of war, however, the services of married women in the labor force became essential to the successful functioning of the economy. Personnel managers attempted to hire single women first, but as *Fortune* magazine observed in 1943, "there are practically no unmarried women left to draw upon." The urban housewife became the principal source of labor supply, her services as assiduously cultivated during the war as they had been shunned in the Depression.

As the manpower crisis intensified, wives of all ages and from all parts of the country flocked to take jobs. Seventy-five percent of the new women workers were married, and the number of wives in the labor force doubled. To some extent, the dramatic increase reflected a shift in marriage patterns. The outbreak of war prompted a rash of weddings, and by 1944 there were 2.5 million more married women and 830,000 fewer single women in the population than there had been in 1940. Many of the recently wedded spouses of young soldiers took jobs near military centers while waiting for their husbands to return from the front; moreover, the wives of servicemen who were away were three times more likely to be employed than married women whose husbands were at home.

A great many working wives, however, were older women who had been married for a number of years. Over 3.7 million of the 6.5 million female newcomers to the labor force listed themselves as former housewives. Many had children of school and pre-school age, including 60 percent of those hired by the War Department. Their employment exemplified a drastic change in policy by business and government. In Connecticut and Ohio, unofficial bans against employment of married women office workers in public positions were discarded. Swift and Company lifted a ninety-year rule against hiring wives. And the large insurance companies, each of which had previously discriminated against married women, began to recruit them actively.

A similar change occurred in the policy of employers toward middle-aged women. In January 1941, many firms refused to consider hiring any women over thirty-five years of age. At the beginning of the war, the majority of women workers were thirty-two or under. Within the next four years, however, 60 percent of all the women added to the labor force were over thirty-five. Mary Anderson persuaded government arsenals to begin hiring women over forty in early 1942, and private business quickly followed suit. By the end of the war, the proportion of women thirty-five to forty-four in the labor force had jumped from 27 percent to 38 percent, and the number over forty-five had grown from 16 to 24 percent. Almost all the older workers were also married. For the first time in their lives, they played an important part in the economic processes of the country. And four out of five indicated in a Women's Bureau survey that they wished to stay in the labor force after the war.

None of the changes in women's work could have occurred without the active approval and encouragement of the principal instruments of public opinion, at least for the duration of the war. While necessity required the employment of millions of new female workers, the mass media cooperated by praising women who joined the labor force. A few years earlier, newspapers and magazines had discouraged women from leaving the home and had supported restrictions on the hiring of married women. Now, radio stations and periodicals glamorized war work and pleaded with women to hurry and enlist at their local employment office. Portland, Oregon, stations sponsored a "Working Women Win Wars Weeks," and a national network gave time each week to a broadcast by "Commando Mary" on how women could assist in defeating the enemy. In one radio script, the announcer declared that women possessed "a limitless, ever-flowing source of moral and physical energy, working for victory." Why do we need women workers, the broadcast asked? "You know why," came the answer. "You can't build ships and planes and guns without [them]."

Newspapers and magazines did their part in the publicity build-up by depicting Rosie the Riveter as a national heroine and exhorting others to join her. The woman with an acetylene torch became almost as familiar a figure to magazine readers as the "girl" with the Palmolive smile. *Life* featured a pigtailed pilot on its cover and detailed the exploits of Jacqueline Cochran's air ferry service, while Ruth Sulzberger in the *New York Times* testified to the "Adventures of a [Female] Hackie." Almost every issue of a national publication contained some laudatory article on women's war contribution, whether it concerned a female oboeist in a symphony orchestra, a woman parachute maker in California, or the wives and mothers who ruled a Cumberland town.

The government provided the impetus for the campaign to attract women workers. Acknowledging that "getting these women into industry is a tremendous sales proposition," Paul McNutt, head of the War Manpower Commission, directed defense agencies to make an all-out effort to secure female employees. General Hershey of Selective Service urged industry and agriculture to hire women in factories, farms, and offices; and Henry Stimson, secretary of war, issued a pamphlet entitled "You're Going to Employ Women," which made recruitment of females into government service almost a military order. "The War Department," the pamphlet declared, "must fully utilize, immediately and effectively, the largest and potentially the finest single source of labor available today—the vast reserve of woman-power." Local United States Employment Service offices sometimes even banned the hiring of men, insisting that women be employed for every job that did not absolutely require a man.

The War Manpower Commission (WMC) itself attempted to facilitate the process by issuing guidelines designed to end sex discrimination. Employers were told to hire and train women "on a basis of equality with men," to "remove all barriers to the employment of women in any occupation for which they are or can be fitted," and to use "every method available" to ensure women's complete acceptance. The Office of War Information conducted a vigorous public relations campaign in support of the WMC's policies and urged both employers and women to answer the call to national service. Although the government's pronouncements about nondiscrimination were often not followed in practice, the war and the effort to legitimize women's work did succeed in changing the average citizen's attitude toward female employment. At the height of the Depression, over 80 percent of the American people strongly opposed work by married women. By 1942, in contrast, 60 percent believed that wives should be employed in war industries (only 13 percent were opposed), and 71 percent asserted that there was a need for more married women to take jobs.

—— III ——

As a result of the aggressive campaign to recruit female workers and the urgency of the wartime crisis, women's economic possibilities improved for the first time in thirty years. During the war, the proportion of women who were employed jumped from slightly over 25 percent to 36 percent—a rise greater than that of the preceding four decades. By V-E Day, the female labor force had increased by more than six million, or approximately 50 percent. For the first time, more wives were employed than single women, more women over thirty-five than under thirty-five. Manufacturing took the largest number of new workers—2.5 million—but an additional 2 million entered the clerical field, and the only areas of female employment to suffer a relative decline were those of domestic service and the professions. At the close of hostilities, nearly 20 million women were in the labor force—35 percent of all workers in contrast to 25 percent in 1940.

In the eyes of many observers, women's experience during the war years amounted to a revolution. The Women's Bureau called the increase in female employment "one of the most fundamental social and economic changes in our time." Erwin Canham of the *Christian Science Monitor* declared that "in the long years ahead, we will remember these short years of ordeal as the period when women rose to full stature." Others commented on change in woman herself. Instead of being treated as "a social inferior living on the fringe of American life," Rose Schneiderman said, the woman worker had become a first-class citizen whose contribution was recognized by everyone as indispensable to national survival. In a similar vein, Margaret Culkin Banning asserted that women would never again be dependent on men for their bread and butter. Able to earn their own keep, they could even support a husband who was wounded or ill.

In part, the economic activities of women in the war years provided support for such conclusions. The exigencies of the crisis had swept away some established ways of doing things. Women substituted for men in many fields of endeavor, and barriers against the employment of middle-aged and married women had been shattered. Millions of women found out for the first time how it felt to receive a paycheck, and with growing frequency, wives assumed equal responsibility with husbands for earning the family income. Most important, the public's attitude toward women's work changed, at least temporarily, from outright condemnation to tolerant sanction. "[W]e are building up an entirely different social climate," Jennie Matyas, a labor leader, commented in 1943; "what we didn't consider the nice thing to do after the last war will become the regular thing to do after this one."

There were other signs, however, that such optimism was both premature and exaggerated. Female employment provoked opposition as well as praise, especially as it affected people's perceptions of the stability of family life. The war had been accompanied by severe social dislocations, many of them attributed by critics to women's work. The Connecticut Child Welfare Association reported a startling increase in childhood neurosis, and "latch-key" children who had no supervision during the day while their mothers were at work became a subject of national concern. Those hostile to women's new roles seized on issues of delinquency and child neglect to lambaste women's participation in the work force. Clare Booth Luce demanded that women return to the home to care for their children, and the Children's Bureau called the growing employment of mothers "a hazard to the security of the child in his family." For some Americans at least, women working represented a threat to the cohesion and sanity of social life. It might be tolerated as a temporary necessity but not as a permanent reality. Added to this was evidence that even the progress women had made was accompanied by unyielding discrimination. Such attitudes provided ample reason for skepticism.

The critical question, in the end, was how deeply the wartime changes had gone and whether the advances made at a time of crisis would continue into peacetime. The war, by its very nature, had disrupted the established order and forced an adjustment in the patterns of national living. As a result, many of the most overt forms of discrimination were ameliorated, at least for the moment. A permanent change in women's economic status, however, required a continued redefinition of sexual roles, a more profound shift in public attitudes, a substantial improvement in the treatment afforded women workers, and a new ideological assault on traditional values and sex stereotypes. On those scores, there was considerably less reason for optimism. Although the evidence suggested that a dramatic change had occurred for the moment in the status of women workers, a closer look at the nation's economic institutions indicated that some of the deeper structural manifestations of female inequality remained, having been only partially mitigated by the impact of the war.

CHAPTER 8

The Persistence of Inequality

THE BURGEONING EMPLOYMENT of women may have been essential to victory in the war, but it also raised challenging questions about the future direction of male-female relationships and the perpetuation of the existing social order. It was one thing to encourage women to work as a temporary device to meet a war-induced labor shortage; it was quite another to view women as permanent jobholders. The achievement of economic equality required more than simply hiring women as replacements for men gone to war. It also entailed the establishment of a uniform standard of pay, equal access to the higher ranks of business and government, and, most difficult of all, the development of community services to ease the conflicts between the multiple roles of homemaker, parent, and worker. American women and men had to decide, for example, whether it was more important for a mother to care for her children all day long or be able to join men as an equal contributor to the work force. Not surprisingly, such issues involved substantial controversy and were not resolved easily. But they also highlighted the profound nature of the questions raised by changing gender roles. Thus, while women's economic activity may have altered significantly during the war years, the larger problem that remained was whether steps would be taken to root out the basic causes of persistent inequality between the sexes.

— I —

Discrimination against business and professional women constituted a primary example of enduring prejudice based on sex. The government had urged all women to sign up for jobs, regardless of their occupational background, but for the professional desiring to serve her country, few positions existed. Despite the urgent need for medical personnel, the army refused to commission women doctors until 1943, and it took an act of Congress to correct the injustice. The attitude of private industry was often no better. Businesswomen complained bitterly that they were denied management posts commensurate with their ability and were expected to serve as trainees rather than executives.

Women were also excluded from most of the top policy-making bodies concerned with running the war. Mary Van Kleeck, a prominent social-welfare worker, charged that the government had totally ignored the experience of women leaders in setting up its production, manpower, and food agencies. The same accusation was made by Minnie Maffett, head of the National Federation of Business and Professional Women. With the exception of Anna Rosenberg, she pointed out, not a single woman had been appointed to an important executive position in the various war agencies. Mary Anderson, director of the Women's Bureau, reported that her experts were never consulted by defense officials on questions involving female employment. Throughout the history of the Office of Defense Production, she observed, "the women had very little chance to be even thought of." When the president finally appointed a Women's Advisory Commission (WAC) as an adjunct to the War Manpower Commission (WMC), it was only after the WMC's chairman had expressed his opposition and the members of at least one all-male committee had threatened to resign if a woman joined them. Mary Anderson concluded that the WAC had been created as a calculated device to put women "off in a corner" while denying them any real power.

To a large extent, the WAC's subsequent history confirmed Anderson's initial judgment. Established to evaluate the problems of women war workers and make recommendations for remedial action, the committee met constant frustration in attempting to carry out its mandate. Despite repeated requests, it had no staff to set up studies and prepare position papers. Frequently, it was not consulted on issues affecting women workers. And more often than not, its recommendations—when made—were ignored. Significantly, the WAC was told only in August 1943 about a government plan to mount a public relations drive in September to attract women to war jobs. By the time the committee was notified, copy had already been written and sent to the printer. The campaign itself testified to the government's commitment to recruit women workers, but the manner in which it was planned indicated that women leaders were not valued to the same degree as the workers themselves.

Under such circumstances, the WAC rapidly developed a sense of its own futility. "If we are an advisory committee," one member declared, "somebody ought to ask us for advice sometimes." The women resented having to travel to Washington each month only to sit around a table and hear each other talk. They had hoped to become a vital force in determining government policy toward the woman worker but found instead that they constituted a "token" body. Complaining that women were tired of being treated as "assistants to assistants," the WAC demanded that the War Manpower Commission appoint women to executive positions where they could exercise some real influence. A woman was finally named as assistant to the deputy chairman, but most members of the committee were not mollified. One member resigned in frustration, complaining that women should be "unwilling to accept such subordinate and ineffective positions," and others contemplated the same course of action.

The WAC's relations with the War Manpower Commission's Labor Management Committee (LMC) illustrated the reason for such discontent. The LMC was established in March 1943 to coordinate all policy regarding the use of manpower in the nation's factories. Mary Anderson, among others, had been assured that the head of the WAC would serve as a full member of the new committee. To her consternation, however, she discovered that, while the head of the WAC, Margaret Hickey, could sit in on committee deliberations, she had neither a vote nor a voice in its decisions. When the WAC protested and asked that its leader be given a vote, the LMC unanimously rejected the request, claiming that no special representation could be granted to minority groups. In fact, the new committee consistently demeaned Hickey, barring her from one emergency meeting on the forty-eight-hour week and permitting her only fifteen minutes to present her case for the appointment of women to regional Labor Management Committees.

The WAC's experience highlighted the extent to which inequality persisted in the higher ranks of business and government. The WAC was forced to meet as a "woman's" committee because its members were not allowed to participate in other deliberative bodies. Yet all the decisions affecting women were made in a committee composed entirely of men. "The only place you can make yourself felt is if you are where a thing happens," WAC member Elizabeth Christman observed, "[and] they apparently don't happen [here]." Paul McNutt assured the WAC that it enjoyed the same status in the eyes of the War Manpower Commission as the LMC, but committee members learned from bitter experience that separate did not mean equal. "The more I work in government," Margaret Hickey said early in 1943, "the more I know that in the policy there is nothing discriminatory, but in the practice— that is where we have difficulty."

―――― II ――――

The gap between promise and performance was perhaps best illustrated in those areas where women continued to receive less pay than men. The government could not be faulted on its formal commitment to equal wages. The War Manpower Commission had repeatedly urged a uniform pay scale for men and women, and in a series of decisions handed down in the fall of 1942, the National War Labor Board (NWLB) appeared to give substance to the WMC's policy. In the Brown and Sharp Manufacturing case, the NWLB rejected the company's practice of paying women 20 percent less than men for the same work and endorsed the principle of equal pay "for female employees who in comparable jobs produce work of the same quantity and quality as that performed by men." The nation had an obligation, the board declared, "to provide the utmost assurance that women will not be subject to discriminatory treatment in their compensation."

Some industries, at least, conformed to the NWLB's policy, generating substantial gains for women workers. Newer businesses, with a shorter history of discrimination against women, offered female employees a better chance for equal treatment than older ones, and most aircraft plants, munitions factories, and shipyards had "pay for the job" policies. In addition, a number of CIO unions wrote equal-pay provisions into their contracts and brought suits before the NWLB to correct wage inequities. The electrical workers, with 280,000 female members, succeeded in writing equal-pay clauses into contracts covering 460,000 workers in 1944. A Women's Bureau survey of eighty contracts in three Midwestern states showed that half had equal-pay provisions, with the highest percentage in the radio, electrical, aircraft, and machine industries where CIO unions predominated.

In a series of subsequent decisions, however, the NWLB weakened its initial ruling on equal pay and gave employers a series of loopholes through which they could continue to discriminate in their wage scales. One company was allowed to pay women less than men for the same work because the women were given an extra rest period. In other cases, the board determined that the equal-pay doctrine did not apply to jobs which were "historically" women's, nor to inequalities that existed between two plants owned by the same company. Wage rates for jobs to which women alone were assigned, the board declared, were "presumed to be correct." By the time the NWLB had completed its revisions, employers enjoyed wide latitude in devising ways to avoid the equal-pay principle. General Motors, for example, continued to pay women less than men simply by substituting the categories "heavy" and "light" for "male" and "female."

The government's concern with controlling inflation further deterred implementation of the equal-pay doctrine. Fearing that an across-the-board wage hike would start an inflationary wage-price spiral, the NWLB *permitted*, but did not require, industry to raise women's wages to the same level as men's. Board chairman William Davis declared that the order was addressed primarily to employers who wished voluntarily to equalize the pay received by their female employees. The wording of the directive hardly seemed designed to encourage a rash of pay increases for women. Moreover, President Roosevelt's executive order to "Hold the Line" on spending appeared to countermand even the permissive clause of the NWLB's ruling. Under the president's order, the board could grant wage increases to correct substandard conditions but not to eliminate inequalities. As a result, the NWLB postponed thirty cases involving wage parity, declaring that it had no more power to grant equal pay for equal work. Subsequently, the NWLB's authority to order pay increases under the equality doctrine was restored, but in the meantime, the movement to establish uniform standards of pay had suffered a severe setback.

In the face of government equivocation over the equal-pay question, a great many employers continued to discriminate against women. Only one out of four Bridgeport, Connecticut, manufacturers offered both sexes the same starting rate. In one Eastern war plant, male trainees received a higher wage than the women training them, while in forty-one steel companies surveyed by the Women's Bureau, women clerical workers averaged $60 a month less than men doing comparable work. Employers frequently skirted the issue entirely by placing women in separate job categories from men. When the Brooklyn Navy Yard began to use women to replace men, it called them "helper trainees" instead of "mechanic learners" and assigned them a commensurately lower wage. Other companies simply substituted the words "light and repetitive" for "skilled." Under the former category, a female gauge inspector in one plant earned 55 cents an hour, while her male counterpart took home $1.20.

Yet job segregation was precisely the problem. The worst form of discrimination against women workers was the rate paid for historically female jobs, and the NWLB had specifically refused to regulate the wages for such positions. No class of work exhibited more profound prejudice, but under existing regulations, nothing could be done about it. A Fort Wayne, Indiana, General Electric plant, for example, had fourteen classifications of male employees and five classifications of females. Many of the jobs required comparable skill and training, yet only the women in the highest female grouping received as much as the men in the lowest male category.

At the root of the disparity was the pervasive assumption that any job historically filled by women must have less intrinsic value than a comparable position held by men. In contrast to men, the National Metal Trades Association explained, "women are more patient, industrious, painstaking, and efficient about doing the same thing over and over again." More to the point was the comment of a Connecticut Valley industrialist. "Women," he said, "do the monotonous, repetitive work . . . that drives a man nuts." The two remarks beautifully illustrate how the dynamic of job segregation by sex functioned: women had distinctive qualities that conformed to pre-existing sex stereotypes, and the sex stereotypes justified unequal pay.

Although it was true that many women took jobs during the war that had previously been held by men, the actual incidence of occupational segregation by sex failed to diminish. As Ruth Milkman has shown, even in the "progressive" auto industry separate categories of employment remained the rule rather than the exception. "Rosie the Riveter did a man's job," Milkman writes, "but more often than not she worked in a predominantly female department or job classification." Such classifications, in turn, served as a basis for perpetuating inequality. The premise of women's lower worth prevailed even where "objective" evaluations showed that a woman's occupation required more skill than a man's. General Electric, for example, assessed the job of janitor at thirty-six points and the job of inspector at sixty-eight points; but because the first position was held by a man and the second by a woman, it paid twelve cents an hour more to the male. Asked to explain the contradiction, the company asserted that the point totals were not comparable, since men's work and women's work were classified separately. Thus, the vicious cycle continued. Men and women were arbitrarily assigned to separate labor categories on the basis of sex, just as women were assigned separate jobs and responsibilities in the home; in both cases, it was presumed that women's tasks were worth less, at least monetarily, and the result in the labor market was an entrenched two-tier system that barely changed at all, notwithstanding the disruptions of war.

The perpetuation of such categories often represented a tacit alliance between labor and management to keep women in their place. Although industrial unions fought for equal pay when women took jobs left by men, they frequently insisted that women be assigned to separate seniority lists and grouped together in distinct job classifications. A 1944 United Auto Workers' contract declared that "men and women shall be divided into separate, non-interchangeable occupational groups unless otherwise negotiated locally." Similar contracts specified that women's membership in a union, and their seniority, should last only for the duration of the war. A legal brief presented by the United Electrical Workers (UEW) to the NWLB in 1945 suggested that many unions supported equal pay less out of a commitment to justice for women workers than out of concern for preserving a high wage for the returning veteran. If females replaced males at a lower rate of pay, the UEW asserted, the soldier coming back from war would find his job reclassified as women's work with a woman's wage.

Despite some important advances, therefore, many women workers continued to suffer from wage discrimination. In 1945, as in 1940, women who were employed in manufacturing earned only 65 percent of what men received. The NWLB made a brave start toward redressing some of the inequalities that women experienced, but subsequent decisions weakened the impact of the board's action. In addition, the government's anti-inflationary policies discouraged aggressive implementation of the equal-pay doctrine. Significantly, the NWLB refused to consider the most important source of discrimination against women—the differential in wage rates paid for "women's work." Impressive gains had been made in some war industries, especially those with strong unions, but as long as women's employment was judged by a different standard than men's inequality was inevitable. A wage geared to the job rather than the sex of the worker offered the best solution, but at the end of the war, such a goal remained almost as far away as it had been at the beginning.

—— III ——

The only issue more important than wages was the development of community services to ease the woman worker's household burden. From the time of the first women's right convention at Seneca Falls, women's rights activists had protested against women being saddled with exclusive responsibility for the domestic sphere of life. Charlotte Perkins Gilman pointed out that women could never achieve economic equality until methods were devised for relieving the woman of some of her cooking, housekeeping, and child-rearing tasks. Pursuing the same line of thought, Marguerite Zapoleon, a Women's Bureau official, wrote that equal job opportunities for women depended on the creation of public institutions such as child-care centers which would "expand rather than contract the possible areas of female usefulness." The arguments of both women had a compelling logic. The wife who worked outside the home and also took care of her family carried two full-time jobs. Her dual responsibility prevented her from functioning on the same basis as a man in the world of business and labor. A strong case could thus be made that substantial modification of the existing domestic pattern was essential if women were to gain economic equality. Either men had to thoroughly redefine their domestic roles, or alternative social institutions would have to be created.

The issue of community services, however, involved complicated questions of values and immediately stirred up controversy. The creation of surrogate domestic institutions such as child-care centers challenged deeply held convictions about the integrity of the family and the importance of a woman's role in the home. Most Americans, female as well as male, believed that the primary responsibility of wives and mothers was to care for the household and to rear children. The development of community services threatened such beliefs by assuming that it was just as valuable and proper for a wife to work outside the home as for her to retain full responsibility for domestic tasks. Furthermore, the establishment of child-care centers or central kitchens required a willingness to provide families with a special form of subsidy to enable both husbands and wives to participate more freely in the job market. In effect, society was asked to give women some compensatory treatment so that they could have the possibility of achieving "equality." The issue thus entailed a fundamental clash of values concerning woman's proper place and illustrated better than anything else the difficulty and complexity of achieving full equality between the sexes.

The question of community services first emerged as a result of the high turnover and absenteeism among women in war industries. Women workers changed jobs twice as often as men and stayed home twice as much. For every two women workers hired in war-production factories in June 1943, one quit. The turnover rate in aircraft plants reached 35,000 a month, and Boeing had to employ 250,000 women over a four-year period to maintain a labor force of 39,000. After surveying the manpower crisis in war industries, Bernard Baruch commented that female turnover and absenteeism in one factory alone caused the loss of forty planes a month. In Elizabeth Hawes's case history of a woman war worker, the fictional foreman asked, "Why is Alma always absent?" The same query echoed in defense plants and government offices throughout the country, posing a critical problem for those in charge of winning the war on the home front.

Although part of the difficulty could be traced to lack of adequate training for wartime jobs, a more important cause was woman's dual role as worker and homemaker. Seventy-five percent of the new women workers were married, and over 3 million were full-time housewives. Their responsibilities in the home inevitably affected their performance on the job. Some husbands might help with the household work, but the principal burden rested on the wives. A 1943 survey of war plants showed that 40 percent of all women who left work cited marital, household, and allied difficulties as the reason, while only 9 percent spoke of poor wages or working conditions. In a parallel study, the National Industrial Conference Board reported that family needs ranked as the cause most often given for female absenteeism, after illness. The Sperry Gyroscope Company summarized the problem in a quick acronym. Women, it said, suffered from a bad case of the "d.t.'s"—domestic and transportation difficulties.

Put in the simplest terms, many women workers who were full-time housewives and had not worked prior to the war found it impossible to do both jobs without either succumbing to exhaustion or taking time off from work. After toiling eight hours a day on an assembly line, they had to shop for food and buy clothes for themselves and their families. In some areas, merchants accommodated their needs, but more often, grocery and department stores closed before the woman worker was free. Rationing boards and banks shut down early. Repair shops were dark. And transportation to and from war plants was poor, making it difficult to reach shopping centers quickly. Cooking, cleaning, and laundering added further to the woman worker's burden, and understaffed commercial establishments provided little relief. In some cases at least, the woman worker was forced to take time off to catch up with her household chores. The result was a mounting rate of absenteeism and turnover and the loss of precious hours needed to produce more ships, planes, and war supplies.

Faced with a similar problem, Britain eased the difficulties of its working women by creating special community services for their benefit. "Priority certificates" permitted women workers to order food in the morning and pick it up at night, thus avoiding long lines and stale groceries. Industry gave women one afternoon a week to shop, and stores remained open in the evening for the convenience of female employees. Welfare officers were assigned to each war plant to handle any problems that arose, and rest centers in the country were provided for those workers who needed a holiday. Every factory with over 250 employees was required to install a cafeteria, and the Food Ministry set up over 2,000 "Central Kitchens" that each week prepared over 3 million meals—at cost—for women to carry home to their families.

The United States, however, did relatively little to provide special services for women workers. War-production centers shot up overnight, many of them without restaurants, laundries, banking facilities, or decent transportation systems. The nearest restaurant to one munitions factory in the Midwest was a dirty crossroads café, and buses to and from the plant were scheduled so that workers had no time to eat at the company cafeteria. Men as well as women suffered from the shortage of decent facilities, but the fact that many women had the major responsibility for the care of their homes made their burden heavier. The president called for more public help for women workers and the War Manpower Commission urged stores and banks to stay open at night. Yet with the exception of sporadic efforts by individual companies, no programs approaching the British model emerged on a national level. "The essential difference in the way the war effort is organized in Great Britain and the United States," the journalist Agnes Meyer said in a 1943 speech, "lies in the fact that the British are using necessity to conquer their social weaknesses whereas our endeavor to achieve maximum production has gone forward with brutal disregard of the human beings involved, and with a consequent intensification of our social problems."

The question of whether or not to build child-care centers crystallized the conflicts involved in the community-services issue. The need for such centers was clear from the beginning of the war. Over half of the new women workers came from the home, and although women with small children at home were the least likely to be employed, many, nevertheless, left behind their preschool and young school-age children. In Bridgeport, one-quarter of the students in the elementary and junior-high schools reported that both their parents were employed, while in Detroit, 35,000 of 138,000 prospective women war workers declared that they had young children who needed care. Surveys of Buffalo, San Diego, Los Angeles, and Baltimore confirmed that approximately 25 percent of the new members of the female labor force had at least one child who required supervision during the day, and the War Manpower Commission estimated in 1943 that as many as two million youngsters needed some form of assistance.

The lack of child-care facilities directly affected war production. In Los Angeles, aircraft manufacturers petitioned the city to re-open schools for the summer of 1943 because women workers had departed *en masse* to supervise vacationing children. Repeated studies by the Women's Bureau and other government agencies showed that the need to care for children represented an important cause of high turnover and absenteeism. A California survey revealed that women were absent most often on Saturday—the day children had no school—and Washington, D.C., officials estimated that two million working hours a year were lost in government agencies as a result of women who stayed at home to care for children. Although precise statistics were hard to come by, most studies indicated that approximately 20 percent of all female absenteeism was due to the need to supervise infant and young school-age youngsters. The West Coast Air Production Council summarized the consequences for the defense industry: "one child-care center—adds up to 8,000 man hours a month, in ten weeks equal to one four-engine bomber. Lack of twenty-five child-care centers can cost ten bombers a month."

In some areas, industry itself made notable strides toward coping with the problems. In Portland, Oregon, for example, the Kaiser Company staffed and financed a twenty-four-hour-a-day community school for children from eighteen months to six years. Designed to save time and expense for working families, it was located on the edge of Portland harbor. Structured like a wheel's spokes with entrances on every side for easy access by workers, it featured a swimming pool, brightly colored playrooms, and ready-cooked meals, which weary employees could carry home for their families. The cost per day was seventy-five cents a family.

On a community basis, Vancouver, Washington, demonstrated how existing facilities could be stretched to accommodate after-school activities for older children. The city's population multiplied five times in the first two years of the war, and its school enrollment soared from 4,000 to 12,000. With working parents unable to supervise the after-school activities of their children, business, industry, and civic leaders developed an extended school program of athletics, dancing, and drama. Using classrooms and recreation halls of housing projects for space, faculty wives and student teachers supervised over 3,000 children a day at a cost of a little over seven cents a child.

Elsewhere, however, the cost of creating adequate facilities far exceeded the financial resources of many local governments. Minneapolis, for example, opened an experimental center in 1942 which offered professional supervision, medical care, and three meals a day for pre-school children. Projected expenses for twenty such centers, however, amounted to $224,000, or $198,000 more than the revenue anticipated from the fees paid by parents. Many communities across the country faced a similar dilemma. With school populations skyrocketing, housing needs increasing, and the cost of municipal services mounting, they were unwilling to commit the financial resources necessary to initiate vast new child-care programs. As a result, most observers agreed that the problem could be handled only through national planning and financing. "The fact is that a war is a national emergency," the head of the Michigan Child Care Committee wrote, "and that its effects on community life are too big and too drastic for [local governments] to handle . . . on their own."

Money represented only one of the obstacles to an effective solution, however. Far more important was the issue of whether the government or community should sanction the employment of mothers by providing public facilities for the care of children. Even if financial resources were available, there was a substantial question in many people's minds of whether the benefits of maternal employment outweighed the costs involved. For most Americans, a close relationship between mother and child was essential to family health and stability. A woman might take a job after her children were grown, but employment prior to that time was viewed as violation of a sacred trust and a direct threat to the future of society. As one journalist wrote, "No informed American needs a psychologist to tell him that children separated from home ties and without constant care . . . are the troublemakers, the neurotics and the spiritual and emotional cripples of a generation hence."

Many officials in Washington shared the same concern and emphasized the importance of maintaining women's traditional role in the family. "[A] mother's primary duty is to her home and children," the Children's Bureau declared. "This duty is one she cannot lay aside, no matter what the emergency." Pursuing a similar theme, the Women's Bureau observed that "in this time of crisis . . . mothers of young children can make no finer contribution to the strength of the nation than to assure their children the security of the home, individual care and affection." To an extent, child-care centers encouraged the employment of mothers and threatened the perpetuation of such values, and many social-welfare workers questioned their efficacy. "We have what amounts to a national policy," one WPA official declared, "that the best service a mother can do is to rear her children in the home."

In addition, many mothers resisted the idea of placing their children in the care of strangers. When George Gallup asked a cross section of women in 1943 whether they would take a job in a war plant if their children were cared for in a day nursery free of charge, only 29 percent said yes, while 56 percent said no. Even mothers who were already employed preferred that their children be cared for by relatives and friends rather than a public nursery. Charles Taft, a social-welfare official in Washington, noted in 1943 that many mothers whose children needed care distrusted the idea of institutional supervision and associated child-care centers with charity of relief.

Frequently, these mothers preferred to seek private arrangements for their children, using friends or family members. Karen Anderson and D'Ann Campbell have demonstrated in their studies of wartime women that the urgent need for child care was perhaps exceeded only by the ambivalence of mothers about utilizing public facilities. In Seattle, one after-school center never even opened because it had no enrollment (despite hundreds of requests for such a center), and two others signed up only four children. A Baltimore war worker, in turn, reported that her decision to send her child to day care elicited acid comments, because day care "sounds like the Spartans binding their children over to the state." One survey of women workers in North Carolina showed that most simply had no information about the availability of such centers and lacked confidence about the option even if it existed. Citing the same attitude, a West Virginia official wrote that "the whole thing boils down to the fact that West Virginians think nursery schools and kindergartens are frills."

Yet whatever one's opinion on the wisdom of mothers working, the fact remained that millions were employed and that a large number of children were not receiving adequate care. The press was filled with stories of youngsters penned in basement corrals or exiled to neighborhood movie houses. A social worker in the San Fernando Valley counted forty-five infants locked in cars in a single war-plant parking lot, and the number of child-neglect cases in Norfolk, Virginia, tripled. Although the War Manpower Commission did not encourage others to seek employment, it viewed them as an indispensable labor reserve and urged other departments to develop "special provisions" to aid those who were at work. Brigadier General Louis McSherry of the War Production Board wrote Katherine Lenroot of the Children's Bureau that "one of the most important programs before us is the development of adequate facilities for the care of children of working mothers." Similarly, the War Manpower Commission placed primary importance on helping the female worker meet her family responsibilities so that she could remain in the labor market. The Women's Advisory Committee devoted more time to child care than to any other issue, and nine of the largest women's organizations joined in a concerted campaign to force the federal government into action.

Faced with a profound clash of opinion among its own officials, the Roosevelt administration reacted initially by insisting that responsibility for child care rested with the local community. "We don't want the possibility of federal funds to discourage state and local initiative," Katherine Lenroot of the Children's Bureau declared. Charles Taft wrote a New York official that the government opposed any national movement to set up day-care centers, and the Bureau of the Budget asserted that a bill sponsored by Senator Claude Pepper of Florida to provide federal aid for the establishment of kindergartens and nursery schools did not conform to administration policy. President Roosevelt, in effect, bridged the gap between his advisers when he allotted $400,000 in August 1942 to help local communities ascertain the need for child-care centers. Although the president's action gave the appearance of a national commitment to day care, it actually postponed such a commitment. No funds were set aside for operating existing facilities, or even for hiring supervisory personnel. The average grant was only $7,000—a minuscule sum compared to the dimension of the need—and the principal result of the program was to multiply the studies indicating the necessity for day care, while delaying aid for those states that had made their studies and were prepared to move forward. The administration's approach outraged most day-care advocates and prompted severe criticism from manpower experts. "There are entirely too many agencies studying these problems," Bernard Baruch declared; "What must be done is known. Action alone remains necessary."

As the pressure for federal help mounted, the administration ruled in 1943 that Lanham Act funds for construction of wartime facilities could be used to build and operate day-care centers as well. The decision was no solution, however. Georgia congressman Fritz Lanham thoroughly disapproved of the expenditure of money under his act for child-care facilities and made his opinion known by intervening to obstruct the application process. In addition, the grants to the various communities were made on a matching basis, with local governments required to put up 50 percent of the actual cost. The Lanham Act contained a deficit clause, whereby local authorities had to prove to federal officials that they could not themselves afford to build the centers. If at the end of the fiscal year Washington determined that sufficient local funds were available, it could force the cities and towns to repay the federal contribution. For most local governments, the prospect of having to dip into financial reserves to fund a program which was already controversial seemed a risk too great to take, and relatively few sought help under the Budget Bureau's conditions.

More important, those who did apply encountered a bureaucratic maze which often made the effort hardly worthwhile. Seven separate agencies were involved in the overall program, each with its own sense of priorities and values. Lanham Act funds were administered by the Federal Works Administration (FWA), but before an application could be approved, it had to be recommended by either the education or the welfare department of the local community, the corresponding state agency, the regional FWA office, the Office of Education or Children's Bureau in Washington, and the national FWA office. "What actually happens," one New York representative said, "is that you just don't get the projects under way." The federal program gave the appearance of progress, without the substance. "I'm active," one state official wrote, "but it is pretty much like a horse forever prancing around at his starting place. I am not getting far." Local communities bridled at the delays caused by federal policy and blamed the national government for not being more responsive to their needs. After visiting public nurseries in California, Agnes Meyer reported that "the mere fact that I came from Washington made me a target for violent reproaches." She concluded that the Lanham Act had "delayed more than it had . . . furthered" the development of day-care facilities.

At least in part, the infighting of competing federal agencies reflected a simple contest for control over the federal program. The principal antagonists were the FWA, a construction agency headed by General Philip Fleming, and the Federal Security Agency (FSA), an amalgam of social-welfare departments including the Office of Education and the Children's Bureau. Although the Children's Bureau consistently objected to maternal employment and cautioned against federal involvement in the child-care field in late 1941 and 1942, Katherine Lenroot, the bureau's chief, had herself proposed a national day-care project in August 1941 to be supervised by her own agency and the Office of Education. Ironically, the reasons she offered at the time were precisely those she opposed a few months later. Small communities, she insisted, would lack the facilities and personnel necessary for a large-scale program. Only a national effort could cope with "the constantly changing nature of the problem, with population shifts as well as military population changes." John Studebaker, head of the Office of Education, made a similar appeal for federal staffing and financing of child care. The fact that both officials reversed position when their own proposals were turned down suggested that considerations of power were not irrelevant in the dispute.

Basically, however, the conflict symbolized a far-reaching difference of opinion between the various departments over how to approach the problem of child care. The FWA viewed public nurseries as an "emergency" device to meet a temporary wartime need. Concerned primarily with problems of physical construction, it paid little attention to education and welfare officials who emphasized the need for high-quality centers and instead sought to build the maximum number of facilities in the shortest possible time. The FSA, on the other hand, focused primarily on developing a program that would serve the best long-term interests of children. As one government official noted, the FSA was more concerned with securing a good location and qualified personnel "than with trying to blast through red tape and get on with the program." It envisioned day-care centers as a permanent addition to the nation's social-welfare institutions and went out of its way to ensure that each project measured up to the highest professional standards. In particular, it insisted that child-care proposals receive the approval of local education and welfare officials (the people with whom the Children's Bureau and Office of Education had to work on a daily basis) and represent prevailing community sentiment.

Although the Lanham Act placed operational control in the hands of the FWA, the FSA was deeply involved in the application process, and the result was constant bickering. The FSA accused the FWA of bypassing its agencies, belittling its staff, and ignoring its professional expertise. Instead of requiring complete, in-depth investigations of each application, the FSA charged, the FWA wanted canned paragraphs of support for any and every project. Charles Taft accused FWA officials of being engineers who knew nothing about children and demanded that all FWA instructions on child care be cleared with his office. The FWA, in response, refused to share its files on day care, failed to consult local FSA representatives, and dismissed the Office of Education and Children's Bureau as meddling interlopers. Since every application for federal assistance had to be approved by each agency, the internecine conflict caused even further delay in getting day-care centers established. The only answer was to concentrate all control in one department, and it seemed that the FSA was the best qualified for the job. But as long as the Lanham Act remained the principal vehicle for dispensing federal wartime aid, such a solution appeared impossible.

The controversy reached a peak in the debate over legislation setting up permanent authority in the child-care field. The FSA's point of view was embodied in a bill by Senator Elbert D. Thomas of Oklahoma appropriating $20 million to be administered on a grant-in-aid basis under the supervision of the Office of Education and the Children's Bureau. In support of the Thomas bill, FSA officials argued that the Lanham Act had been completely ineffective, that it was designed to construct buildings, not care for children, and that Congressman Lanham himself had repeatedly interfered to stop the use of federal funds for child-care projects, especially those administered by welfare agencies. The FWA, on the other hand, claimed that it had already solved the problem. Charging that the Thomas bill would "create confusion and overlapping delay," it implied that what the FSA really sought was federal control over the entire educational process. Although the FSA had the better of the argument, the principal effect of the debate was to underline the profound divisions within the administration over how to proceed with a child-care program.

Finally, the conflict between the two sides became so bitter that the president was forced to intervene. In a July 1943 letter to the FSA, he described the controversy as "unfortunate" and announced that he had asked General Fleming of the FWA to institute revised procedures. The chief executive's letter forecast the outcome of the battle, and a month later in a memo to Roosevelt, the FWA, FSA, and Bureau of the Budget declared a "treaty of peace" which in effect ceded all control over child care to the FWA. The power of Congressman Lanham and the fact that the FWA had already established its authority in the field proved too strong a combination to overcome. Although the Thomas bill received the unanimous backing of the Senate in June and was endorsed by most child-care experts, the president's action destroyed any chance for its passage by the House. In the fall of 1943, Congress enacted an amendment offered by Mary Norton which provided that funding for child-care facilities should remain within the Lanham Act and be administered by the FWA.

By the time Congress acted, the problem of child care had reached severe proportions. One journalist estimated that out of 662 war areas needing child-care facilities in the summer of 1943, only 66 had operating programs. The FWA told the Senate in June that it had already provided care for 250,000 children and would help an additional 750,000 within six months, but both claims were vastly exaggerated. As of February 2, 1944, some 65,717 children were enrolled in federally supported facilities, and at the height of its effectiveness in the spring of 1945, the Lanham Act offered assistance to only 100,000. From one point of view, the figures represented significant progress, especially given the suspicion with which many Americans viewed child-care centers and the unprecedented nature of the program. On the other hand, the number of children receiving supervision in federal centers represented less than 10 percent of those needing it and only one-third of the number cared for in Great Britain, a country with less than half the population of the United States. Despite the government's belated effort, a Women's Bureau survey of ten war areas showed that only one out of ten working mothers with children sent them to a day-care center. "[I]n a substantial proportion of the households," the bureau concluded, "no real provision was made for [child] care while the woman worker was absent."

—— IV ——

The history of the child-care issue dramatized the difficulty of achieving economic equality for women. On the one hand, it seemed clear that women could not compete in the job market on the same basis with men as long as they were expected to bear the principal share of responsibility for the home. Frieda Miller of the Women's Bureau observed in 1947 that "freedom of choice [for married women] to enter or not to enter the labor market is conditioned by the community services available." On the other hand, the decision to build central kitchens or public nurseries entailed a commitment to modify traditional sexual roles and encouraged married women to take jobs. The creation of surrogate domestic institutions provoked serious opposition from those who believed that the well-being of society depended on the maintenance of women's role as mother. Many Americans might agree that women deserved a position of equality in the work force, but that did not mean they believed as well in the government subsidizing such equality, especially if the price was the destruction of the family and existing patterns of male-female relationships.

Under more pressing circumstances, Great Britain demonstrated that the problem of child care could be handled, at least in wartime. There, the bombing of London forced public officials to evacuate children and assume direct responsibility for their care. Faced with the prospect of imminent defeat, the government drafted wives and mothers into the labor force and "went out of its way to provide amenities to reorganize social services, and to overcome traditional prejudices." In the United States, however, the crisis was never so urgent. Wives and mothers were recruited as war workers, but they were not drafted. Throughout the period of fighting, most Americans retained a strong belief in the integrity of the family and were reluctant to see women's position in the home taken over by public institutions. In the absence of a preeminent national emergency that required the immediate enlistment of mothers in the work force, it was at least debatable (in most people eyes) whether the government should encourage the disruption of family life by taking over some of the responsibilities of the woman in the home. If workplace requirements had been the only consideration, the United States might have followed the British example. But profound social issues were involved as well, and the conflict between wartime needs and traditional values placed a serious obstacle in the path of decisive action. As a result, the Roosevelt administration at first equivocated on the issue of child care and then permitted the rivalry of competing agencies to retard development of an effective program. With strong, determined leadership, a solution might have been found. Without such leadership, however, a massive child-care program could not be implemented, and most mothers who worked continued to suffer the disadvantage of being responsible for two full-time jobs.

The absence of greater progress in the areas of equal pay, job segregation, community services, and recognition of women leaders raised profound doubts about the war's permanent impact on underlying attitudes toward woman's place. There could be little question that the economic role of women had expanded during the years of fighting. The sharp increase in employment of married and middle-aged women provided just one measure of the extent to which the war had changed women's lives. On the other hand, the hiring of millions of women did not itself signify that women had gained the right to be treated as equals with men in the job market. Economic equality could be achieved only through a substantial revision of social values and a lasting modification in the nature of male-female relationships. By that criterion, it appeared that less change had occurred than might have been expected on the basis of women's participation in the labor force. Female leaders were often denied a voice in policy-making councils; many women workers were still paid unequal wages; and wives and mothers who were employed received inadequate public assistance in the area of child-care and community services.

In the end, therefore, the war's ultimate impact on women's status would not be determined until the fighting stopped and "normalcy" returned. Deeply rooted social values are rarely altered overnight, especially when they are so thoroughly ingrained in society. It seemed likely that any permanent shift in the social order would depend on two things: whether women workers retained the positions in the labor force that they had gained during the war and whether the institutions and ideological assumptions that governed women's "place" would prove amenable to change as well. In the short term, it could be argued that change more than continuity had characterized women's experience during the years between 1940 and 1945. But the long-term verdict would have to await the postwar period, when the soldiers came home, the economy returned to a peacetime level of production, and the country's citizens determined what they believed about the centrality of traditional gender roles to the existing social order.

CHAPTER 9

The Paradox of Change

WHEN JAPAN SURRENDERED in August 1945, the American people rejoiced in the victorious end to their long struggle. Church bells pealed, families prepared to welcome back loved ones who had been at the front, and national leaders praised the dedication of soldiers and war workers who had made the victory possible. No one knew for sure, however, what would happen to women in a world at peace. The nation had experienced fifteen years of uninterrupted turbulence, moving from a decade of depression through nearly half a decade of war. In that time span, attitudes toward women had fluctuated dramatically. In 1938, over 80 percent of the American people strongly opposed work by married women. Five years later, over 60 percent approved of such employment. In each case, public opinion had been shaped in large part by the exigencies of a crisis situation. Now with the return of peace, the future social and economic roles of women became a focal point for controversy. Anxious soldiers wondered whether the war had permanently changed their wives. Parents waited to see if their daughters would come back home and settle down in a nearby community. And social scientists speculated about the war's impact on marriage, the family, and morals. The postwar years thus became a period of testing, a time of transition, in which women themselves and the society at large sought to determine whether women still had a prescribed sphere, and if so, what its boundaries were.

— I —

The fate of women workers provided one obvious and critical measure of the war's effect on women's overall status. Despite the persistence of discrimination, women in the labor force had made significant gains in wages, union-ization, and job opportunities during the war years. With enthusiasm and dedication (as well as economic self-interest), they had taken the place of men and earned the respect and gratitude of the nation. Now, munitions industries were shutting down; eleven million soldiers were speeding home; and many experts doubted whether there were enough jobs to give both women *and* the returning veterans employment. The movement from a wartime to a peace-time economy threatened the advances women had made and raised directly the question of women's future economic role. Would most women who were not poor automatically return home, or, if they wished to do so, would they remain on the job? What would social attitudes be toward wives or mothers working outside the home, especially if jobs were scarce? And if women did continue to work in numbers comparable to those of wartime, would they do so as equals with men or as a separate category of workers considered to be worth less and limited to jobs with low wages and few possibilities for advancement?

In anticipation of the postwar employment squeeze, the Women's Advi-sory Committee (WAC) and other government officials sought to protect the rights of women workers. "Prospects for job security and other new job opportunities after the war are as important to women as to men," the WAC declared. "The American people therefore must demand consideration of the status of women in all postwar plans." The WAC urged government econo-mists to define full employment "to include all women now at work" and lobbied for the establishment of a family assistance program and child-care facilities to help women workers. "No society can boast of democratic ideals if it utilizes womanpower in a crisis and neglects it in peace," the committee asserted. "To take for granted that a woman does not need work and use this assumption as a basis for dismissal is no less unfair than if the same as-sumption were used as a basis for dismissal of a man."

Other government agencies echoed the WAC's pronouncements. In a de-mocracy, the War Manpower Commission emphasized, every citizen regard-less of race or sex enjoys a "fundamental right to choose whether to work or not." The Department of Labor issued a directive specifically prohibiting em-ployers from discriminating against workers because of race or sex, and the secretary of labor warned against any restriction on the hiring of married women. Focusing on the attitudes of returning veterans, the War Department distributed a pamphlet urging soldiers to share housework and support an extension of community services as a way of helping wives who wished to continue on the job. "Family problems are produced by social change," the pamphlet declared, "and often can be solved only by further changes." Administration spokesmen in Congress adopted a similar tone. "Many women who have gone into factories and done such splendid work . . . will want to continue working," Senator Harry Truman said in 1944, "and they are entitled to the chance to earn a good living at jobs they have shown they can do."

Despite such rhetoric, however, a substantial number of Americans, believed that the time had come for women to return to the home. Many observers viewed women's working as a primary cause of juvenile delinquency and believed that the continued presence of wives and mothers in the labor force directly threatened the stability of the nation's social institutions. In a widely circulated article reflecting popular concern, the anthropologist Margaret Mead asked, "What's Wrong with the Family?" Mead concluded that despite troubled times, the family was still a flourishing institution, but others were not so sure. Willard Waller, a Barnard sociologist, charged that during the war, women had gotten "out of hand," with the result that children were neglected and the very survival of the home was endangered. The only solution, he asserted, was the restoration and strengthening of the patriarchal family. "Women must bear and rear children; husbands must support them." In less blunt terms, others took the same position. Frederick Crawford, head of the National Association of Manufacturers, praised women for their wartime contribution but declared that "from a humanitarian point of view, too many women should not stay in the labor force. The home is the basic American institution."

In part, the desire to restore old patterns of economic responsibility was motivated by fear of recession. The spectre of massive unemployment haunted politicians, economists, and workers who remembered all too well the Depression that had preceded the outbreak of fighting. If the war had eliminated bread lines and relief rolls, peace threatened to reestablish them. In the eyes of many leaders, a cutback in women's employment offered no guarantee against the possibility of a new economic downturn. A Southern senator, for example, urged Congress to force "wives and mothers back to the kitchen" in order to ensure jobs for the millions of veterans who would be seeking new positions. Labor leaders, with their separate seniority lists and contract clauses providing for an end to women's employment after the war, sought the same end, failing repeatedly to defend women's rights during demobilization layoffs.

Just as important, however, was the persistence of hostility toward the idea of women participating as equals in the economic world. Magazines were full of articles which revived shibboleths about women's inferiority and questioned the ability of women to compete with men. Margaret Pickel, dean of Barnard, declared in the *New York Times Magazine* that women "had less physical strength, a lower fatigue point, and a less stable nervous system" than men. For that reason, she claimed, employers found female workers more demanding, more emotional, and less reliable. "By middle age, when men are at their best, a devoted woman worker is apt to degenerate into fussiness or worse." Union leaders also exhibited a distrust of women workers. R. J. Thomas, president of the United Auto Workers (UAW), charged that women accepted the advantages of union membership but not the responsibilities. Many women were reluctant to pay dues, he reported, and few showed any interest in fighting for their own needs. On the other hand, when women union leaders protested such attitudes and asked for support from the UAW's International Executive Board, they were arbitrarily turned down. Thomas predicted that at the end of the war, almost all women would lose their jobs—a prospect which seemed more to please than disturb him.

Public opinion surveys, moreover, indicated that most Americans—women as well as men—believed in perpetuating a sharp division of labor between the sexes. Men were expected to earn a living and to make the "big" decisions, while women were expected to take care of the home. Both *Fortune* magazine and the American Institute of Public Opinion found that a sizable majority of the American people were opposed to a wife working if her husband could support her. The people surveyed by *Fortune* asserted that women should be in charge of rearing children and caring for the family but that men should determine where a family lived and how it spent its money. Less than 2 percent of the respondents believed that a woman was as qualified as a man was to serve as a mayor.

Despite the changes engendered by war, then, traditional ideas about "woman's place" retained a strong following. Female workers had been assiduously cultivated in the midst of the military crisis, but now the courtship appeared to be over. "Perhaps intentions were never honorable," Margaret Hickey of the WAC observed. Frieda Miller, chief of the Women's Bureau, remarked that public opinion had shifted from a period of "excessive admiration for women's capacity to do anything, over to the idea . . . that women ought to be delighted to give up any job and return to their proper sphere—the kitchen." At least one woman supervisor in an aircraft factory shared such ideas. "[Women] will go back to their homes, and to their beauty parlors," Ida Dumars of Boeing said, "and they love the idea. They've done a grand job, . . . but they are glad it's over." Even those women leaders who had been most skeptical of the gains made in wartime were stunned by "the toboggan in public esteem."

If public opinion had turned against female employment, however, women workers themselves gave every indication of desiring to stay on the job. A Women's Bureau survey of ten areas showed that three out of four women who had taken jobs in the midst of the war wanted to continue working. In

New York, the figure was 80 percent; in Detroit, 75 percent. A UAW survey of women workers in the Glenn Martin factory in Baltimore showed that 98 percent wanted to stay on the job; among UAW women members in Detroit, the figure was 85 percent.

If all the women actually worked who wanted to, the numbers employed would far exceed the 1940 totals—by 55 percent in Detroit and 150 percent in Mobile. "War jobs have uncovered unsuspected abilities in American women," one worker said in explaining her desire to remain employed. "Why lose all these abilities because of a belief that 'a woman's place is in the home.' For some it is, for others not." A female steelworker agreed. "If [women] are capable," she declared, "I don't see why they should give up their position to men. . . . The old theory that a woman's place is in the home no longer exists. Those days are gone forever." The testimony of the women workers seemed to vindicate the predictions of those who said that the war had changed the fundamental outlook of women. "Used to money of their own," the *Saturday Evening Post* observed, "millions of the sex are going to sniff at postwar bromides about women's place."

Although some women workers were undoubtedly more committed than others, the desire for employment appeared to characterize women of every age group. Within the labor force, the greatest enthusiasm was expressed by women over forty-five, of whom 80 percent indicated an interest in a permanent job. "These are the women who have been developing new skills during the war," the Women's Bureau observed. With husbands off at work and children grown, they had no pressing tasks in the home to prevent them from remaining in the work force. A job offered both personal satisfaction and financial rewards. The wish for employment extended to the young as well, however. Of 33,000 female students sampled in a *Senior Scholastic* poll, 88 percent wanted a career in addition to homemaking, while only 4 percent chose homemaking exclusively. Even the *Ladies' Home Journal*, whose writers preached that "the ideal of every woman is to find the right husband, bear and rear his children, and make . . . for them a cozy, gay, happy home," reported that more women workers wanted to continue on the job than quit and return to the home. As the war hurtled to a climax in the spring of 1945, many women clearly wished to retain an active role in the labor force. The question was, as Mary Anderson phrased it, "[would the nation] meet the days to come in terms of the future, or [would it] try to keep the world bound to an outworn order?"

—— II ——

Demobilization and the return home of servicemen determined part of the answer. Under the Selective Service Act, veterans took priority over wartime workers in the competition for their old jobs. As war plants reconverted to peacetime production, women who were last hired were also first fired. Since large numbers of employers had been reluctant to hire women in the beginning, women had low seniority and throughout the war had been the first to be laid off during job changeovers. Moreover, many industries now folded overnight as victory approached. The Springfield Arsenal, where 81 percent of the women hoped to continue working, dismissed every employee within a week of V-J Day. The changeover hit women in heavy industry especially hard. In California, where producers of durable goods employed 144,700 women in October 1944, the number plummeted to 37,000 a year later. The aircraft industry laid off 800,000 workers in the two months after V-J Day—most of them women—and the auto industry went through a similar transition. The number of women auto workers fell from 25 percent of all auto workers in 1944 to 7.5 percent in April 1946. The last figure was only one point higher than the percentage employed in October 1939. Overall, women comprised 60 percent of all workers released from employment in the early months after the war and were laid off at a rate of 75 percent higher than men. With the manpower crisis over, some employers revised their age requirements, throwing women over forty-five out of work, and large companies like Detroit Edison, Thompson Aircraft, and IBM reimposed earlier restrictions on the hiring of wives.

But if countless women were thrown out of work at war's end, an appreciable number were either rehired in other jobs or retained their wartime positions, confounding the expectations of those who believed that the situation would revert immediately to the prewar status quo. Unfortunately, very few of those who stayed in the work force remained in "Rosie the Riveter" jobs. Many women welders tried desperately to keep their skilled positions, protesting bitterly when they were refused. As one woman poignantly observed of her own shattered occupational dream, "All I wanted to do was to make an ornamental gate. Was that so much to ask?" But being rejected as a welder did not mean leaving the labor force. The Bureau of Labor Statistics had predicted that six million people would lose their jobs in the year after the war, a substantial proportion of them women. In fact, only a small percentage of that number remained permanently out of work.

The process by which the female work force was redistributed after the war spoke volumes about both the systemic prejudice that existed against women and women's willingness to persist in the quest for employment, notwithstanding these constraints. Many women war workers, of course, simply accepted demobilization and were happy to go back home, so joyful at the war's termination and at the return of the soldiers that they did not mind losing their jobs. But many also protested, demanding that their seniority rights be protected and that they be given first choice when reconversion jobs opened up in the auto industry and elsewhere. Usually, labor leaders shunned their protests, in one case accidentally "losing" copies of 100 grievances (all in *triplicate*) before action could be taken on them. For these and other skilled war workers, the next step was to join the employment lines at the United States Employment Service. There, sex discrimination again took over. Women with skills in welding or machinery were offered jobs as waitresses or clerks. If they turned down the jobs on the grounds that the positions did not match their skills, the women were often denied unemployment compensation and taken off the government rolls. Men, by contrast, were allowed to insist on jobs appropriate to their skill level and could reject numerous job openings while continuing to receive unemployment compensation. Through such a process, it did not take long for women to get the message that they could return to "women's" work but not to the skilled positions they had held during the war.

As a result, the most striking feature of women's employment picture in the years after the war was the number of women who rejoined the labor force, but in sex-segregated and sex-typed occupations. Between September 1945 and November 1946, for example, 2.25 million women left work, and another million were laid off. But in the same period, nearly 2.75 million were hired. The number of women in heavy industry declined substantially, yet women's employment in clerical, sales, and service positions continued to grow, suggesting that many of the women who had joined the labor force during the war were continuing to work, but now in lower-paying, less open-ended positions.

The experience of women workers in Baltimore represented one barometer of the direction of postwar female employment. In a Women's Bureau survey conducted in 1944, three out of four Baltimore war workers had expressed an interest in staying on the job. Two years later, four out of five were still employed, nearly half of them in the same position. Fifty percent of those who planned to quit were also working, and overall, one of every two members of the female labor force had joined the working population in the years after Pearl Harbor. The average wage had fallen from $50 to $37, but the Women's Bureau concluded that "for a surprisingly large proportion of women . . . wartime plans [had] materialized."

Two years after the war ended, women had regained many of the statistical losses suffered in the immediate postwar period. The overall number of women in manufacturing declined by nearly a million, but there were still one million more women in the nation's factories in late 1946 than there had been in 1940. In October 1946, women's hiring rate was greater than men's for the fifth month out of six, and their layoff rate was down. Aircraft factories in San Diego and Hartford began to call some women back to work, and the postwar economic boom resulted in a huge demand for female workers in sales and service jobs. Almost all of the wartime clerical employees stayed at work; women still constituted 40 percent of the operatives in consumer industry; and female participation in heavy industry had grown from 9 to 13 percent. In addition, severe shortages of stenographers, typists, teachers, and nurses were reported across the nation.

As the decade drew to a close, therefore, the imprint of the war remained strong, albeit ambiguous. Twice as many women were employed in California in 1949 as had been employed in 1940. Nationwide, the female labor force had increased by over 5.25 million—substantially more than the increase that might have been expected without the war. The number of female clerical workers had nearly doubled; women in manufacturing had increased by 50 percent; and the proportion of women who worked had jumped from 27 percent to 32 percent—a change greater than that for the preceding three decades. The nation, Frieda Miller of the Women's Bureau speculated, was "approaching a period when for women to work is an act of conformism." Most of this employment, of course, reflected none of the progress that had been made in wages and job possibilities during the war itself. Karen Anderson has noted that at the end of the decade women "remained a cheap labor force to be kept in reserve in anticipation of future needs," with discrimination continuing to shape the jobs, pay, and promotion possibilities available to women.

Still, important changes had occurred. The most important of these was reflected in the continued growth in employment among married women who had joined the work force in large numbers during the war. By 1952, some ten million wives held jobs—two million more than at the peak of World War II and almost three times the number employed in 1940. During the 1940s, the proportion of married women at work jumped more than 50 percent (from 15.2 percent to 24 percent), and for the first time, wives comprised a majority of the women employed (52.1 percent in 1950 versus 36.4 percent in 1940). The number of married couples working leaped from three million, or 11 percent, in 1940 to almost seven million, or 20 percent, in 1948, and approximately four and a half million mothers of children under eighteen were employed—nearly 25 percent of the total female labor force.

The same type of dramatic shift took place in the age distribution of women workers. At the end of the decade, the greatest proportion of new workers were in their early forties, and women in their fifties entered the labor force in the same numbers as those in their twenties. Two and a half million women over thirty-five went to work from 1940 to 1950, and the median age of female workers rose from thirty-two to thirty-six and a half.

While the number of women workers aged eighteen to twenty-four declined 8 percent, the number from thirty-five to forty-four grew 51 percent, and those from forty-five to fifty-four gained 77 percent. By 1950, there were five and a half million women over forty-five years of age in the labor force, and women between thirty-five and fifty-four constituted 40 percent of the total number of women at work.

Equally important, the war helped women's work to become an increasingly accepted part of middle-class life. In the past, wives from the middle class had been discouraged from taking a job by the fear of social ostracism. If a woman entered an occupation that was competitive with that of her husband, she posed a threat to traditional notions of male superiority and challenged the image of the man as provider. On the other hand, if she took a job that was inappropriate to her class standing, she brought social embarrassment to her family and created a problem of status inconsistency. The war aided in resolving both dilemmas. First, it helped to legitimize work for women of all classes by defining employment as a patriotic necessity. And second, it prompted a boom in white-collar occupations which were "respectable" for women of middle-class status to hold—a boom which continued throughout the postwar era. During the 1940s, the proportion of female workers filling clerical and sales positions jumped from 31 to 37 percent—a gain matched only in the decade of 1910 to 1920—and by 1950, over half of all women workers were employed in white-collar jobs, including 66 percent of native white women. The evidence suggested that as the decade of the 1950s began, work for married women had become an integral element in the lives of many middle-class families. Sociologists observed that more wives were seeking jobs even though their husbands earned enough to support the family, and the National Manpower Council reported in 1954 that in 40 percent of all families receiving a total income of from $6,000 to $10,000 a year both the husband and wife worked. Indeed, a strong argument could be made that female employment was the crucial means by which many families achieved middle-class status.

By these criteria, the war represented a significant turning point for many women workers. It had enabled millions of women to take jobs who otherwise might not have sought employment. It forced the substantial weakening of barriers to the employment of wives. And it opened up the opportunity for a second vocation to thousands of older women whose primary homemaking duties were over. Although structural discrimination based on sex was pervasive, the experience of work for women had become an institution in many households where it had not been before. Moreover, despite the built-in obstacle of demobilization, women succeeded in surprising numbers in finding jobs to replace their wartime positions, albeit in occupations that reflected all the inherent deficiencies of sex-typing and sex-segregation. Many people still opposed the idea of women working outside the home, and it was at least debatable whether the life of a filing clerk or salesperson was more rewarding than that of a full-time housewife. But now the option to work outside the home existed, and however limited the option was, it represented a change of potentially dramatic proportions.

—— III ——

The success of women in holding onto some of their wartime economic gains made all the more inexplicable the relative absence of progress in the fight for equality. One might have expected the expansion of women's sphere to be accompanied by a growing recognition of women as equal participants with men in the job market. Such was not the case, however. While the war produced important changes in women's numerical representation in the labor force, it failed to bring a parallel improvement in the economic opportunities most women enjoyed. Instead, discrimination persisted in professional employment, wage scales, and community services. Ironically, the areas of traditional concern to the women's rights movement received little attention, even at a time when women's involvement in activities outside the home was increasing dramatically.

The area of business and professional employment illustrated the absence of progress on wider issues of equal rights. Despite the shortage of highly trained personnel during the war, the proportion of women entering the professions continued to decline. In a 1948 article in the *Saturday Evening Post*, Susan B. Anthony IV cited the decrease in the number of women lawyers and superintendents of schools as evidence of the "crack-up" of the American woman's movement. Medical schools continued to impose a quota of 5 percent on female admissions; 70 percent of all hospitals refused to accept female interns; and medical associations like the New York Obstetrical Society barred women members. Although women comprised 25 percent of all women workers in government, they represented only 3 percent of those who held high-level positions, and Margaret Hickey charged that a "campaign of undercover methods and trumped up excuses" was being used to drive women even further out of upper-bracket public jobs. The same disparity existed in other fields. A survey of Chattanooga banks showed that while women and men served in equal numbers as bank tellers, men were called senior tellers; women, junior tellers. Furthermore, business executives professed little confidence in women's ability to hold management positions. In response to a *Fortune* poll, 53 percent of the executives said that women handled people less well than men, and 65.8 percent asserted that women were less able to make decisions. (The figures for the average man were 43.6 percent and 49.7 percent respectively.) Whether or not discrimination was solely to blame, the evidence clearly indicated that most barriers to women's employment in business and the professions remained intact.

Women workers also continued to receive appreciably lower wages than men. At the end of the war, the National Industrial Conference Board reported that women in manufacturing earned 66 percent of what men were paid. A female laundry worker in Illinois took home $0.55 an hour; a man, $1.10. Five years later, the Bureau of Labor Statistics disclosed that women's median earnings were only 53 percent of men's. Women in public administration received 74 percent as much as their male co-workers, but those in retail trade earned only 48 percent as much. A survey of all industries in 1951 showed that wherever women constituted more than 50 percent of the labor force, the industry paid a wage that fell below the national average. In short, there was little reason to believe that *any* change had occurred in the basic assumption that women's work was worth less than men's, and there was some evidence that with the passage of time women's earnings were declining relative to men's.

Senator Wayne Morse of Oregon attempted to eliminate the worst discrepancies by sponsoring a federal equal-pay bill that geared wages to job content, but his legislation failed to gain the support necessary for passage. Although both parties endorsed the measure in principle, the opposition prevented it from coming to a vote. The Chamber of Commerce declared that the problem of equal pay should be handled voluntarily by employers, and George Meany of the AF of L asserted that the issue of wages fell "within the province of collective bargaining, and not of police action by government." A few states had corrective laws on the books, but most of the statutes contained massive loopholes and provided little enforcement power. Industry and labor, meanwhile, failed to deliver on their promise to solve the problem voluntarily. A Women's Bureau survey of 2,044 collective bargaining agreements showed that only 17 percent had equal-pay clauses.

Advocates of child care met with even more frustration. The Federal Works Administration announced in August 1945 that grants under the Lanham Act would end as soon as the war crisis was over. Most experts agreed that the large number of mothers in the labor force made a continuation of such facilities essential, but since the federal enabling legislation was for the duration of the military conflict only, entreaties for help received little encouragement from administration officials. When Earl Warren, governor of California, wrote that closing the 530 centers in his state would cause "a great wrench in our community life," the FWA responded that the future of child-care centers rested with the states themselves, not with the federal government. Mary Norton and others finally persuaded Congress to extend the Lanham Act for six months, but after March 1, 1946, all federal support for child-care facilities ended.

The history of day care in New York exemplified the difficulties facing those who sought to establish a meaningful permanent program. During the war, the state had been forced to step in to provide funds for hard-pressed local communities that had been unsuccessful in their efforts to get money under the Lanham Act. After the war, however, Governor Thomas Dewey and the state assembly killed legislation designed to fund the centers on a permanent basis. State authorities agreed to temporary appropriations for New York City but insisted that the prime purpose of the limited program was to combat juvenile delinquency in hard-core poverty areas. Mothers who wished to use the centers had to submit to "means" tests to establish their need for public assistance, and the state youth commissioner suggested that working mothers might better go on relief so that they could care for their children in their own homes.

Although a survey showed that seven out of eight families using the centers could not earn a living wage unless the mother worked, state officials continued to discredit the program. The welfare commissioner claimed that many mothers worked "only to satisfy their desire for a career," and others insisted that the Aid to Dependent Children program more faithfully protected the family unit. In 1947, the *New York World Telegram* entered the controversy, charging that child care was conceived by leftists operating out of Communist "social work cells." The campaign for day-care centers, the *Telegram* said, had "all the trappings of a Red drive, including leaflets, letters, telegrams, petitions, protest demonstrations, mass meetings, and hat-passing." Those who benefited from the program, it claimed, were often "furcoated mothers" who arrived with their children in taxicabs. Such charges were absurd on their face and said as much about the tendency of conservatives to use the "Red Scare" as a device to kill social reforms as anything else; but the disagreement over publicly supported day care also testified to the depth of feeling on the issue of wives and mothers working. Throughout the Progressive era and the New Deal, enormous energy had been expended in the effort to secure social-welfare measures that would protect the mother's place in the home, and there was great reluctance to reverse that emphasis. As a result, the child-care program fell into disrepute, and all state aid to child care ended on January 1, 1948.

In the meantime, women activists continued to divide over the ongoing effort by the National Woman's Party to win adoption of the Equal Rights Amendment. For a brief period during and after the war, the outlook appeared promising. Congressmen talked of approving the amendment as a vote of thanks to women for their "magnificent wartime performance"; both parties endorsed the measure; and luminaries such as Homer Cummings, Henry Wallace, and Harry Truman added their voices in support. The amendment involved a fundamental division of opinion over the meaning of equality, however, and provoked as much opposition as praise. Prominent women like Eleanor Roosevelt and Mary Anderson insisted that protective legislation was more valuable than the establishment of an abstract principle of legal rights, and in the end, their viewpoint prevailed despite the increased backing won by the N.W.P. The Senate first considered the amendment in August 1946 and by a margin of 38 to 35 denied it the two-thirds approval needed for adoption. (The *New York Times* praised the vote, saying "motherhood cannot be amended.") Four years later, the measure passed by a sweeping majority of 63 to 11, but this time it contained a rider introduced by Senator Carl Hayden of Arizona specifying that no protective legislation was to be affected. The Hayden rider in effect voided the operative intent of the feminist bill and rendered it meaningless. "My amendment is a revolving door," Hayden boasted. "We come in one side and go out the other." One Washington reporter observed that Hayden "could put a rider on the Ten Commandments and nullify them completely." Although the Equal Rights Amendment was passed by the Senate one more time in 1953, with the Hayden rider, the Senate's action effectively buried hopes for its adoption until the late 1960s.

—— IV ——

The experience of women during the 1940s thus presented a strange paradox. On the one hand, large numbers of women joined the labor force, substantially altering the existing distribution of economic roles. On the other hand, only minimal progress was made in the areas of greatest concern to women's rights advocates—professional employment, child-care centers, a uniform wage scale, and occupational segregation. Women's sphere had been expanded, yet traditional attitudes toward woman's place remained largely unchanged. A job for a wife over thirty-five became normal—at least by a statistical standard—but most Americans continued to subscribe to the belief that women were (and should remain) primarily homemakers.

Although the paradox seemed inexplicable on the surface, it contained the key to understanding the amount of change that did occur during the decade. The events of the war years suggested that most Americans could accept a significant shift in women's economic activity as long as the shift was viewed as "temporary" and did not entail a conscious commitment to approve the goals of a sexual revolution. On the other hand, when the issue was one of preserving a division of labor between the sexes, they demonstrated their adherence to traditional values. Ironically, then, the less people saw women's work as a threat to conventional views about woman's place, the greater was the possibility that sex roles could continue to change. In that light, the "lag" between cultural norms and everyday behavior said a great deal about what happened (and did not happen) in the 1940s.

Public opinion surveys provided one clue to the dynamics of the paradox. When the nation's citizens were asked whether a wife should work if jobs were scarce and her husband could support her, 86 percent said no. The question, in effect, tested the respondents' loyalty to the idea of the man as the principal wage earner in the family and implied that if a wife worked, she would be depriving a man of a job. On the other hand, after the query was rephrased to eliminate the issue of job scarcity, the number of people opposed to the employment of married women fell to 63 percent. The greatest change, however, occurred when *Fortune* modified the wording a third time and asked whether a wife should hold a job if she had no children under sixteen. In response to the final version of the question, only 46 percent of the men and 38 percent of the women still rejected the idea of a wife working. Thus, toleration of female employment increased precisely to the extent that traditional definitions of sexual roles were not challenged. When the salient issue was man's role as provider or a mother's responsibility to rear children, opposition to married women working remained high. When neither issue was present, on the other hand, antagonism toward the employment of wives dropped substantially.

Other polls, meanwhile, indicated that women's economic potential, if measured by itself, was viewed as an asset rather than a liability. When *Fortune* asked a group of men whom they would choose to marry among three equally attractive women, only 16.8 percent selected a woman who had never held a job, while over 55 percent chose one who had worked and been either moderately or extremely successful. In addition, a majority of those expressing a clear opinion asserted that if a young couple did not have enough money to get married, the prospective wife should take a job rather than wait until the man could earn more on his own. Thus, it appeared that public attitudes toward women working depended in large measure on how the issue was defined. On an economic basis alone, female employment seemed to be acceptable, while when the question became one of social values, opposition grew.

Against such a background, the conditions which prevailed in postwar American assumed decisive importance. In the years immediately following the war, inflation racked the nation. Meat prices rose by 122 percent between 1945 and 1947, and repeated strikes in major industries sent the cost of basic purchases skyrocketing. The inflationary spiral created a severe economic pinch for almost everyone, but it especially affected those families, that had postponed their desire for consumer products during the war. At just the moment when husbands and wives were planning to build new homes, buy new cars, and purchase improved appliances, a series of arbitrary price hikes stood in the way. Many couples found it impossible to fulfill their quest for a higher standard of living on one income alone. Furthermore, many of the younger couples who had just gotten married and were about to start a life together could not survive on the benefits of the GI Bill or veterans assistance alone. For them, a wife's employment was indispensable.

The combination of inflation and rising aspirations cast the issue of women's work in a special light. Husbands who might have opposed married women holding jobs as a matter of principle were able to rationalize employment by their own wives as a necessary device to get more money for family needs. The married woman, it now appeared, was seeking by working to give her children a better life and a healthier environment, not attempting to strike out on her own in the selfish pursuit of personal ambition. Frieda Miller commented that women's work had become essential to "the quality of family life," and a national conference on work in the lives of married women concluded that the increased economic activity of wives constituted a pivotal element in the improvement of family living standards, the growth of real income, and the rising rate of social mobility. In short, women's work become a critical component for millions of families seeking to join the middle class.

Significantly, women workers interpreted their role in the same way—at least publicly—thereby reinforcing the sense that female employment was directed primarily to helping the family. When women war workers were asked why they wished to continue on the job, a total of 84 percent cited "economic need" or the desire to assist with family support. Only 8 percent, in contrast, gave what could be described as such "feminist" explanations as the desire for self-expression or dissatisfaction with the traditional role of women in the home. Thus, women workers themselves were—apparently—not seeking to challenge existing sexual roles. Instead, they were fulfilling the sanctioned function of "helpmate" in a new way. One plant psychologist at Lockheed Aircraft noted that morale among married women employees was high because "they seem to feel they are contributing to home life, not detracting from it."

It would be wrong, of course, to underestimate the changes that were taking place beneath the surface,. Frieda Miller pointed out that although the vast majority of women workers cited "economic need" as a primary motivation, the desire for self-expression was often present also. For many women, the justification of financial need provided a convenient (and acceptable) substitute for more complicated responses. A *Ladies' Home Journal* poll, for example, showed that 79 percent of the workers interviewed enjoyed the experience of being employed, especially the chance to meet new people. More important, it seemed clear that the definition of "economic need" was undergoing a substantial transformation. In the years prior to 1940, married women held jobs only if their husbands received an income below the poverty level, thus assuring that the highest percentage of married women workers would be black or foreign-born. By 1950, on the other hand, a growing number worked in order to purchase new homes or finance the education of their youngsters, rationales that for the first time legitimated employment for white wives and also those from the middle class and above. As one woman told Gertrude Samuels of the *New York Times*, "the children get more things by my working; it's easier to buy them clothes and pay for school. We get more out of life." Both the census and the National Manpower Council's study of families earning from $6,000 to $10,000 indicated that many middle-class wives were employed. Far from meaning just family survival, therefore, the phrase "economic need" had come to include the quest for a better life. As female employment became a vehicle for upward mobility, a new element of voluntarism entered the equation of women's work.

Nevertheless, what remained most significant was the *impression* that women went to work out of "necessity." If a woman had declared that she sought employment in order to gratify a personal desire or prove her equality with men, she would immediately have come into conflict with the social norm that a wife should be happy to stay in the home. A large number of such responses, in all likelihood, would have prompted a campaign to discourage married women from working. A wife who sought employment to help the household, on the other hand, complemented rather than challenged conventional perceptions of the female role. The function of inflation, in such a context, was to make the argument of "economic necessity" both convenient and credible. As long as the married woman was working to help pay the bills or move the family ahead, there was little basis for attacking her. A person might question the consequences of her employment but not the motivation.

To clinch the argument, it was important that the women most directly involved in the expansion of the female labor force—wives over thirty-five— had already finished their primary homemaking responsibilities. The 1940 census revealed that the average woman married at twenty-one years of age, had her first child at twenty-three, and had her last when she was twenty-seven. All her children attended school by the time she reached her mid-thirties, and all had left home when she was forty-five. With the cares of child rearing over, and the duties of housekeeping reduced by electrical appliances, she was "ready" to work. Margaret Mead observed that many middle-aged women felt "restless and discontented . . . unwanted and rudder-less" after the task of raising a family was over. For such women, a job—even as a file clerk or saleswoman—frequently offered a new focus of activity, a welcome respite from the loneliness of an empty home. The war had made employment for women over thirty-five an increasingly viable possibility, and it was not surprising that the bulk of new female workers during the 1940s came from the middle-aged segment of the population.

From a social point of view, however, the most significant fact about such women was that they had already fulfilled what society defined as their primary role—to be mothers. Their employment did not represent a "feminist" threat to the existing distribution of sexual roles because they had already seen their children through the pre-school years. Nor did their work seem to disturb most people's sense of propriety. A 1946 *Fortune* poll showed that a majority of citizens had no specific objection to married women holding jobs if they had no children under sixteen. Thus, the one group best suited to lead the growth of the female labor force without engendering controversy actually comprised the largest body of women workers during the 1940s. Such women performed the unique service of setting a precedent for female involvement outside the home, while keeping to a minimum the social conflict which such involvement ultimately entailed.

In a profound sense, then, the expansion of women's economic role depended on circumstances that prevented female employment from being perceived as a feminist threat. During the early 1940s, the war helped to legitimize women working by making the issue a question of national necessity. After the war, inflation and rising consumer demands served much the same function. In neither case could female employment be interpreted as part of an overt revolt against traditional values or a self-conscious movement for equality. Many Americans were deeply concerned about the future of women—a concern at least partially inspired by women working—but female participation in the labor force was defined so as to mitigate the clash of values. Women workers sought jobs, not careers—an extra paycheck for the family rather than a reputation as a success in business or the professions. Indeed, every aspect of women's employment—including their sex-segregated jobs and low pay—seemed designed to mute the suggestion that traditional modes of female behavior were under attack.

In such a situation, it was hardly surprising that so little progress took place on issues involving women's rights. The world of social ideals existed on one level of reality, the world of economic practice on another. A solution to the problem of child care or community services required some connection between the two—a conscious commitment to guarantee women the same opportunity as men in the job market, even at the cost of altering traditional family patterns. Yet there was no evidence that the nation was prepared to tolerate such a sweeping change in values. The poll data showed that most citizens preferred to retain traditional definitions of masculine and feminine spheres, even while modifying the content of those spheres in practice. A married woman might work after her children were in school, but she was not thought of as an equal in the labor force, and almost no one believed that her right to a job was more important than her duty to the home.

The same circumstances help to explain why there was no major "feminist" protest from women about the reimposition of the old order once the war had ended. Some women did find a collective voice to express their anger, especially in the union movement; but for the most part, their petitions went unanswered. "It was the environment," said one woman union leader; "it created a lot of pressures on women not to pursue their grievances." Indeed, the "environment" worked consistently to undermine any possibility of mass demonstrations or protests. Layoffs did not all happen on one day or to all workers in a plant simultaneously. Many women, in turn, initially welcomed the chance to go home and resume a more normal existence, especially given the propaganda that described such a life as Nirvana. Then there was the mood of jubilation at the return of brothers and husbands who were soldiers and the sense that it was somehow inappropriate to mar their homecoming by expressing discontent at being laid off from jobs that the soldiers presumably had come back to fill. When we add to this the fact that feminism *per se* had little popular following and was dismissed by many as an anachronistic social idea, it becomes easier to understand why the displacement of women from their skilled wartime positions did not create militant protest and why—in the context of the times—accepting lower pay in more sex-stereotyped jobs became prevalent. Everything in the social and cultural atmosphere militated *against* ideological and political confrontation and *in support of* accommodation to traditional values, at least on the surface.

If little progress was made toward equality between the sexes as a result of the war, however, the changes that had occurred were very important, especially in their long-term behavioral consequences. The American people were clearly not ready to dispense with a sexual division of labor or to accept the demise of traditional values. But within that set of values, women's economic activities had significantly increased. Millions of women left the home to take part in the nation's economic life who otherwise would have remained out of the labor force. Of particular importance was the extent to which these women were married, middle-aged, and—to a growing degree—of the middle class. To be sure, their entry into the work force simply accelerated trends in women's employment that had been there before the war. And the persistence of occupational segregation, low wages, and limited opportunities certainly belied any notion of the war as a source of progress toward feminist goals. Nevertheless, the war had provided a critical lever that significantly facilitated the institutionalization of long-term trends and offered a decisive impetus toward legitimizing employment for married women of the middle class.

Carl Degler has observed that social change is more likely to occur as a practical response to specific events than as the implementation of a well-developed ideology. The events of the 1940s testify to the validity of that hypothesis. Some women may have been "ready" to assume a new economic role, but the outbreak of fighting gave them the opportunity and acted as a crucial catalyst. Moreover, having entered the job market, most women decided to remain. Their activity outside the home expanded rather than contracted with the passage of time, and by 1950, the wife who worked had become a permanent feature of American life. It could be argued that the growth of the female labor force simply increased the ranks of the victimized. But a shift of such dimensions inevitably affected the whole structure of roles played by men and women, with the potential of creating long-term changes that would challenge the very values that justified sex inequality.

Despite the persistence of traditional ideas on woman's place, therefore, the decade of the 1940s—paradoxically—marked a turning point in the history of American women. Economic equality clearly remained a distant goal. But the content of women's lives had changed, and an important new area of potential activity had opened up to them, with side effects that could not yet be measured. At the turn of the century, the young, the single, and the poor had dominated the female labor force. Fifty years later, the majority of women workers were married and middle-aged, and a substantial minority came from the middle class. In the story of the dramatic change, World War II represented a pivotal moment. For that reason, if for no other, the war and its aftermath constituted a milestone for women in America.

PART FOUR

THE POSTWAR YEARS
AND THE REVIVAL
OF FEMINISM

CHAPTER 10

The Debate on Woman's Place

IN THE SUMMER of 1947, *Life* magazine featured a special thirteen-page spread on the "American Woman's Dilemma." The title of the piece summed up its central thesis. A growing number of modern women, the editors claimed, were confused and frustrated by the conflict between traditional ideas about woman's place and the increasing reality of female involvement in activities outside the home. At an earlier time, the editors asserted, such a conflict had not existed. A woman had been required to make only one big decision—her choice of a husband. Thereafter, her life revolved exclusively about the duties of the household. The woman of 1947, however, faced a more complicated set of options. She still wanted to get married and have children, but she also wished to participate in the world beyond the home, especially after the early years of child rearing were over. The problem was that cultural norms made little provision for women who were not homemakers. One of the by-products of the war, it seemed, was a deepening sense of bewilderment among many American women over how to define their identity in a society that failed to offer adequate alternatives.

Although the editors of *Life* undoubtedly exaggerated the scope of the problem and confined their concern to the dilemma of white, middle-class women, the evidence indicated that many women were disturbed by the absence of an up-to-date consensus about the roles women and men should play. The wife who worked from nine to five and who was still expected to be a full-time homemaker experienced understandable difficulty in resolving the conflicting priorities in her life. She needed guidance to sort out her diverse roles, but the view of femininity handed down by tradition offered little help. The extent to which many women were dissatisfied with their social identity was dramatically revealed in a 1946 *Fortune* poll. When Elmo Roper asked American women whether they would prefer to be born again as women or men, a startling 25 percent declared that they would prefer to be men (only 3.3 percent of the men preferred to be women). A few years later, a third of the 1934 graduates of the best women's colleges confessed to a feeling of stagnation and frustration in their lives.

In large part, of course, such overt dissatisfaction was limited to a narrow segment of middle-class, well-educated women. Black, Hispanic and working-class white women gave less indication of desiring a redistribution of sexual roles. A number of studies suggested that many women in black families longed for the opportunity to devote full-time to the conventional roles of wives and mothers. For such women, a world in which men were able to provide for the family and women had the option of tending the home represented a goal to be sought rather than a fate to be avoided. Similarly, studies of working-class white families found that most wives neither expected nor desired to be treated the same as men. Women exerted a considerable influence over the family, but within a context of a rigid division of labor that both men and women accepted as a given. Social and economic activities were segregated into distinct sexual spheres, and there was little overlapping.

Even though discontent with sexual roles was limited to a minority of middle-class women, however, the "woman problem" quickly became a subject of nationwide controversy. Hardly a week went by without some new treatise on "the trouble with women," the "manners of women," or the drinking problem of women. A housewife could skim any magazine on the newsstand and find herself "castigated, praised, worried over and analyzed." Every side offered its own interpretation of the dilemma. Feminists claimed that women were unhappy because they were still tied to the home. Anti-feminists blamed the upsurge of discontent on the fact that women had ventured too far from their traditional role. But persons of all ideological persuasions agreed that a problem existed. "Choose any set of criteria you like," Margaret Mead wrote, "and the answer is the same: women—and men—are confused, uncertain and discontented with the present definition of women's place in America."

—— I ——

The phenomenon of "momism" served as the jumping-off point for the controversy over women's proper role. First articulated by Philip Wylie in 1942, the concept described the fetish of mother worship in the United States. In no other country, Wylie declared, did veneration of motherhood go to such extremes. Mom was toasted by politicians, feted with a national holiday, and celebrated in song. Marching bands spelled out her name in formation, and young men allegedly used her as the standard by which to choose their own marriage partner. The excess of adoration, in Wylie's opinion, symbolized a pathological emptiness in women's lives. With nothing else to occupy them, women preyed on their children, smothering them with affection so that they would remain tied to the home. The result was a nation crisscrossed with apron strings. Mom's love of her children was in fact "love of herself," the vehicle by which she prevented them from growing up and leaving her. Indeed, women had devolved into a race of parasites—"an idle class, a spending class, a candy-craving class"—devoted to consuming all the money, affection, and virility which men could offer. Mother worship was ostensibly based on the endless self-sacrifice of "mom," but in reality, it was rooted in her insatiable appetite for devouring her young and preventing them from developing into independent adults.

Although Wylie clearly bore a substantial grudge against "mom," the experience of military doctors with army recruits during World War II seems to give his analysis some support. Psychiatrists administering tests to inductees found a disturbingly high rate of nervous disorders. A total of three million men avoided military service for reasons associated with emotional instability, and Dr. Edward Strecker, a psychiatric consultant to the secretary of war, placed the blame squarely on women who had "failed in the elementary mother function of weaning [their] offspring emotionally as well as physically." Strecker's "mom" was not quite the villain Wylie had depicted, but she exhibited most of the same qualities, overprotecting her sons and creating such emotional dependency that they were unable to grow up and accept the responsibilities of manhood. Strecker's analysis focused renewed attention on the phenomenon described by Wylie a few years earlier and gave it the added credibility of professional endorsement. As one reviewer commented in 1947, "Mom' is on the spot." Newspapers and magazines seized on her plight as one more indication that deep trouble was brewing among American women, and feminists and anti-feminists alike used "momism" to support their explanations for the puzzle of women's discontent.

The anti-feminist point of view received its most sophisticated presentation in the 1947 publication of *Modern Woman: The Lost Sex* by Ferdinand Lundberg and Marynia Farnham. As Wylie had done, Lundberg and Farnham attributed part of the "woman problem" to the decline of the home as a social institution. After the Copernican revolution, they argued, men had turned their energies outward, away from the home, in an effort to recoup their sense of importance by conquering the universe through reason and science. The ethos of Calvinism encouraged the drive for material accomplishment and established a convincing rationale for the entrepreneurial thrusts of the industrial revolution. In the modern world which resulted, the home had been "reduced to much the same function as a crossroads bus station, wherein people tarried for a brief while until more pressing matters demanded their attention." Men left the home to work in factories and offices, families decreased in size, and children went off to school at the age of six. Man's striving for power had left woman without a valued purpose. Events had passed her by, and she became a peripheral observer rather than a central participant in life. With her primary role reduced to that of caretaker for a family of transients, she had no focal point for her existence, "no certainty of status . . . no security . . . *as a woman, a female being.*"

In Lundberg and Farnham's view, however, the rise of industrialism provided only a necessary pre-condition for women's discontent. The real cause was the feminist response to the industrial revolution. The women's rights movement, they argued, represented a neurotic reaction to male dominance, a "deep illness" that encouraged women to reject their natural, sex-based instincts in a futile attempt to become imitation men. Instead of urging women to develop a new way of life based on their true identity, feminists had attempted to persuade women to seize a share of masculine power and to beat men at their own game. The result was to obliterate the distinctions between the sexes, to cast women adrift from their biological and psychological moorings, and to generate a collective cultural pathology of which "momism" was but one manifestation.

In contrast to the feminist aberration, the true woman stood forth as an example of self-acceptance and fulfillment. While feminism "bade women commit suicide as women," the normal women exulted in her sexual distinctiveness and found in it her deepest source of happiness. The independent woman was a "contradiction in terms," Lundberg and Farnham declared. Women had been created to be biologically and psychologically dependent on man. The sex act itself constituted a paradigm for female happiness. During intercourse, they argued, woman's role was passive, receptive, and accepting, based on the recognition that sexual pleasure could come only from welcoming the male phallus. (The woman could "deliver a masterly performance by doing nothing . . . except being duly appreciative," Lundberg and Farnham said. Her part was easier than rolling off a log. It was as easy as being the log itself.) The only prerequisite for female happiness was that the woman "accept with deep inwardness and readiness . . . the final goal of [intercourse]—impregnation." The desire to be a mother constituted the key to sexual pleasure, and the culmination of the sex act really occurred when the mother nursed the child who had been conceived. The woman who wished complete fulfillment had only to extend the attributes displayed during intercourse to the rest of her life. Passivity, dependence, and the desire to raise children comprised the formula for female contentment.

Since the disaster precipitated by feminism could be ended only by curbing the influence of the "masculine woman," Lundberg and Farnham proposed a concerted program to restore the prestige of the sexually ordained roles of wife and mother. Specifically, they urged a government-sponsored propaganda campaign to bolster the family, subsidized psychotherapy for feminist neurotics, cash subsidies to encourage women to bear more children, and annual awards to mothers who excelled at child rearing. Lundberg and Farnham insisted that women could achieve mental sanity only if they reclaimed the home as the central focus of their existence. Housewives had to repossess the duties from which they had been displaced and to revive such lost arts as canning, preserving, and interior decorating. If the woman who viewed cooking as a pedestrian task rededicated herself to becoming a gourmet chef (and a food chemist), what had once been a tiresome chore could be transformed into a creative adventure. The key was willpower. Government could help by discriminating against feminists, but women themselves had to take the lead in reconstructing their own identity. If they cared enough about achieving happiness, they could move away from an era of discontent into an era of fulfillment in their "higher roles" as modern wives and mothers.

Lundberg and Farnham had clearly touched on an issue of great interest, for within a brief period of time, the theme they established was echoed by others. As might have been expected, women's magazines led the list of supporters, and the joys of "femininity" and "togetherness" became the staple motifs of periodicals like *McCall's* and the *Ladies' Home Journal*. But the cry for women to return to the home was taken up by other authors and journals as well, not all of them with the same vested interest in domesticity as women's magazines. Agnes Meyer, the muckraking critic of government community services during the war, argued in *Atlantic* that while women "had many careers, they had only one vocation—motherhood." Women served as the "cement of society," Meyer claimed, its preservation against the "competitive, materialistic world" of men. If they followed the example of feminist businesswomen, their natural instincts would be sterilized. "What modern woman has to recapture," she concluded, "is the wisdom that just being a woman is her central task and her greatest honor. . . . Women must boldly announce that no job is more exacting, more necessary, or more rewarding than that of housewife and mother." A few years later, Ashley Montagu expressed the same opinion in the *Saturday Review*. "Being a good wife, a good mother, in short a good homemaker," he wrote, "is the most important of all the occupations in the world. . . . I put it down as an axiom that no woman with a husband and small children can hold a full-time job and be a good homemaker at one and the same time."

The anti-feminist attack also extended to traditional conceptions of women's education. Lynn White, president of Mills College in California, called on women's schools to "shake off their subservience to masculine values" and create a "distinctively feminine curriculum." Citing letters from women graduates complaining of the irrelevance of women's education to the tasks of homemaking and motherhood, White delivered a blistering attack against feminists for insisting that women receive exactly the same kind of schooling as men. "The great blunder of the old women's rights movement," he told the American Association of University Women, "was its acceptance of the masculine scale of values as the human scale." By declaring that "we are people *too*," feminists had implied that maleness constituted the norm for women to follow if they desired equality. Women's colleges had fallen into the trap and had become obsessed with the idea of duplicating the educational experience of men. In doing so, however, they had guaranteed that women would remain unequal. Men were naturally better suited to achieve success in the sciences, fine arts, mathematics, and areas of learning that placed a premium on the ability to think abstractly. By forcing women to compete in the same disciplines, women's colleges had established the groundwork for women's failure. More important, by "masculinizing" their students, women's colleges had cut their students off from their true identity as wives and mothers. College women bore fewer children than average, and according to early returns from the Kinsey survey, they experienced markedly greater difficulty in achieving orgasm. (Final results from the Kinsey survey showed exactly the opposite results.) Instead of creating equality and happiness, then, feminist education had produced misery among women and destroyed their opportunity for self-fulfillment.

To solve the dilemma, White and other like-minded educators suggested that women's colleges emphasize rather than obliterate the sex differences between men and women. "Only by recognizing and insisting on the importance of such differences," White wrote, "can women save themselves, in their own eyes, of conviction as inferiors." Specifically, White proposed that female students take courses oriented to their sexual aptitudes. "Women love beauty as much as men do," he asserted, "but they want a beauty connected with the process of living." Women's instincts were "practical and earthy." Consequently, they should study such "minor" or applied arts as ceramics, textiles, weaving, leatherwork, and flower arrangement. More important, they should prepare themselves for the tasks of motherhood and homemaker which lay ahead. James Madison Wood, president of Stephens College in Missouri, urged women to specialize in disciplines like home economics, child development, and interior decorating. "If [homemaking] roles are to be played with distinction," he wrote, "the college years must be rehearsal periods for the major performance." In a similar vein, Anne Parnell, head of Sweet Briar College, advocated that "the task of creating a good home and raising good children" be raised to the dignity of a profession and made the primary purpose of women's colleges. Why not study the "theory and preparation of a Basque paella," White asked, instead of a course in post-Kantian philosophy? With such an education, women could learn how to develop to the fullest their sexually distinctive attributes and acquire skill and expertise in their appointed vocation.

The anti-feminist attack on women's education and employment generated substantial support. At a time when the nation was experiencing severe social tension, it called forth the image of a simpler era when each person knew his or her own place. The anti-feminists described woman in terms designed to take advantage of traditional cultural stereotypes. She was "soft" rather than "tough," passive rather than aggressive. Devoted to "conserving and cherishing," she offered an attractive counterpoint to the harsh, masculine world of wars and competition. In the home, her inborn proclivity for nurture and love found a creative outlet. Outside the home, her instincts were destroyed by the "masculine" rat race. For the sake of her own fulfillment and the salvation of the race, she needed to renounce the false god of feminism and revitalize the dormant virtues of femininity.

The greatest advantage of anti-feminist analysis, however, rested in its simplicity and clarity. All the anti-feminist thinkers presented woman as a static creature, eternal in her attributes and unchanged by events. They assumed that women were polar opposites of men and that the spheres of the two sexes were ordained to remain permanently separate. Although not all anti-feminists consciously used Freud to bolster their case, his assertion that "anatomy is destiny" served as the underlying premise of their argument. Anti-feminists believed that a woman's psychic life was permanently shaped by her biological status. Whether that status was traced to her lack of a penis or the fact that she bore the children of the race was less important than the conclusion that her options in life were determined by immutable physical characteristics. If a woman followed the path of "normal femininity," the Freudian psychiatrist Helene Deutsch declared, she accepted her distinctive sexuality, repressed her masculine strivings, and related to the outside world through identification with her husband and children. On the other hand, if she rejected her femininity, she developed a "masculinity complex," sacrificed the "warm, intuitive knowledge" of womanhood to the "cold, unproductive thinking" of manhood, and betrayed her basic sexual identity. There was no middle ground, no way to combine marriage and a career, a job and motherhood. A woman became either a well-adjusted homemaker or a feminist neurotic.

Given the popularity of such ideas, it is not surprising that the 1950s have frequently been viewed as the embodiment of traditional family life and the "feminine mystique." From TV situation comedies like *Ozzie and Harriet* to Doris Day/Rock Hudson movies, the age seemed dedicated to the celebration of conventional sex roles, with men taking on the task of conquering the world and women content to infuse the home with warmth and happiness.

—— II ——

There was another side to the debate over woman's place, however. While Lundberg and Farnham were urging a return to the "eternal feminine," a growing number of social scientists rejected the argument of biological determinism and emphasized the impact of environment and society on personality formation. At the core of the sociological approach was the belief that women's lives were molded as much by shifting expectations of their role behavior as by immutable characteristics of sex or psychology. "Identity," Peter Berger has written, "is not something 'given,' but is bestowed in acts of social recognition." Since personality development was a response to cultural norms and social circumstances, there was no reason why individuals and groups should not change over time. Margaret Mead, in her observations of life in the South Sea Islands, found that qualities such as aggressiveness, independence, gentleness, and passivity were not sex-linked at all but rather resulted from social conditioning. "There is no evidence that suggests women are naturally better at caring for children [than men]," she said in 1946; "with the fact of childbearing out of the center of attention, there is even more reason for treating girls first as human beings, then as women." If the observations of Mead and others were correct, it made more sense to look for the cause of women's discontent in the changing nature of women's roles, than in the doctrines of feminism itself.

In an early postwar article, the sociologist Elizabeth Nottingham indicated the direction of the social-science approach by attributing the dilemma of modern women to the "precipitating effects of alternating war and depression upon long-term trends that were already making for a recasting of the feminine role in the Western culture." Nottingham contrasted woman's family and sexual roles, with her economic and social roles. The former focused on maintaining harmony in interpersonal relationships, while the later emphasized achievement in a competitive, individualistic society. Through most of history, the first two roles, had clearly been dominant, since "unlimited competitiveness [was] inimical to smooth functioning in both the family and sexual roles of women." Under the impact of two world wars, however, women had increasingly added the third and fourth competitive roles to the first two conciliatory ones. Nottingham noted that World War II in particular had "acted as a stimulus to the . . . flagging aspirations of middle-class women in their political, community and vocational roles." Inflation and greater job opportunities facilitated an ever-increasing expansion of female employment, and the conflict between women's two life-styles intensified. Fundamentally, then, women's discontent was rooted in the changing definition of their sphere, and the only solution was to create a new concept that would give as much recognition to their economic and public roles as to their family and sexual roles.

From an anthropological point of view, Florence Kluckhohn arrived at much the same conclusion. Society conferred its greatest rewards, she pointed out, on persons who succeeded as individuals in their own right. Within such a system of values, women suffered from severe "structural strain." On the one hand, they were educated as equals and trained for the same independent, autonomous role as that assumed by men. On the other hand, they were expected after their school years to revert to the "lonely," unstimulating role of homemaker—a role allotted little prestige or value and depicted by advertisers as a bore from which the lucky housewife could escape with the right kind of automatic stove or dishwasher. Confusion was thus built into a woman's life in a modern industrial society. Kluckhohn herself believed that the wife who worked was better off than the one who stayed at home "in a state of frustration," but she recognized the tension involved in making such a decision. In effect, American culture had subjected women to a barrage of conflicting images and expectations, and women could achieve security of status only when an entirely new definition of sexual spheres was developed.

The Barnard sociologist Mirra Komarovsky elaborated the theory of role conflict most fully. Addressing herself specifically to the argument of antifeminists, she rejected the contention that the discontent among American women could be traced to collective psychological maladjustment or the predisposition of an entire sex for one set of activities rather than another. Despite differences between the sexes at the extreme ends of the scale in aptitude tests, she pointed out, the vast majority of men and women shared a common ability to master most academic subjects. Furthermore, women who were involved in the culturally approved activities of service clubs displayed the same traits of aggressiveness and assertiveness denounced by antifeminists as "masculine" in intellectuals and career women. The "woman problem" was thus grounded not in congenital personality differences but in the conflict that resulted from the increased overlapping of masculine and feminine spheres. Women's status had changed with such lightning speed that their "modern" role contradicted their "feminine" role. "Society confronts the girl with powerful challenges and strong pressure to excel in certain lines of endeavor," Komarovsky noted, "but then, quite suddenly . . . the very success in meeting these challenges begins to cause anxiety." Traits which were defined as "assets" in one role became "liabilities" in the other, generating widespread confusion and conflict.

The tension between the "modern" and "feminine" roles followed a woman through every stage of her life. As a child, she was urged to "select girls toys, and to be more restrained, sedentary, quiet and neat" than her brothers. When she started school, however, her parents stressed the need for achievement. The contradiction reached a peak in college. On the one hand, she was told to work hard and get good grades. On the other hand, she was warned against being "too smart" and scaring off prospective suitors. Almost a third of the students at Barnard complained about the inconsistent goals articulated by their parents. "My father expects me to get an 'A' in every subject," one young woman said, "[but] my mother says,' . . . don't become so deep that no man will be good enough for you.' " The contradiction especially affected women's behavior in relation to men. Two out of five Barnard students admitted that they "played dumb" on dates in order to get along with boys. "When a girl asks me what marks I got last semester," a student reported, "I answer, 'Not so good—only one A.' When a boy asks the same question, I say very brightly, with a note of surprise, 'Imagine, I got an A.' " Urged to be competitive on the one hand and docile on the other, the students faced a bewildering choice of options which inevitably created ambivalence.

The conflict persisted even after college and was heightened by the discontinuity of a woman's life. Just as black male college graduates were frustrated when treated like porters or bellboys, female graduates were disturbed by the ordeal of transferring from the life of a scholar to the task of scrubbing floors and washing diapers. "The plunge from the strictly intellectual college life to the 24-hour-a-day domestic one is a terrible shock," one alumna wrote. "We stagger through our first years of child-rearing wondering what our values are and struggling to find some compromise between our intellectual ambition and the reality of everyday living." Even if a woman resolved her conflict temporarily, the cycle of role confusion appeared again when the mother sent her last child off to school. With no full-time task to fill the day, her desire to use her education revived, and she often sought a job. But she was still expected to serve as a full-time homemaker, and the confusion over the priorities in her life remained.

Within Komarovsky's point of view, discontent was clearly not limited to the "morally defective" or "emotionally sick" women in America but rather represented an endemic condition of female life, rooted in the contradictions of the social structure. As the society changed, women's activities changed also. But the new roles women assumed were added on to the old ones, and the conflict between the two guaranteed that discontent would persist. Women could not resolve their identity crisis by seeking massive psychotherapy or devoting their energies to canning and preserving fruit. A solution would come only when "the adult sex roles of women are redefined in greater harmony with the socioeconomic and ideological character of modern society."

The sociological perspective was adopted by a growing number of observers as a sensible analysis of women's plight. *Life*, for example, blamed the high rate of divorce in America on the narrowness of women's role in the home and the absence of companionship with their husbands. Americans divided up their "spheres of interest too sharply after marriage," the magazine declared, and the sharp separation between home and work tended "to freeze women in their subservient social role." As an answer to the problem, *Life* urged that "some means . . . be found to open the door to a fuller life [for women]." The magazine acknowledged that full-time employment would be difficult for a wife when her children were small, but work had the advantage of leaving "her well-rounded in interests and experience when she reached the free years after forty." On the other hand, the woman who devoted herself exclusively to the home found it almost impossible to keep up with the interest of her husband, and "once her children have grown, a housewife . . . lacking outside interests and training, is faced with a vacant years." In the end, *Life* found the employment of married women a more attractive alternative than the spectre of twenty million idle women over forty, "bored stiff" with "numbing rounds of club-meetings and card-playing."* However patronizing the analysis, *Life* certainly seemed less than complacent about leaving the status quo unchanged.

Taking up the same theme, the feminist Della Cyrus attributed "momism" to the fact that most women were too little involved in the world outside the home. Philip Wylie had never made clear his own attitude toward women's rights, but his description of "mom" in many ways lent itself more to a feminist than an anti-feminist position. Using Wylie's portrayal of women as a reference, Cyrus charged that housewives were segregated from reality and denied the opportunity to develop into mature, well-rounded individuals. With no other focal point for their lives, they devoted all their attention to their children and destroyed them with over-affection. The answer to "momism," Cyrus declared, consisted of liberating women from the home, not

---

*Once again, it needs to be said that all this discussion focused on middle- and upper-class white women.

forcing them further into a domestic routine. If society crippled women psychologically by foreclosing their options, women would continue to cripple their children. Freedom and autonomy represented the answer for both.

In the end, the debate over women's place could be resolved only by the behavior of women themselves. To a large extent, both sides agreed on the symptoms of the problem. Each noted that the rise of modern technology had reduced some of the immediate responsibilities of women in the home, and both commented on the dilemma posed for those women who were in the process of shifting roles. But the intellectual controversy, for the most part, occurred in a vacuum. Many women were unaware of any overt conflict in their own lives, and for those who were troubled, the principal contribution of the debate was to outline—abstractly—a set of opposing alternatives. The important question was how women—in this case, middle-class, educated women—acted in practice. Did they continue to expand their sphere of activities, or did they find new meaning and significance in their traditional roles?

—— III ——

In some ways, it seemed that the 1950s witnessed precisely the revitalization of family life which people like Lundberg and Farnham had advocated. During the years after World War II, the nation experienced a gigantic "baby boom." The birthrate for third children doubled between 1940 and 1960—that for fourth children tripled. Advertisements in mass-circulation magazines ceased to show a three-person household and began to feature pictures of five and six-person-families. The editor of *Mademoiselle* declared that women in their teens and twenties had decided to eschew careers and raise as many youngsters as the "good Lord" gave them. As households increased in size, "togetherness" became a watchword. "A family is like a corporation," one writer observed. "We all have to work for it." A plethora of articles celebrated the virtues of families which engaged in "creative" activities together, and the cross-country camping trip and outdoor barbecue became a vogue in family recreation.

The revival of popular concern with the home coincided with a substantial exodus to the suburbs. Between 1950 and 1968, towns and villages within commuting distances of large cities grew more than five times faster than urban areas, and the number of people living in such communities increased from 24 to 35 percent of the total population. The suburban way of life added a new dimension to women's traditional role. The nationwide "do-it-yourself" craze infected women as well as men, and wives took pride in redecorating their homes, planting gardens, and making their own clothes. The duties of child rearing also underwent expansion. Suburban mothers volunteered for library work in the school, took part in PTA activities, and chauffeured their children from music lessons to scout meetings. Perhaps most important, the suburban wife was expected to make the home an oasis of comfort and serenity for her harried husband. "Modern man needs an old-fashioned woman around the house," the novelist Sloan Wilson declared. *Newsweek* stressed the importance of a woman understanding the tensions of her husband's job, and in its "Blueprint for a Wife" emphasized how crucial it was for her to be a "model of efficiency, patience and charm." If popular literature was any index, it appeared that many modern women had found a solution to their "problem" by discovering new meaning in their traditional role in the home and family.

The new "cult of domesticity" reflected an apparently intense preoccupation with conformism in the 1950s. All the "ticky-tacky" houses in the Levittowns of the world looked alike; consumer housewives outdid each other in trying to purchase the latest cookout gadgetry; and couples herded together in what one theologian called "the suburban captivity of the churches," seeking through collective involvement in religious social life some kind of common salvation. Individual rebelliousness was frowned upon. Perhaps out of fear that there were so few roots in modern America and things were changing so fast, people found solace in doing what they were supposed to do, whether as "gray-flannel Organization Men" climbing the corporate ladder together or as "organization women" holding down the home front and providing a bedrock of security in a world of competition and chaos.

There was also a link between the suburban family mystique and the external world of cold-war confrontation and potential nuclear annihilation. Elaine May has shown that the international situation in postwar America induced widespread anxiety. Everything seemed to be going wrong. China had "fallen" to the enemy. Korea had exploded in flames, causing President Truman to brood about the onset of a third world war. And people like Joseph McCarthy insisted that the whole process was due to internal subversion of the "American way" by disloyal Communist sympathizers seeking to erode and poison American confidence. In such a context, the country had to hold on to its most cherished institutions and fight back against the forces of anarchy and amorality. Where better to start than with the family, the oldest and most important institution of all.

Thus, in some ways the new focus on conforming to traditional sex roles represented an act of "domestic containment" that paralleled the act of "international containment" whereby the Free World said no to the spread of Communism. The Truman Doctrine and Marshall Plan were designed to stop the Red Menace in Eastern Europe, and a similar commitment was necessary to "contain" the threat of moral decay and social deviance at home. By revitalizing the American family, accentuating the values of "togetherness," and rejecting challenges to traditional religiosity and patriotism, the American middle class could do its part to protect and preserve a way of life under attack from internal as well as external enemies. All of the propaganda and rhetoric made sense from this perspective: Whether the maudlin injunction against women having careers in TV sitcoms like *Life with Father* or the celebration of red-blooded patriotism in radio shows like *Counterspy*, the message was to cleave to traditional values lest the world at home become as frightening as the world outside.

Yet the shrillness of the campaign went too far, suggesting the schizophrenia of American culture and society as much as any uniformity of purpose. While countless suburban housewives (and husbands) carried out their roles as written, there were just as many others who sought new options and wanted to go on changing the world. Whether in their Kaffeeklatsches, church groups, or neighborhood gatherings, these women were questioning their lives and the direction of their society, sharing some of their disquietude at being confined to certain "feminine" spheres. Some became active in political groups—"Women Strike for Peace," for example, was an early case of a middle-class group of women expressing their protest about the ways the world (and men) tried to solve problems. Others pursued jobs outside the home, in practice if not in ideology rejecting the notion that the sole path to fulfillment lay in domesticity.

Indeed, one of the most striking features of the 1950s in retrospect was the degree to which women continued to enter the job market and expand their sphere. The pace of female employment quickened rather than slowed during the postwar years. In 1960, twice as many women were at work as in 1940, and 40 percent of all women over sixteen held a job. Female employment was increasing at a rate four times faster than that of men's. The median age of women workers had risen to forty-one, and the proportion of wives at work had doubled from 15 percent in 1940 to 30 percent in 1960. While the number of single women in the labor force declined over a twenty-year span, the number of mothers at work leaped 400 percent—from 1.5 million to 6.6 million—and 39 percent of women with children aged six to seventeen had jobs. By 1960, both the husband and wife worked in over ten million homes (an increase of 333 percent over 1940), and mothers of children under eighteen comprised almost a third of all women workers.

Significantly, the greatest growth in the female labor force took place among well-educated married women from families with moderate incomes. In households where the husbands earned from $7,000 to $10,000 a year, the rate of female participation in the job market rose from 7 percent in 1950 to

25 percent in 1960. Although before World War II married women workers had come almost exclusively from working-class families, by 1960 it was just as likely for a middle-class wife to be employed. Of the wives twenty to forty-four years old with no children under eighteen, the women whose husbands earned from $4,000 to $10,000 a year worked in almost exactly the same proportion as those whose husbands earned from $1,000 to $4,000. Mothers with children six to seventeen years of age were still employed more frequently at lower income levels, but 37 percent of those whose husbands received from $6,000 to $7,000 also worked, and the direction of change was clear. By 1964, a larger proportion of wives worked when their husbands received from $7,500 to $10,000 (42 percent) than when their spouses earned under $3,000 (37 percent), and by 1970, almost 60 percent of all nonfarm wives in families with incomes over $10,000 were employed. In addition, a growing number of working women were well-educated. Over 53 percent of female college graduates held jobs in 1962, in contrast to 36.2 percent of those with only a high-school diploma, and among women with more than five years of higher education, the employment figure was 70 percent. Wives with husbands in white-collar occupations sought jobs more frequently than those whose spouses worked in factories, and female workers in clerical positions showed a stronger commitment to stay in the labor force than women in industry. In short, not only was the revolution in female employment continuing, it was also spearheaded by the same middle-class wives and mothers who allegedly had found new contentment in domesticity.

At least in part, the expansion of women's economic role reflected the ongoing impact of inflation and rising expectations. The new connotation of "economic need" which first began to appear in the late 1940s seemed to have spread even further by the 1950s. Clearly, women whose husbands earned between $7,000 and $10,000 a year were not seeking jobs for bread and rent money alone. Rather, their employment provided a vehicle by which the family could buy a new home, afford luxuries, and send the children to decent colleges. A survey in Illinois showed that families in which both the husband and the wife worked spent 45 percent more on gifts and recreation, 95 percent more on restaurant meals for husband and wife, and 23 percent more on household equipment than did single-wage families. The quest for a better living standard obviously remained one impetus to women's employment. It was also no accident that the greatest increases in women's employment were in clerical and sales jobs—almost by definition, "women's" work.

In addition, however, a growing number of women appeared to value a job for its own sake and for the personal rewards it conferred. Almost 90 percent of working women interviewed in Greensboro, North Carolina, and Champaign-Urbana, Illinois, stated that they liked their jobs, especially being with other people and receiving recognition for their work. In a University of Michigan study in 1955, about 48 percent of working women still gave financial necessity as a reason for seeking employment, but 21 percent asserted that they worked because of a desire for a sense of accomplishment, and even those who cited economic need mentioned the ancillary benefits of social companionship and the sense of independence represented by a paycheck. In a culture oriented to the cash nexus, the idea of tangible remuneration for performing a task seemed to carry special meaning.

The same basic syndrome appeared in Mirra Komarovsky's study of blue-collar-wives. The women who worked enjoyed the "self-esteem" which an independent income brought, welcomed the opportunity to "get out of the house," and appreciated being able to tell their husbands something interesting about their day. Even those who performed the most menial tasks gained a sense of achievement from their work. "I'm strong and do a good job," one cafeteria worker explained. "They tell me I help digestion because I make cracks and laugh, and they like it." Significantly, a large number of women seemed to derive more gratification from their occupational roles than from more traditional female roles. In one survey, almost two-thirds of married women workers referred to their jobs as a basis for feeling "important" or "useful," while only one-third cited the socially sanctioned activity of house-keeping as giving those feelings. In a great many cases, it seemed, gainful employment provided women with a sense of personal and social worth which they did not find elsewhere.

The results of such studies provided at least indirect confirmation for those who traced female employment to deeper social causes. Social scientists in Britain, for example, asserted that the isolation of housewives, the desire for company, and the wish for financial independence all played a part in prompting women to seek jobs. Pursuing a related theme, American sociologists emphasized the particular problems of married women whose children were grown or in school. Describing the plight of one such prototypical woman, Margaret Mead wrote: "Some day, while she is still . . . young . . . she will have to face a breakfast table with only one face across it, her husband's, and she will be quite alone, in a home of their own. She is out of a job. . . . " In a world where housework was given little prestige, Arnold Rose noted, the mother whose offspring no longer needed constant care felt "partly function-less." Volunteer activities remained an option for some, but many charitable endeavors had been professionalized by social workers, leaving energetic women without a constructive outlet. In such a situation, David Reisman observed, many women viewed a "culturally defined job" as a path of liber-ation, the only alternative to boredom and a sense of uselessness. Although there was no hard evidence to support Riesman's hypothesis, it did seem consistent with the employment statistics. Most of the increase in the female labor force came from married women over thirty-five—precisely the group whose children were reaching maturity—and many of the workers specifically mentioned the rewards of companionship and recognition which came from holding a job.

Among the potentially important consequences of the continued growth in women's employment were some that were unanticipated and, at the time, generally unacknowledged. For example, sociologists had long observed how traditional family life was tied to an economic division of labor. Men—the "breadwinners"—were expected to dominate women and take charge of activities outside the home; women—the "homemakers"—were expected to follow their husbands' lead and to tend the house. But when women worked and men were unemployed, some role reversal occurred as well. Mirra Komarovsky and Herman Lantz found that a husband's sense of efficacy declined if he had no job and could not fulfill his ordained role as "provider." Conversely, a woman's sense of efficacy could increase if she did have a job. David Heer's study of Irish Catholic couples in Boston showed that in both working-class and middle-class families, women who worked enjoyed more influence over "really important decisions" than did wives who were not employed. Deborah Kligler concluded the same in her study of middle-class households in New York, where employed women substantially affected decisions on "major purchases, loans, savings, and investments."

The key, Robert Blood hypothesized, was the experience of participating in the world beyond the home. A woman's contribution to the decision-making process, he reasoned, correlated with her value as measured by the outside world. Within that system, the working wife possessed more "resources" than her nonworking sister. She had a moral right to help determine how her earnings were spent, she enjoyed the benefit of outside contact that she might use as a source of ideas in pressing her position, and she could draw upon the social skills and confidence which came from functioning effectively in an occupational setting. The housewife, in contrast, provided no monetary assistance to the household and performed a job that was accorded little prestige or status. In some cases, then, one of the consequences of women's employment was to lessen the dominance of the man by breaking his monopoly on control of the outside world and giving his spouse some of the authority derived from participating in an "external environment." Although the patriarchal family remained a dominant norm, it seemed that employment by married women mitigated to some extent the sharpness of the division of labor and authority in the home. "A working wife's husband listens to her more," Robert Blood has written. "She expresses herself and has more opinions. Instead of looking up into her husband's eyes and worshipping him, she levels with him. . . . Thus her power increases, and relatively speaking, the husband's falls."

In all of this, a certain cultural logic held sway. Married women's employment increased, but primarily among older women whose children no longer were at home during the day. The increase, in turn, took place in sex-segregated jobs that were defined, culturally, as "women's" work. In no way could the women who went out to fill the clerical and sales positions of the consumer society be viewed as "competing" with men or as seeking sex equality. Moreover, the "helping" jobs they took were completely consistent with women's "helping" role in the home; indeed, these jobs became central to the success of the home, since women's second paychecks provided the income by which their families could enjoy better recreation, additions to their homes, or more affluent life-styles. If minor and gradual changes occurred in domestic decision-making patterns because of women's employment, that was coincidental and "only fair" given women's new roles. But none of this suggested any revolt. Rather, it became an almost organically functional way of giving women some broader role than simply that of homemaker, while never even having to acknowledge that the old roles were no longer satisfying or adequate—and it all occurred in complete harmony with the employment and social needs of a rapidly growing consumer economy that required, simultaneously, relatively cheap secretarial and sales help and more spending customers.

—— IV ——

In the end, therefore, those who examined American sex roles and saw continued change seemed more on the mark than anti-feminist psychoanalysts and popularizers. Although the normative ideology of middle-class America remained committed to a polarization between "masculine" and "feminine" spheres and a rigid division of labor by sex, middle-class women themselves were continuing in practice to add new roles to their lives, albeit in a social and economic structure that was totally sex-biased in job availability, pay, and services. The statisticians of the Metropolitan Life Insurance Company observed in 1955 that the average wife in America was employed before her first baby was born and went back to work shortly after her children started school. The company's assessment in no way signified that the family had assumed less importance in American culture. Indeed, the key was that—as framed by participants and observers—there was no necessary contradiction between female employment and the new emphasis on the home reflected in popular literature. Most women went to work only after their children no longer required full-time supervision, and the income they earned contributed directly to higher family living standards. Still, the growth of the female labor force did point to an ongoing modification in women's activities in American society—a modification that, however consistent with traditional ideas, had the unintended consequence of diluting the strength of those ideas. Once women were propelled out of their traditional role—even in jobs and with treatment that were "traditionally" female—they would not go back, and the continued changes promised ultimately to erode the material basis for claiming that women's "place" should be in the home.

At the same time, other women were beginning to raise questions and pursue activities that would inaugurate a new era of female activism. Although women's church organizations and peace groups were not "feminist" *per se*, they continued to explore larger issues of politics and ideology that would grow in importance in the new decade. League of Women Voters organizations did the same, often initiating discussions of school desegregation or international peace in their local communities. And it was black middle-class women who organized and carried out the Montgomery bus boycott, the first massive civil-rights campaign of the postwar period, with Rosa Parks precipitating the action by refusing to give up her seat to a white person and Jo Ann Robinson and her Women's Political Council mobilizing the workers to put the boycott into effect.

Even as the debate over the appropriate roles of men and women continued, therefore, signs were multiplying that a new stage of female activism was on the way. And although the debate itself did not resolve anything, it did highlight the extent to which society was in transition and provided a framework within which to judge the actions of women themselves. Women, especially middle-class married women, were continuing to expand beyond their traditional roles; but they did so in a cultural, economic, and social environment that was still governed by anachronistic definitions of women's worth and possibilities. During the 1950s, these conflicting propositions remained in tenuous balance. In fact, they co-existed almost symbiotically, since change could be tolerated only if it did not foretell challenge and transformation. But ultimately, a collision would occur that would create the context for a new drive for equality and ideological transformation during the 1960s and 1970s.

CHAPTER 11

The Revival of Feminism

HELMAN   Before all else, you are a wife and mother.

NORA   That I no longer believe. I believe that before all else, I am a human being, just as much as you are— or at least that I should try to become one.

Henrik Ibsen, *A Doll's House* (1879)

IN THE FALL of 1962, the editors of *Harper's* observed a curious phenomenon. An extraordinary number of women seemed "ardently determined to extend their vocation beyond the bedroom, kitchen and nursery," but very few showed any interest in feminism. Both observations were essentially correct. In the years during and after World War II, millions of women had joined the labor force, many of them leaving the home to take jobs; but the expansion of their "sphere" occurred without fanfare and was not accompanied either by progress toward equality or an organized effort to protest traditional definitions of "woman's place." If many women were dissatisfied with what one housewife called the endless routine of "dishwashing, picking up, ironing and folding diapers," they had no collective forum to express their grievances. Women examined their futures privately and with an unmilitant air. There seemed to be no sanctioned alternative.

Eight years later, feminism competed with the war in Vietnam, student revolts, and inflation for headlines in the daily press. Women activists picketed the Miss America pageant, demonstrated at meetings of professional associations to demand equal employment opportunities, and insisted on equal access to previously all-male bars and restaurants in New York. They called a national strike to commemorate the 50th anniversary of woman suffrage, wrote about the oppression of "sexual politics," and sat in at the editorial offices of *Newsweek* and the *Ladies' Home Journal*. In an era punctuated by protest, feminism had once again come into its own. If not all women enlisted in the new struggle for equality, few could claim to be unaffected by it.

The evolution of any protest movement, of course, is a complicated process. In general, however, a series of preconditions are necessary: political currency and sanction for the ideas around which a movement grows; a catalyst to initiate protest; support from an energetic minority, at least, of the aggrieved group; and a social atmosphere that is conducive to reform. To an extent unmatched since the last days of the suffrage fight, all these elements were present during the 1960s. The accumulated grievances of individual women found expression in a growing number of feminist voices whose writings gave focus to the movement; the civil-rights struggle helped to trigger a renewal of women's rights activism; a substantial number of women, young and old, were ready to respond; and the society at large was more sensitive than at any time in the twentieth century to the quest for social justice. No one development could have fostered the resurgence of feminism, but the several acting together created a context in which, for the first time in five decades, feminism became again a force to be reckoned with.

—— I ——

The most widely noted indictment of America's system of sex inequality came from the pen of Betty Friedan. Although other books and articles exerted just as much influence on key groups of women activists, Friedan's acerbic look at *The Feminine Mystique* (1963) generated the kind of attention that made feminism a popular topic of conversation once again. According to Friedan, American women had been held captive by a set of ideas that defined female happiness as total involvement in the roles of wife and mother. Advertisers manipulated women into believing that they could achieve fulfillment by using the latest model vacuum cleaner or bleaching their clothes a purer white. Women's magazines romanticized domesticity and presented an image of women as "gaily content in a world of bedroom, kitchen, sex, babies and home." And psychiatrists popularized the notion that any woman unhappy with a full-time occupation as housewife must be neurotic. As a result, Friedan charged, a woman's horizons were circumscribed from childhood on by the assumption that her highest calling in life was to be a servant to her husband and children. In effect, the home had become a "comfortable concentration camp" that infantilized its female inhabitants and forced them to "give up their adult frame of reference." Just as Victorian culture had repressed women's sexual instincts, modern American culture had destroyed their minds and emotions.

Other observers came to the same conclusions. Adopting a more academic perspective, Ellen and Kenneth Keniston pointed out that young women had no positive models of independent women to emulate and that with no culturally approved alternative to homemaking, many women accepted a "voluntary servitude" in the home rather than risk losing their femininity. The sociologist Alice Rossi made the same point. "There are few Noras in contemporary society," she observed, "because women have deluded themselves that a doll's house is large enough to find complete fulfillment within it." As a result, however, children were treated like "hothouse plants," women over-identified with their offspring, and a vicious cycle of repression and frustration ensured. The family became a breeding ground for discontent and unhappiness, with suburban bliss exploding into skyrocketing divorce rates, addiction to pills and alcohol, and an epidemic of mental illness.

At the heart of this diagnosis was the assertion that women had been deprived of the chance to develop an identity of their own. Assigned to a "place" solely on the basis of their sex, women were kept from seeing themselves as unique human beings. All women participated equally in the undifferentiated roles of housewife and mother, but many lacked a more precise image of themselves as individuals. As one young mother wrote to Friedan:

> I've tried everything women are supposed to do—hobbies, gardening, pickling, canning, and being very social with my neighbors. . . . I can do it all, and I like it, but it doesn't leave you anything to think about—any feeling of who you are. . . . I love the kids and Bob and my home. . . . But I'm desperate. I begin to feel that I have no personality. I'm a server of food and putter-on of pants and a bedmaker, somebody who can be called on when you want something. But who am I?

To Friedan and others like her, the question struck at the core of the alienation of modern women and could be answered only if wives and mothers rejected cultural stereotypes and developed lives of their own. If women pursued their own careers, Alice Rossi noted, they would demand less of their husbands, provide a "living model" of independence and responsibility to their children, and regain a sense of their own worth as persons. With an independent existence outside the home, they would cease to be parasites living off the activities of those around them and, instead, became full and equal partners in the family community.

There were a number of problems with this analysis. First, it reflected an extraordinary middle- and upper-class bias, ignoring both the circumstances and aspirations of those women who were not white and not affluent. Second, it failed to do justice to those women who were content with their lives—three out of five according to a 1962 Gallup poll. And third, it presumed that the ideas of "the feminine mystique" were a post-World War II phenomenon, when in fact they went even further back than the "cult of true womanhood" in the nineteenth century. Nor could it fairly be said that women in the 1950s were more "victimized" than they had been at other times in history.

Nevertheless, the fact that a feminist analysis had gained political currency proved to be enormously important. For years, talk about women's discontent had been rife, but now there was an assessment of that discontent that compelled attention. With eloquence and passion, Friedan had dramatized through case studies the boredom and alienation of those afflicted by "the problem that has no name." In addition, she was able to take her readers behind the scenes to editorial offices and advertising firms where they could see firsthand the way in which the image of the feminine mystique was formed. It was hard not to be outraged after reading how advertising men—who themselves viewed housework as menial—tried to sell cleaning products as an answer to drudgery and as a means of expressing creativity. If, as Friedan claimed, the women frustrated by such manipulation were legion, her book helped to crystallize a sense of grievance and to provide an ideological explanation with which the discontented could identify. *The Feminine Mystique* sold more than a million copies, and if not all its readers agreed with the conclusions, they could not help but reexamine their own lives in light of the questions it raised.

No protest movement occurs in a vacuum, however, and it is unlikely that feminism could have gained the energy it did during the 1960s had it not been for the catalyst provided by the civil-rights movement. Race had always constituted a central theme of American history, and in the 1960s, as in the 1830s and 1840s, the struggle to end racial discrimination caused women to develop a heightened consciousness of their own oppression. Throughout the 1950s, the civil-rights movement had swelled, growing in confidence and vision. Black women had played a major role in that effort, from the actions of Rosa Parks and Jo Ann Robinson in sparking the Montgomery bus boycott in 1955 to Ella Baker's help in giving birth to the Student Non-violent Coordinating Committee in 1960. As the civil-rights movement became a daily front-page story in the nation's newspapers, it alerted an entire generation to the existence of profound social and economic inequalities in America and highlighted the immorality of discriminating against any group of people on the basis of a physical characteristic like sex or race. Like their abolitionist ancestors, many women who became active in the civil-rights movement fully realized the extent to which they too were victims of discrimination only when they experienced the "sexism" of their own male civil-rights colleagues.

Whenever America became sensitive to the issue of human rights, it seemed, the woman's movement acquired new support in one way or another, and the 1960s proved no exception to the rule. The civil-rights movement did not cause the revival of feminism, but it did help to create a set of favorable circumstances.

One group of women who perceived the connection between sex and race discrimination were young Southern activists who took part in the direct-action civil-rights struggle of the Student Non-Violent Coordinating Committee (SNCC). Both black and white, they found their voices in the civil-rights crusade. As one white woman who joined the sit-ins later testified, "to this day I am amazed. I just did it." Countless others had the same experience of empowerment. A younger generation of black and white women sought to emulate the strength and courage of older black women like Fannie Lou Hamer, who were pillars of the church and community. For white women in particular, such role models for independence were scarce in their own background.

These younger women also encountered what at times appeared to be pervasive attitudes of male supremacy. Whether in their attitudes toward housework and decision making or their expectations that women would automatically acquiesce when they asked them to sleep with them, men displayed little evidence of egalitarianism when it came to gender roles. One woman participant wrote in her diary: "the attitude around here toward keeping the house neat (as well as the general attitude toward the inferiority and 'proper place' of women) is disgusting and also terribly depressing." As the historian Sara Evans recounts the story, more and more of these young women began to talk with each other about their common experiences. In the beginning, they hoped that simply pointing out the problem would bring change. With the passing of time they concluded that they must fight just as assertively for their own rights as they would fight—together with men—for racial equality.

Increasingly, the two causes were linked directly. In a "kind of memo" addressed to women in the peace and freedom movements, Casey Hayden and Mary King declared in the fall of 1965 that women, like blacks, "seem to be caught in a common-law caste system that operates, sometimes subtly, forcing them to work around or outside hierarchical structures of power which may exclude them. Women seem to be placed in the same position of assumed subordination in personal situations too. It is a caste system which, at its worst, uses and exploits women." As the Black Power movement made it more and more difficult for white and black women to unite across racial lines, the white women veterans of the civil-rights struggle took such sentiments into the student movement, the anti-war movement, and other activities associated with the New Left, becoming in the process the vanguard of the white women's liberation movement. A direct product of the civil-rights struggle, the movement for women's liberation became the radical cutting edge of the new feminism.

The second group of women affected by the civil-rights movement were older and more experienced. Academics, lawyers, business and professional women, as well as veterans of social welfare and voluntary organizations had been active in women's issues throughout the 1940s and 1950s. Many were members of groups such as the League of Women Voters, the American Association of University Women, or Business and Professional Women's Clubs. Some had also served on various state commissions that were established as counterparts to the federal commission on the status of women initiated by John F. Kennedy in 1961. As Cynthia Harrison has shown, those federal and state commissions helped define the reform agenda for women in the 1960s, documenting the second-class treatment women had always received and evolving a set of recommendations on social security, equal pay, and economic discrimination that would guide the legislative program of women's groups for nearly a decade.

For these women, the civil-rights movement offered a powerful and relevant model on how to proceed to secure change. Indeed, virtually every act of legislation, every judicial decree, every executive order that applied to race could easily be applied to sex as well. Hence, it was logical that the 1964 Civil Rights Act should prohibit discrimination in employment on the basis of sex as well as race. Although the sponsor of the amendment was a conservative who hoped to cripple the entire bill by adding what, in his eyes, was a ludicrous clause, supporters of women's right used the logic of the connection between race and sex to persuade a majority to support the new language.

The civil-rights movement also provided an example of how to implement the changes legislation had decreed. When it became clear that the ban on sex discrimination in employment was not being enforced, women who had served on the various state commissions on the status of women came together with activists like Betty Friedan to form the National Organization for Women (NOW), a civil-rights type of organization that vowed to use lobbying, litigation, and other political means to force the Equal Employment Opportunities Commission (EEOC) to make women's issues as much a part of its mandate as racial issues. Such groups as NOW, and the Women's Equity Action League (WEAL) assumed the responsibility for maintaining progress already made on women's rights while initiating new fights to secure additional victories in the struggle for gender equality.

In all of this, the civil-rights movement was not only a direct impetus for women organizing themselves but also proved indispensable to moving the public toward greater concern for social justice. In the 1950s, as Elaine May has shown, conservatism on women's rights went hand in and with McCarthyism, the Cold War, and ideological orthodoxy. Any threat to the family, woman's "place," or traditional definitions of sexuality was perceived as part of a larger "plot" to destroy America. But now, with the church-based civil-rights struggle as the path breaker, it became possible to raise profound questions about social equity. Social reform and patriotism no longer appeared to be at odds; youthful idealism was sanctioned from the White House on down; and it was once more permissible to criticize the status quo, even on such pivotal issues as relations between the races and between the sexes.

Still, the final precondition for the resurgence of the woman's movement was the amount of change that had already occurred among American women. If the situation had been as pervasively oppressive as Friedan and some others said, it is unlikely that feminists would have found an audience. But the combination of some change with the continuation of structural barriers to real equality created the chemistry that made a social insurgency possible. In effect, the stereotype of woman's place in the home no longer had a material base in reality, and the absence of such a base made both possible and necessary the ideological challenge to develop new norms of relations between the sexes.

Although the shifts in women's economic roles in no way caused the revival of feminism, they did help to create the foundation for that revival. To begin with, over 40 percent of all women—including wives—held jobs by the end of the 1960s. Included in that number were a substantial number of middle-class women (41 percent of those whose husbands earned from 8,000 to 10,000) and approximately 50 percent of all mothers with children six to eighteen years old. For the first time in the nation's history, almost half of the adolescent girls in the country were growing up with examples in their own homes of women who combined outside employment with marriage.

In addition, the evidence suggested that many working mothers already provided a positive model for their children. Repeated surveys of elementary and high-school students showed that children of mothers who held jobs approved of maternal employment and that the daughters intended to work after they married and had children as well. Significantly, an adolescent female was more likely to name her mother as the person she most admired if she worked than if she did not work. "The [employed] mother," sociologist Lois Hoffman wrote, "may represent to her daughter a person who has achieved success in areas that are, in some respects, more salient to a growing girl than household skills." Daughters of working mothers also scored lower on tests that measured traditional femininity and tended to view the female role as less restricted to the home, believing that both men and women should participate in and enjoy a variety of work, household, and recreational experiences.

On the other hand, young women who later became active in feminist causes were also upset about the extent to which their mothers were still restricted by traditional ideas of "woman's place." In her study of feminist activists, the historian Ruth Rosen found that the women she interviewed were bitter about seeing their mothers barred from high achievement positions while being expected to fulfill all the subservient roles of the perfect housewife and mother. Although Rosen's sample was selective, her evidence suggests that the special compound of some change, mediated by even greater conformity to anachronistic norms, created a readiness to respond as soon as a powerful feminist alternative presented itself.

For all these reasons, the time was right in the mid-1960s for feminism to make a profound impact, with substantial support from both younger and older women. Fortuitously, the woman's movement of the 1960s and 1970s was operating in tandem with rather than in opposition to long-term social developments. During the 1910s and 1920s, suffragist calls for greater economic and social independence for women ran counter to patterns of behavior that found most married and middle-class women still conforming to traditional norms. Now, feminist calls for the same kind of independence coincided with women leaving the home in ever greater numbers and learning firsthand how pervasive sex discrimination was. Fertility rates, attitudes toward sexuality and the double standard, changes in long-term employment curves— all these seemed to be working *for*, not against, the demands of women activists.

Thus by the end of the 1960s, it became clear that feminism was going to be one of the most vigorous, dynamic, and far-reaching social movements to come out of a decade of already unparalleled activism. The new feminism embraced a multiplicity of concerns and issues, from abortion rights to equal pay to the ERA. It was also decentralized, drawing its strength from grassroots groups in countless local communities rather than taking its identity solely from a national, single-issue focus such as the suffrage. And it brought together enough potential supporters so that there seemed at least a possibility that Americans might agree to the proposition that women should be as free as men to make choices about jobs, family, sex, and personal fulfillment. The question was whether, in seeking that victory, the new feminism could also overcome the barriers that had frustrated and perplexed previous efforts to win equality.

—— II ——

Although outside observers were impressed by the apparent fervor with which large numbers of activists supported abortion reform, ERA, and child care, there existed beneath the surface of the women's movement an ongoing set of conflicts over the tactics, goals, and values of the new feminism. From the nineteenth century onward, women's rights activists had struggled with a series of troubling dilemmas. Were women different from men or similar to them? *Should* women accept or seek differential treatment from society? Was the best method of securing equality to assimilate into the society, adopting integration as a means as well as an end, or did separatism make more sense as a strategy and tactic? Should women join in coalition with others in behalf of shared goals, or should women act only on their own behalf and pursue their own agenda regardless of potential alliances? Was reform or revolution the goal, and if revolution, who was the enemy to be overthrown? Obviously, such questions were not easy to answer, nor did they pose the kind of choices that could readily be solved by compromise. Yet the endurance of these problems after more than a century of efforts to achieve equality testified to the importance of the issues to be addressed.

Most scholars of contemporary feminism trace the conflict over these questions to the different origins of the women's liberation movement on the one hand and the women's rights movement on the other. Because the women's liberation movement drew its primary support from younger participants in the civil-rights struggle and the New Left, it logically reflected a more radical political perspective—peculiar to that generation—than might be found among the older, more-established women who came to the feminist movement through their participation in business and professional activities or commissions investigating the status of women. Although such an explanation contains substantial truth, it runs the risk of attributing total causation to age and of obscuring other sources of ideological and political difference. In fact, women of different political persuasions moved in and out of a variety of feminist alliances during the late 1960s and early 1970s, seeking the particular organization that most effectively represented their assessment of the causes and solutions for women's condition. Rather than place sole responsibility for these shifts on a generational explanation, therefore, it seems more sensible to outline—albeit schematically—the most striking differences in approach to these underlying issues.

At least three different kinds of feminism competed during the early 1970s for the allegiance of women activists. Broadly defined, these can be labeled as liberal feminism, radical feminism, and socialist feminism. Each in its own way developed a different analysis and set of answers to the key questions of the sources of women's oppression, the possibilities of coalition to end that oppression, and the goal of reform or revolution. Radical feminism and socialist feminism shared in common a collectivist approach to women's dilemma and an antipathy to the individualist priorities of liberal feminism. Yet both radicals and socialists at different times shared a commitment to some of the programmatic goals of liberal feminism and might join the ranks of such liberal organizations as NOW and WEAL. The conflicts were stark, but it was not at all unlikely that the same person could—at different stages of ideological perception—be identified with all three kinds of feminism.

To casual observers, liberal feminism was clearly the dominant force in women's rights activity in the years after 1968. Associated primarily with personalities like Betty Friedan and organizations like NOW, liberal feminism sought to work politically within the existing social and economic framework to secure reforms for women and progress toward full equality of opportunity between the sexes. Although the analogy was not perfect, NOW frequently was compared with the NAACP in the black civil-rights coalition—that is, it sought change from *within* established structures and did not question the legitimacy or soundness of those structures.

Ultimately, then, the goal of liberal feminism was complete integration of women into American society. Assimilation, not separatism, was the desired end, with victory being defined as the total acceptance of women—as individuals—in all jobs, political organizations, and voluntary associations *without regard to their sex*. Implicitly, then, NOW and other liberal feminist groups embraced a natural-rights philosophy that all individuals should be treated the same, that sex and gender should be discounted, and that eradication of a "separate-sphere" ideology was a *sine qua non* for progress toward equality.

Within this framework, liberal feminists concentrated on a series of pragmatic reforms. Recognizing that equal access for women into the "opportunity structure" necessitated at least acknowledging past barriers, NOW and other similar groups endorsed affirmative-action programs to promote women in compensation for prior neglect and the creation of social institutions such as federally funded child-care centers to ease conflicts between family and work. Liberal feminists emphasized compliance with equal-opportunity legislation, enactment of the ERA to guarantee that women would be treated exactly like men under the law, and advancement of women into careers that previously had been dominated by men. Typical of NOW's initiatives in the late 1960s were campaigns to eliminate sex identification from employment advertisements in newspapers ("Male Only Jobs," "Female Only Jobs"), a blistering indictment of one airline that offered "Men only" executive flights from Chicago to New York at the end of the business day, and insistence on open admission to clubs and bars previously off-limits to women. Clearly, the message was that women wanted to join, as individuals with equal rights, all the institutions of the society and that separate classification of spheres by sex was no longer acceptable.

Although for many Americans at the time these positions seemed extreme, liberal feminists themselves were—within the overall women's movement—perceived to be pragmatic and even conservative. They were "liberals," after all, who believed in incremental change and the possibility of persuading individuals through reason of the need for reform. They neither wished to topple the power structure nor to create their own. Rather, they wanted to join the existing social and economic system. As a consequence, they were more likely to eschew radical rhetoric and shy away from controversy, lest they alienate some of those *within* the structure of power whom they needed as allies. Thus, in the early years at least, NOW preferred to avoid the issue of sexual preference, lest lesbian-baiting be used to defeat their other goals. When NOW did take a strong stand in favor of abortion reform and reproductive freedom, some of its members were distressed enough to form the women's Equity Action League (WEAL) in 1969, a group that would concentrate exclusively on economic and political issues in an effort to avoid losing the backing of those who adamantly opposed abortion and gay rights.

Within the overall spectrum of women's activism, then, the position of liberal feminists was fairly clear. They were political, and they were activist— but their activism focused on reform of mainstream institutions, often through the existing electoral system, with the goal of integration by women as individuals within the prevailing social and economic order. Groups like the National Women's Political Caucus might be formed to promote women's issues and women politicians, but any such "separatist" tactics were premised on acceptance of the fundamental health of American institutions and on a belief that reform would eventually eliminate the need for such separate organizations. Although NOW and other liberal feminist groups espoused programs that would benefit poor and minority women as well as the middle class, it was clear that their primary constituency consisted of well-educated, upwardly mobile and independent women who wished to take their place next to men in America's dominant social and economic institutions.

Radical feminists, by contrast, saw men as the enemy, patriarchy as a system that must be overthrown, and separatism as an important strategy and tactic—for achieving the revolution. The adjective "radical" naturally evokes an association with the New Left or the student movements of the late 1960s but in reality it speaks more to the position of activists on a woman-defined scale, not one dictated by male political affiliations—that is, feminists were radical vis à vis their diagnosis of women's oppression as a function of male supremacy rather than vis à vis their position on the war in Vietnam or capitalism.

At the same time, it would be a mistake not to recognize the extent to which New Left machismo played a role in shaping radical feminism. In the early stages of the women's liberation movement, for example, women participants in the civil-rights struggle and the anti-war movement sought repeatedly to bring their concerns before male-dominated New Left organizations. Yet when they did so, they were treated with disdain, contempt, and outrageous sexism. *Ramparts* magazine, one journalistic voice of the New Left, dismissed women petitioners at a Students for a Democratic Society (SDS) conference as a "mini-skirted caucus." When Jo Freeman and Shulamith Firestone brought resolutions on women's rights to the National Conference on New Politics in December 1967, they were told that their concerns were irrelevant. "Calm down, little girl," the man presiding at the convention said. And when a representative of women's groups sought to present two statements on women's issues to the anti-Vietnam War mobilization rally in November 1968, she was greeted with raucous heckling. "Take it off," men around the platform yelled. "Take her off the stage and fuck her." Eventually, the speaker was forced to leave the stage, a male anti-war leader saying it was "for her own good." "If radical men can be so easily provoked into acting like red-necks," one woman observer noted, "what can we expect from others? What have we gotten ourselves into?"

Such experiences simply reinforced the inclination of many women to organize separate groups, free of interruption and domination by men. "We need not only separate groups, but a separate movement, free of preconceptions," Ellen Willis wrote. "It is also clear that a genuine alliance with male radicals will not be possible until sexism sickens them as much as racism. This will not be accomplished through persuasion, conciliation or love, but through independence and solidarity." Convinced of just such an analysis, two Florida activists noted that every group in history was forced to struggle for its own freedom, its members identifying with their own group (being woman-identified) and not using the values and rules of the enemy. "For their own salvation and for the good of the movement," they wrote, "women must form their own group and work primarily for female liberation." Using the analogy of black power, these activists argued that "the best thing that ever happened to potential white radicals in civil rights happened when they got thrown out of SNCC and were forced to face their own oppression in their own world, . . . and the best thing that may yet happen to potentially radical women is that they will be driven out of both of these groups, they will be forced to stop fighting for the 'movement' and start fighting primarily for women.''

But direct experience with the machismo of New Left men was in no way a mandatory prerequisite for radical feminism. Countless other, older women came to a similar diagnosis of the problem without any direct encounters with SDS sexism. Ti-Grace Atkinson, initially the president of New York's NOW chapter, broke with NOW because of its refusal to name the enemy. Women, she said, were by definition a class. "This class is political in nature," she argued, and "this political class is oppressed." The oppressor, in turn, was "the class of men, or the male role." Since women collectively comprised a majority of the world's population, the only way that men were able to stay in control was through dividing and conquering women by establishing individual relationships with them, thereby shattering their solidarity. "The key to maintaining the oppressor role," Atkinson wrote, "is to prevent the oppressed from uniting." This, in turn, was accomplished through the phenomenon of "love," wherein romantic attachments between women and men in marriage and elsewhere allowed women to be co-opted into the oppressive male system. As a result, women became victims who participated in institutions that perpetuated their oppression—such institutions as the nuclear family, marriage, heterosexuality, love, and religion. Only when women reclaimed their solidarity, Atkinson claimed, could they destroy the institutions that enslaved them, regain their autonomy as a class, and become free.

The implications of such an analysis were clear. Women must cut all ties with male-dominated institutions and values. They should create a new worldview that was "woman-identified" by virtue of beginning and ending with women's distinctive values and experiences. And they should build their own institutions and structures—controlled solely by women—which would provide the wherewithal for maintaining women's autonomy and independence. Women *qua* women constituted the organizing base for radical feminism. It was the collectivity of women as a class that counted, not individual women treated like men or regardless of their sex. Thus, a separate identity for women as a group represented the ideological cornerstone of radical feminism, just as identification of men as the enemy responsible for women's oppression represented the starting point for developing a strategy of change.

By virtue of their analysis and prescription for change, radical feminists were identified with a series of issues and processes that while shared with other groups as well were perhaps more characteristic of radical feminist groups than others. Consciousness-raising, for example, provided an organizational tactic for most women's liberation groups, but the process was especially associated with radical feminists. When groups of ten to fifteen women gathered to share their common concerns about the second-class treatment women were accorded in American society, one of the bonds that united them was the stories they told each other about growing up female, being pressured into subservient roles, responding to sexual pressures from men, having to "perform" for an audience with a preordained script on how women should act. As the stories became more intimate and the sense of solidarity more profound, consciousness-raising became the symbol for women standing together against men and society. They found within their group identity and process the model for separatist institution-building and the empowerment to pursue change. If becoming woman-identified was the philosophical core of radical feminism, what better way to initiate and perpetuate the process than by reinforcing every week the experiences and bonds that tied women to each other.

Similarly, while gay rights represented an issue with which every feminist group eventually identified, radical feminists were more likely than others to see the question of sexual preference as pivotal. Not only did lesbianism embody the politics of being a "woman-identified woman"; it is also clearly celebrated the empowerment of being self-sufficient and free of men in *every* aspect of life, including the sexual. Women who lived together, worked together, and slept together made separatism the pragmatic as well as philosophical *raison d'être* of their lives. In an age of reproductive technology that promised to bypass heterosexuality as a precondition for pregnancy, it was possible to envision an entire life free of men. And if women could thereby establish their freedom from patriarchy, they could create a world where class oppression based on sex no longer existed.

Toward that end, radical feminists also focused their energies on developing women-run institutions. To break the shackles of the male-dominated health professions, especially gynecology, women built their own health clinics, taught self-examination, and with books like *Our Bodies, Our Selves* created a mass-market resource that would liberate countless others from medical views of women that reflected a man's point of view. Feminist publishing houses commissioned, edited, and printed their own literature, from children's books that were nonsexist to literary and political journals. Abortion clinics, child-care centers, separate caucuses in professional associations, and food cooperatives all represented ways in which women could structure their own lives and institutions so that men were not in control. Although usually associated with groups like New York Radical Women (1968) and New York Radical Feminists (1970), the radical feminist perspective was widespread throughout the country and helped substantially to shape the ideological direction of the entire movement. While not political in electoral or legislative terms, radical feminism gave support to causes, institutions, and alliances that reflected the power of separatist thinking and the importance of women's distinctive cultural voice in reshaping gender relations in society at large.

The third major expression of feminist thought was also radical, but more in the mainstream sense than in a "woman-identified" sense. Comprised of people often referred to as "politicos," these women were Marxist, called themselves socialist-feminists, and emphasized the inextricable links between race, class, and gender oppression. Rather than advocating separatism, with men as the enemy, socialist-feminists championed solidarity by oppressed peoples everywhere, male or female, with capitalism as the enemy. Like radical feminists, the socialists were contemptuous of the existing social order and sought revolution, but theirs was a revolution where men were potential allies and where the goal was a complete abolition of race, gender, and class hierarchies, not a separate, woman-defined world.

Socialist-feminists were called "politicos" because they had little use for the introspective, self-discovery focus of some feminist groups. At a workshop in San Francisco in May 1970, for example, socialist-feminists protested against the absence of *"principles* or *programs* for action . . . , [any] overall strategy." There was, they said, "little solidarity with other groups." Yet such solidarity was essential if "the system" were to be overthrown. All agreed on "the necessity of a socialist revolution as an absolute prerequisite for the liberation of women," but they recognized that they had to ally with others to bring about the revolution. "We must take sides in the class struggle," they said, and to that end, they declared their determination to join "with poor and working people of all races and regardless of sex." Acknowledging the sexism of New Left men, they promised to "wage our struggle against sexism within the revolutionary movement as well as without," but concluded that in the end, "as we fight for our liberation we will advance the cause of the revolution at the same time. The cause is one and the same." From the perspective of socialist-feminists, only an alliance that included women and men, black and white, poor and middle class had the possibility of developing a strategy, a program, and a vision that would lead to freedom and justice.

With such an ideological framework, socialist-feminists were deeply critical of the narrow class and race bias of most other feminist groups, radical or liberal. Consciousness-raising might be an excellent vehicle for recruitment and mobilization, but by definition, small groups of women who could talk so intimately with each other were likely to be people from the same background. Although there were some exceptions (for example, the interaction between a predominantly black and a predominantly white group in Mt. Vernon and New Rochelle, New York), few of these groups were able to begin cross-class and cross-race community building. Furthermore, the depth and intensity of interaction which occurred in small groups generated an extraordinary agenda of personal confrontation that often took months or years to work through, while larger political issues remained unaddressed.

For some socialist-feminists, therefore, the small group itself became an object of attack. "We spend the majority of our energies and time feeding on our own needs and not moving outward," Pam Allen wrote. Instead of focusing on political issues, the small group contributed to "isolating ourselves from issues not directly related to our status as women." By focusing on individual problems and short-term change, the structural causes of women's oppression were ignored or minimized, they believed. The retelling of individual experiences might be good therapy, but it did not necessarily translate into group struggle. Ironically, some even charged that the movement's commitment to "sisterhood" could become a vehicle for self-imprisonment, since disruption of meetings to confront profound political battles were viewed as somehow unfeminist and unsisterly.

Socialist-feminists saved their harshest criticism, however, for the reformism of liberal feminist groups like NOW. Marlene Dixon, a Marxist, regretted the extent to which "the political consciousness of women [was frozen] at a very primitive level: the struggle against the attitudinal expression of institutionalized white male supremacy . . . particularly as it impinged upon sexual relationships. The early actions of the movement—bra burnings, Miss America protests, Playboy Club demonstrations—reflected a political consciousness which had been stunted in the long debate confined within personal relationships."

In Dixon's view, the time had come to move beyond symbolic and individualistic actions and to forge a strategy based on collective consciousness, under whose banner oppressed people could unite. Unless such an alliance were created, she warned, the movement for women's liberation would fail:

> The business and professional women represented by NOW form such a tiny (and well-behaved) fraction that the establishment will have no problem whatsoever in assimilating them by meeting their basic demands. For example, in the future, we can expect limited and elitist day-care programs, . . . abortion repeal; an effective end to job discrimination at least on the elite level, . . . and reform centering around divorce and marriage. All of these programs give the illusion of success, while in fact assuring the destruction of any hope for women's liberation.

From this perspective, changes in personal relationships, life-styles, and individual career choices would mean little in light of the overall structure of class, race, and gender inequality. In short, reform was a sop that served the primary purpose of co-opting insurgency, and if the movement were willing to accept such changes, it would be guilty of complicity in one of capitalism's worst tricks, the "gimme some syndrome."

Thus, socialist-feminists adopted perhaps the most visionary scheme of all. Not only should women organize to liberate themselves from oppression, but they should constitute a vanguard revolutionary force who—together with blacks, Hispanics, Indians, the poor, and other "victims" of capitalism— could transform the entire social and economic order. Women could be free only if the reign of capitalism ended, but women's captivity was neither separate nor different from the captivity of other groups. Hence, alliance with these groups, whatever the limitations of *their* sexual politics, was a prerequisite for change. Of all the activist visions that inspired women in the late 1960s and early 1970s, the socialist-feminists' was perhaps the most programmatic and political, and certainly the most collectivist, the most severely critical of traditional liberal individualism. In the process, it risked being the least acceptable to a society being asked by a new conservative Republican president to return to tried and true social values, and renounce the experimentation and ideological deviance of the 1960s.

—— III ——

If nothing else, the conflict between different feminist perspectives reflected the vitality, the political sophistication, and the energy of the contemporary women's movement. Virtually every divisive issue that had ever perplexed women's rights activists became fair game for renewed argument, with predictable bitterness and vituperation among the disputants. Betty Friedan, herself the object of invective from those who thought that one woman should not exercise such extraordinary power, struck back at what she called the "sexual shock-tactics and man-hating and down with motherhood stance" of the radical feminists. Lesbianism became her special object of concern, and in the early 1970s, she warned against the "lavender menace" that threatened to alienate support for other women's rights objectives. When NOW members came under attack from socialist-feminists for being petit-bourgeois conservatives, they retorted, in turn, that while Marxists might indulge in revolutionary rhetoric, liberal activists were engaged in actual organizing efforts that brought results, not just hot air.

Although such internecine attacks persisted and even deepened during the 1970s, there was also a great deal of movement within and between feminist groups that mitigated some of the conflicts. It soon became clear, for example, that NOW could not ignore or avoid the issue of gay rights, notwithstanding Friedan's early concerns, and by 1973 the organization had established a national task force on sexuality and lesbianism, while enthusiastically endorsing gay rights as a primary goal of the women's movement. Gay women played a critical role in all feminist groups, including NOW, and although sensitivities about lesbian representation in NOW's leadership ranks continued, there was clearly accommodation on the issue, with Friedan herself defending a gay-rights resolution at the 1977 Houston conference on International Women's Year. On a variety of issues of significance to liberal feminists, in the meantime, radical and socialist-feminists offered support where appropriate, especially on questions like abortion. One sign of the formal efforts toward détente appeared in 1975 when Karen DeCrow was elected president of NOW on the slogan, "Out of the Mainstream, Into the Revolution."

To outside observers, moreover, the unity, vigor, and enthusiasm of feminism seemed far more impressive (or threatening) than any internal divisions. Although comedians might scorn women's liberation and ridicule women who insisted on being admitted to "men's" bars or who protested the Miss America pageant as a "meat market," the measure of derision was, in fact, a testimony to how effectively feminists were entering the public consciousness with their positions. By the early 1970s, countless Americans were debating what could only be described as "feminist" issues, whether the focus was on the Equal Rights Amendment, child care, abortion, "open marriage," greater sharing of household responsibilities, or the sexual revolution. In every kitchen, living room, and bedroom, feminists contended, women—and men—were facing, for the first time in their lifetimes, the centrality of women's liberation to *all aspects* of daily life.

Indeed, what remained most impressive was the growing support that feminist positions seemed to be gathering in the body politic. In 1962, George Gallup asked a cross-section of American women whether they felt themselves to be victims of discrimination. Two-thirds of the women responding said no. Eight years later—three years after the women's movement began—the same question was asked again. This time, 50 percent of the respondents said that they were victims of discrimination. In 1974, the question was asked a third time. Now, with more than seven years of experience with the women's movement, two out of three respondents said that they were victims of discrimination, and even more supported such feminist policies as the Equal Rights Amendment and the right of a woman to have an abortion.

Younger women in particular proved receptive to the ideas of feminism. In 1970, college men outnumbered college women by nearly eight to one in expressing interest in such traditionally "masculine" careers as engineering, medicine, and law. By 1975, the ratio was only three to one. The number of women applying to law school and medical school soared 500 percent, while the number of those planning to enter traditionally "feminine" professions like elementary school teaching plummeted from 31 to 10 percent. By the early 1970s, the pollster Daniel Yankelovich commented on the "wide and deep" acceptance of women's liberation positions among the young. In two years, the number of students who viewed women as an oppressed group had doubled, and nearly 70 percent of college women declared agreement with the statement that "the idea that a woman's place is in the home is nonsense." The expression of such feminist viewpoints coincided with the greatest period of success in securing support for public policies promoting sex equality that had occurred in more than half a century.

Yet if feminism had become one of the most vibrant and powerful social movements of the 1960s and 1970s, there were still profound problems confronting the movement for equality between the sexes. First and perhaps most important, feminist groups—of whatever persuasion—were overwhelmingly white and middle class in composition. No matter how much socialist-feminists espoused a politics of inclusion or groups like NOW advocated a legislative agenda that addressed the needs of working-class women, feminists seemed, almost by definition, to come from privileged backgrounds, and at least in some instances, those backgrounds led to a kind of feminist imperialism in which bourgeois women activists presumed to speak for all women, as if there *really were* a universal sisterhood embodied in the experience of educated, affluent white women.

Nowhere was this problem more evident than in the negative view of feminism that prevailed in black America. Although black women in fact scored higher in support of feminist issues like equal pay and child care than any other group of women, the "movement" *per se* seemed alien and irrelevant. Black women held important leadership positions in groups like NOW; black intellectuals and writers like Eleanor Holmes Norton and Alice Walker wrote eloquently about why women's rights and black rights were compatible; and there was even a National Black Feminist Organization. But most often, feminist issues still seemed like white issues, geared to the cultural and economic backgrounds of women who were pursuing careers, not jobs, and who boasted of individual triumphs rather than group advancement for the poor. When radical feminists stated that sex oppression was the primary oppression and that separatism among women was the only way to attack the oppressor man, they, in effect, insulted black America, many of whose oppressors were white women who cruelly dictated to black women and men. For most black and Chicano women, sex was not the first or primary oppression, yet too few white feminists seemed to acknowledge that fact or the priority that minority women chose to give to advancement of their entire race or ethnic group. To poor women who were on welfare and struggling to keep a family together, most feminist rhetoric sounded precious and selfish, not inclusive and relevant.

Similarly, different cultural traditions among ethnic or minority women created dissonance in the face of most feminist rhetoric. Family solidarity represented the premier value for Asian, Hispanic, and Afro-American women, as well as for most ethnic groups of European extraction. Talk of women warring against men or seeing fathers, brothers, and husbands as the enemy seemed anomalous and a direct threat to cultural traditions of collective solidarity. Sex roles along traditional lines were more widely accepted in poor and minority communities, and advocacy among some feminists that women become more like men sounded alien and insidious. Thus, if women were to advance as sisters and share a sense of collective obligation to each other, feminists had to find a different way of expressing their viewpoint and recruiting support.

The second and equally important problem faced by feminism was the powerful wave of anti-feminism that developed, then crested, among both women and men who saw women's liberation as a dangerous ideology that was foreign to everything sacred in American life. If there were one other movement as striking in its success during the 1970s as feminism, it was the New Right, pro-family movement which used feminism as its principal foil. Notwithstanding the evidence of pervasive discrimination against women that feminists were seeking to overcome, millions of men—and women—believed that the traditional family and woman's role within it were sacrosanct. Feminism not only represented a hostile personal challenge to women who were proud to be housewives and mothers but also constituted an invasion of collective ideals that seemed central to the survival of a way of life. These women and men also were organized and in some ways more effective in presenting their message than articulate and passionate feminists.

In the end, the story of feminism in the 1960s and early 1970s provided a fitting conclusion to a decade of protest and struggle. Inequality between the sexes was as long lasting and as basic as inequality between the races or between rich and poor; precisely because it was so basic, the crusade to overcome it inevitably confronted the most fundamental issues of how to define equality and determine the path to achieve freedom. During the 1970s and 1980s, Americans—for the first time in half a century—experienced the challenge of a new ideological vision of relations between the sexes. The success of that vision—or more accurately those "visions"—would be determined, at least in part, by what happened to American women and men in the aftermath of the revival of feminism.

CHAPTER 12

The Best of Times,
the Worst of Times

IN MANY RESPECTS, the 1970s and 1980s provided an ideal barometer for measuring the impact on women's status of the changes that had occurred during the postwar era. The 1940s and 1950s had been a time of paradox, with significant behavioral changes in women's economic activities occurring simultaneously with a resurgence of traditional patriarchal attitudes that defined women's "place"—rigidly and anachronistically—as being strictly in the home. With the revitalization of a dynamic feminist movement in the 1960s, however, an opportunity arose for reconciling attitudes and behavior and, potentially at least, for creating an ideological mandate for moving toward substantive equality between the sexes.

As the 1970s and 1980s unfolded, however, it became clear that the relationship between attitudes and practice would remain complicated. The feminist movement careened through its own roller-coaster journey, achieving enormous successes, only to have these followed by disastrous defeats. Extraordinary changes continued to occur in the family and workplace, resulting in giant strides forward for a number of women who, two decades earlier, would have been unable even to conceive of some of the choices they now faced; yet other women, caught in the same vortex of change, saw their opportunities diminish and the degree of their oppression deepen, not diminish. In the end, the story of these two decades was reminiscent of what Charles Dickens wrote in *The Tale of Two Cities*: "it was the best of times, it was the worst of times; it was a spring of hope, a winter of discontent." The fact that both characterizations were true said worlds about the divided mind of American society when it came to women's role in life and about the continuing power of race and class to interact with gender and shape women's possibilities and circumstances. As a result, it was possible to predict that by the beginning of a new century, some white women of decent education and economic security would have more equality with men than women had ever experienced in America before and that many poor women—especially of minority background—would be caught in a cycle of poverty and hopelessness not exceeded at any time before in the twentieth century.

—— I ——

The 1970s began with growing evidence that feminism had made a decisive impact on the public policy agenda. For more than four decades after ratification of the Nineteenth Amendment, women's rights issues had systematically been ignored by politicians and government leaders. Even the enactment of the Equal Pay Act of 1963 and Title VII of the Civil Rights Act of 1964 had occurred without the benefit of a mass-based woman's movement. Now, however, such a movement was cresting, and politicians took notice. After having been bottled up in committee for nearly fifty years, the Equal Rights Amendment to the Constitution was brought before the Congress where it received enthusiastic support, going to the states for ratification in 1972. The Equal Employment Opportunity Commission (EEOC) finally began to pay attention to complaints brought by women against discriminatory employers, and James Hodgson, Richard Nixon's secretary of labor, announced in 1970 that federal contracts would henceforth mandate the employment of a certain quota of women. Even the conservative Attorney General John Mitchell initiated class-action suits to end job discrimination against women in such large firms as Libby-Corning Glass and American Telephone and Telegraph.

With a presidential election forthcoming in 1972, politicians developed still more enthusiasm for women's rights issues and congress enacted (1) Title IX of the Education Amendments Act, which barred sex discrimination of any kind by colleges and universities receiving federal aid; (2) tax benefits for parents of young children benefiting from outside care; (3) the Equal Employment Opportunity Act, which broadened the jurisdiction of the EEOC; and (4) the Child Development Act, which offered federally sponsored free day-care centers for those who could not afford to pay, with a sliding scale of charges for those who could. (President Nixon vetoed the Child Development Act in a move that foreshadowed an anti-feminist counter attack.)

At the same time, women's political presence became notable for the first time in years. Shirley Chisholm, a black congresswoman from Brooklyn, announced her intention to become the first black and female candidate for the presidency. The National Women's Political Caucus championed women's rights issues with both parties and succeeded in getting endorsements for the

ERA, educational equity, and a variety of other "feminist" policies from both the Democratic and Republican platform committees. The number of women delegates to the party conventions soared (from 13 percent in 1968 to 40 percent in 1972 among the Democrats, from 17 percent to 30 percent among the Republicans), and many of those delegates played a prominent role in advocating feminist positions at the two conventions. The Democrats even had the chance to vote for a woman vice presidential nominee, when Texas's Sissy Farenthold mounted a challenge to George McGovern's hand-picked candidate, Senator Thomas Eagleton. One reflection of this new political presence was that the number of women candidates for state legislative positions increased 300 percent between 1972 and 1974.

Court decisions proceeded in tandem with these other political trends. In 1973, the Supreme Court ruled in *Roe v. Wade* that women should be able to decide, in consultation with their physician, on whether to terminate their pregnancy during the first and second trimesters, and that no state could constrain that freedom. Coming in the aftermath of numerous feminist demonstrations for reform of abortion laws, the Court's seven to two decision seemed a powerful affirmation that women's freedom to control their own bodies now had achieved standing as a fundamental human right guaranteed by the Constitution. The Court also struck down provisions that denied women in the armed forces the same benefits and rights as men and increasingly seemed to include women's rights among those civil rights protected by the "equal protection" clause of the Fourteenth Amendment. Summarizing popular attitudes toward feminist positions, one *New York Times Magazine* writer noted, to his dismay, that "everyone seems to agree with them. . . . "

In fact, however, the temporary success of feminists—especially liberal feminists—in winning public support for women's rights simply obscured the depth of opposition that was mounting toward the entire feminist movement. To begin with, many feminists were far less conventional than NOW or WEAL and espoused positions on homosexuality, the tyranny of the nuclear family, or the evils of patriarchal capitalism that alienated virtually all of "mainstream" America. Secondly, a powerful counterforce was building in American society that viewed all the liberation rhetoric of the 1960s as an assault on cherished ideals. This counterforce—dubbed "Middle-America" by some, the "New Right" by others, or simply "The Silent Majority"—found in feminism the epitome of all that was "evil" in the churning radicalism of 1960s-style insurgency. What had made America great, these people believed, was the nuclear family, monogamy, the church, and respect for authority. Feminists seemed to be attacking all of these, and hence the only way to defend family and honor was to destroy feminist ideology and preserve the status quo.

—— II ——

The ERA symbolized the enemy. Its goal, according to anti-feminists, was to make women identical to men, indeed, to abolish difference between the sexes and, hence, to abolish all institutions—like the family—based on differences between women and men. Feminists, according to this argument, valued rampant individualism—or, translated literally, pure selfishness—placing their own interests ahead of those of the family, the society, or the country. As a result, support for the ERA became the equivalent of making war against all the traditional values that had made America a great nation.

The pro-family, anti-ERA coalition powerfully evoked themes of religiosity and patriotism. Feminists were associated with secular humanism, an anti-religious force that placed human beings ahead of God and the selfish individual ahead of society. "The humanist-feminist view of the family," one anti-feminist leader wrote, "is that it is a biological, sociological unit in which the individual happens to reside; it has no meaning and purpose beyond that which each individual chooses to give it. Thus, the autonomous self, freely choosing and acting, must satisfy its own needs. When . . . the family exercises moral authority, . . . [it] becomes an instrument of oppression and denial of individual rights."

Such a perspective not only abolished family roles and responsibilities, according to pro-family advocates, but also enshrined, in Connie Marshner's words, "a drab, macho feminism of hard-faced women who were bound and determined to secure their place in the world, no matter whose bodies they have to climb over to do it." Macho feminism, Marshner went on,

> . . . despises anything which seeks to interfere with the desires of Number One. A relationship which proves burdensome? Drop it! A husband whose needs cannot be conveniently met? Forget him! Children who may wake up in the middle of the night? No way! To this breed of thought, family interferes with self-fulfillment, and given the choice between family and self, the self is going to come out on top.

But if everyone looked out only for Number One, Marshner claimed, the entire society—including women—would be destroyed. Indeed, she insisted, this masculinization of women totally subverted woman's own true nature. At root, she argued, a woman "is simply other-oriented. . . . To the traditional woman, self-centeredness is ugly and sinful as ever. The less time women spend thinking about themselves, the happier they are. . . . Women are ordained by nature to spend themselves in meeting the needs of others. And women, far more than men, will transmit culture and values to the next generation."

Within this worldview, the entire future of civilization—and especially motherhood and child rearing—hinged on the defeat of feminism. The logic was simple and clear. The family depended on clearly demarcated sex roles and responsibilities. It was woman's role to think on behalf of the whole family and to serve others in it. That was what motherhood was all about. But feminism would place selfish and narcissistic influences first, and by vaulting the individual ahead of the family, would subvert the entire process by which values were transmitted, children raised, and society protected. Indeed, the ultimate example of feminist selfishness and individualism within this perspective was the issue of abortion, since a pro-choice position elevated the biological mother's right to abort her fetus to a constitutional right. As one anti-feminist declared, "*Roe v. Wade* . . . gave mothers the right to rid themselves of unwanted children" and thereby to destroy the very foundation of the family by exalting the Self as all-important.

This constellation of arguments clearly drew upon deep reservoirs of emotional strength and fear in America. Conservatism and liberalism each had two kinds of appeal. Liberals could defend certain of their positions on the basis of individual freedom from oppressive interference—for example, the right of black citizens, or women, to be free from laws that discriminated on the basis of sex or race. They could defend other positions on the basis of society's collective responsibility to preserve and protect the general welfare—the need to provide affirmative-action programs to compensate minorities and women for past discrimination by intervening in the economy to promote minority hiring. But conservatives could also use these positions—in the case of individualism, to argue against state-run child-care programs as an undue interference of impersonal government structures with the private realm of family life; or in the case of the general welfare, to argue on behalf of the state's right to preserve and protect basic institutions like the family from insidious forces of individualism by enacting laws against abortion.

Conservatives were extraordinarily skillful at using the collectivist or social-welfare argument. Feminists, they contended, were anarchistic individualists, so committed to rapacious egocentrism that nothing else mattered except the private self. In such a situation, the state must intervene to preserve and protect social institutions like the family by repelling such anti-family forces as feminism and abortion rights and by promoting such institutional reminders of society's strength as prayer in the schools. Of course, they could also revert to the anti-collectivist argument, as they did when Richard Nixon vetoed the Child Development Art on the grounds that it would commit "the vast moral authority of the national Government to the side of communal approaches to child-rearing." But it was the anti-individualist, social-conservatism argument that became the most powerful weapon in the anti-feminist arsenal by the mid–1970s.

Before the decade was over, it became clear that the ascendancy of a liberal-feminist public policy agenda would be short-lived. After winning early support in state ratification fights, the ERA ran into a solid wall of opposition. With conservative Republican Phyllis Schlafly in the lead, the anti-ERA coalition (one group, STOP-ERA, stood for "Stop Taking Our Privileges") brilliantly organized women and men throughout the country around the issues of defending the family and preserving separation between the sexes. As Jane DeHart and Donald Mathews have shown, the anti-feminist coalition used the politics of cultural fundamentalism to identify the ERA with godless attacks on the sacredness of the family. Jerry Falwell, television evangelist and president of the Moral Majority, emphasized that "God almighty created men and women biologically different and with differing needs and roles. . . . Good husbands who are godly men are good leaders. Their wives and children want to follow them and be under their direction." Feminists, by contrast, would confuse the roles of women and men and make the selfish individual triumphant. By insisting that feminists wanted to make men and women the same, the anti-feminist coalition succeeded in raising the spectre that homosexuality would become rife in the nation, that women would join men as combat soldiers, and that even the most private activities, such as going to the toilet, would be shared in common. Unisex toilets, homosexual marriages, and unspeakable sexual perversions became the stock-in-trade of anti-feminist propaganda. Taking advantage of deep-seated racial fears as well—especially the idea of black boys and white girls using the same toilet facilities and coming into sexual contact—some anti-feminists talked about the goal of the ERA as "desexegrating" America. When the issue of abortion was added to the equation, the potency of the anti-feminist argument became overwhelming. The ERA would not only blend the sexes and destroy the authority of the family but also reinforce the drive toward killing fetuses, giving sole authority over human life to selfish individuals. It was hard to imagine a more powerful combination of fears and emotions.

By the early 1980s, feminists appeared to be in steady retreat before these forces of reaction. Even though Congress granted the ERA an additional four years to be ratified, the amendment went down to defeat in crucial states needed to establish the three-fourths total required to make the ERA part of the Constitution. Congress, in the meantime, acted to limit the availability of abortion to poorer citizens. Under the Hyde Amendment, no federal money could be allocated to pay for abortions, no matter how much in need a woman might be who wished to terminate her pregnancy. Individual states could still provide assistance, but in the face of an onslaught from "right-to-life" groups, only a small number did so.

Other feminist oriented programs also came under attack. During the late 1970s and early 1980s, conservative groups made affirmative-action programs a special object of attack. All along, one feminist leader noted, securing implementation of affirmative action had been like "wading through molasses," but now, political leaders turned against those programs that had been instituted and sought to eviscerate them of any substance. The Reagan administration's Justice Department joined conservative private groups in arguing before the Supreme Court against affirmative action, and with increasing regularity, the Court—now with a conservative majority as a consequence of Reagan's appointees—ruled against class-action suits by minorities and women and limited the applicability of affirmative-action orders. By the end of the 1980s, the Court had even moved to restore many of the limitations on abortion that previously had been disallowed—in the process, threatening to overturn its own *Roe v. Wade* decision.

In no way could it be said that the liberal-feminist agenda was dead. On issues of equal pay, discrimination in careers, and especially provision of child care, some important gains had been made, with continuing support coming from many powerful sectors of society. But the optimism of the early 1970s had long since disappeared. Men—and women—were still divided profoundly over what it meant to be male or female, how families should be organized, and what the concept of equal opportunity meant for relations between the sexes. Few issues were more basic to a nation's direction and identity, and few were further from resolution in the 1990s.

—— III ——

The same sense of pervasive contradiction emerged from a careful examination of women's experience in work, family, and community over the two decades of the 1970s and 1980s. On the one hand, considerable evidence existed that women's world (and men's to some extent) had been turned upside down by the radical changes that had transpired in employment, sexuality, divorce, and family relationships. On the other hand, the persistence of sexual inequality, plus some of the losses that accompanied change, made it seem as though little had been gained, with the future offering less reason for hope than for despair.

Change was certainly the dominant motif of demographic patterns. The divorce rate, for example, soared from 35 per 1,000 in 1960 to 121 in 1984. By the latter date, it was predicted that half of all recent marriages would end in divorce by early in the next century, the rate rising to 6 in 10 for women who were in their thirties in the mid-1980s. Habits of sexuality had also altered dramatically. During the early 1960s, nearly 50 percent of American women had delayed having sexual intercourse until marriage. By the mid-1980s, in contrast, 75 percent became sexually active prior to marriage. One of the results was a significant increase in births to unwed mothers; another was a much more tolerant and expressive attitude toward sexuality generally, including much wider acceptance of homosexuality.

Although some observers saw these statistics as testimony to the disintegration of family life, others argued that the changes reflected a healthy realism and allowed a greater chance for happiness for those who stayed together, whatever their family arrangement. Despite the rising divorce rate, for example, a Louis Harris poll revealed that eight of ten families were satisfied with their internal relationships and the balance that existed between work and leisure time. The fertility rate of women had plummeted from 3.7 pregnancies per woman in 1955–1959 to 1.8 in the late 1970s. Except for teenage pregnancies, the greatest increase in childbearing occurred among older women who had their first (and last) child in their thirties rather than their twenties. Yet fewer children, potentially, meant greater attentiveness, higher quality care, and a better set of life chances for each child—not necessarily a decline in family life. Other poll data, moreover, showed more willingness by men to give priority to family concerns. A 1979 Harris survey of men aged eighteen to fifty found that health, love, peace of mind, and family ranked ahead of work as concerns that were rated as "very important"; and a *Psychology Today* poll suggested that women and men were becoming more alike, with men wanting to be more nurturant and loving. Some surveys even suggested that men believed in doing half the household work and child care, though no survey indicated that men actually did nearly that much.

All of these changes, in turn, went hand in hand with an employment rate among women that continued to skyrocket. During the 1970s, women accounted for 60 percent of the total increase in the labor force. By the mid-1980s, nearly two-thirds of all women from twenty to sixty-four were employed—250 percent more (in proportionate terms) than had been employed at the beginning of World War II when only one-quarter of all women worked. Moreover, the greatest increases during the 1970s and 1980s occurred among women in their prime childbearing years, so that the average employment curve for women became almost identical to that for men.

In all of this, the cultural logic that had begun to operate during and after World War II continued to unfold. At first, employment increases had occurred among married women over thirty-five with no children in the home. Then, they had broadened to include mothers with children in school. Now, they expanded to include women of all ages, with children who were infants as well as enrolled in school. For the first time, white married women's employment nearly matched that of black married women. By the mid-1980s, more than half of all married women were in the labor force, in contrast to 15 percent in 1940; 70 percent of mothers with children between six and seventeen were employed, compared to 12 percent in 1950. Nearly 60 percent of mothers with children under six were also employed (double the percentage even in 1970) as were more than half of the mothers of infants under one year. For divorced women, the figures were even higher, nearly 84 percent for mothers of six to seventeen year olds, and 67.5 percent for mothers with children under six. Clearly, a revolution had occurred, at least statistically, with employment for women becoming the rule, not the exception, and women's and men's occupational lives becoming less and less distinguishable in the number of years worked. Just as clearly, a two-income household had become indispensable for family maintenance, with one-earner families bringing home only $354 per week in 1983, as opposed to $646 for two-earner homes. Only the latter figure approximated the median family income for Americans.

Some of the women who participated in this employment change were obvious beneficiaries of the revival of feminism and the new opportunities opened up for women by the social-justice struggles of the 1960s. During the 1940s, 1950s, and 1960s, the entering classes of medical, law, and business schools were 5 to 8 percent female. With the challenge by feminism to discriminatory barriers, however, these figures rose dramatically. By the mid-1980s, more than 40 percent of all students entering traditional professional schools were women. The number of women who were judges and lawyers had increased from 4 to 14 percent between 1971 and 1981, while the figure for women doctors jumped from 9 to 22 percent. Women Ph.D.'s rose from 10 percent of the total in 1971 to 30 percent by the 1980s. Three decades earlier, these women would probably have been channeled into careers as secondary school teachers, nurses, or social workers with a limit on both their salaries and promotions. Now, at least some of them were heavily recruited into the best law firms and corporations, with salaries that were competitive with those of men. The men they married—if they married—claimed to believe in sharing household responsibilities, and although the women were somewhat less sure (in one survey, 40 percent of the men said they shared housecleaning chores equally, but only 24 percent of the women said the same), there clearly seemed to be a new ethos regarding career and home possibilities for young professionally oriented women.

Even controversies about combining motherhood with careers could be construed as positive rather than negative. When Felice Schwartz, a business leader dedicated to making it possible for more women to enter corporate life, suggested that companies make allowances in scheduling and job assignments for young mothers, some feminists denounced the idea as a so-called "Mommy track" (Schwartz had never used the word) that would allow corporations to pay women less and relegate them to second-class jobs. But as columnist Ellen Goodman pointed out, the idea could also be seen as making possible "a dream job that allows women the flexibility to do work they enjoy while still having time for school plays. . . . " After all, women in business and the professions too often were expected to be "superwomen," adding to their business responsibilities all the other activities traditionally associated with women's roles. Was not the effort to address this problem at least an advance over simply ignoring it?

Whatever women's view of "the mommy track," it seemed clear that countless younger women from economically secure homes now had opportunities for education and career achievements that would have been inconceivable a few decades earlier. There were still huge gaps and massive barriers to be overcome. Most professions remained under male control, and on average, even women professionals earned only 73 percent of what men earned. Women still had to cope with anachronistic cultural assumptions about their "place" and with men who failed to do their share at home, regardless of their rhetoric to the contrary. But for a generation of comfortable, well-educated younger women, feminism had helped to make a new world possible, one which—if not a model of sex equality—nevertheless offered richer and more diversified life chances than had ever existed before.

Such a rosy picture for some made all the more grievous the persistent and worsening plight that confronted the majority of women in the labor force. Even women in better-off jobs continued to suffer from discrimination. Only 4 percent of all working women earned more than $28,000 per year in 1984 while 26 percent of white men did. Women lawyers, on average, received $33,000; men, $53,000. But the "regular" working women were far worse off. From 1955 to 1981, women's actual earnings fell from 64 percent of men's to 59 percent, and even in the late 1980s, their earnings had climbed back only to 62 percent—still below the figure thirty years earlier. Women's median earnings in the mid-1980s were $13,000 per year, barely above the poverty level for a family.

Moreover, although some women had broken into male-dominated occupations, most remained clustered in sex-segregated, woman-defined jobs that paid less and offered fewer opportunities for advancement. Eighty percent of all women workers were employed in just 5 percent of all jobs—the lowest paying 5 percent. More than 40 percent of employed women were in clerical and sales jobs; another 17 percent were in service positions. Yet saleswomen made only 50 percent of what salesmen earned; waitresses, only 72 percent of waiters. By contrast, 75 percent of higher-paying jobs were held by men. Thus, women constituted only 6 percent of all engineers, 3 percent of mechanics, and 1 percent of plumbers, but more than 75 percent of teachers and nurses. Indeed, part of the explanation for women's skyrocketing employment was that most of the expansion in the economy after 1950 occurred in the service sector—a set of jobs defined as "appropriate" for women and the lowest paying segment of the economy. Even more frightening, economists predict that *every job* to be created in America from now on will also be in the service sector. "We may be approaching a situation like that in some industrializing third-world countries," one economist has declared, "where there has been a big increase in jobs for women . . . but the jobs don't lead anywhere, they don't lift women out of poverty." Thus, sex segregation, together with the concentration of economic growth in service industries, helped reinforce, not lessen, the degree to which women would suffer from ongoing sex inequality in the workplace.

Many of the women who took these dead-end jobs suffered the additional burden of being separated or divorced. Although some financially secure women may have benefited from the liberalization of divorce laws and the soaring divorce rate in the 1980s, most women did not. Lenore Weitzman's comprehensive survey of divorced couples showed that on average, a man's income *rose* 72 percent after a divorce, while a woman's income *fell* 43 percent. Historian Barbara Ehrenreich has described in vivid detail the stories of some of these women. Avis Parke, the former wife of a Unitarian minister, had devoted her life exclusively to child rearing and volunteer work for her husband's parishioners. When he suddenly left her, she and her children ended up on the welfare rolls, dependent on food stamps for their daily meals and on the Salvation Army for their clothing needs. Ehrenreich estimated that 85 percent of all American women could expect to support themselves at some time, yet without marketable skills, they often ended up in some of the new service jobs that paid a minimum wage and offered no future. Approximately 25 percent of all working women who were heads of households with children earned incomes below the poverty level, largely because of their plight after divorce and their lack of skills for higher-paying jobs. For such people, women's "liberation" seemed laughable. As one of Ehrenreich's divorced women said: "I work in an office with fifteen fantastic women who are suffering exactly as I am. You want to talk about mad? Everyone of these women is divorced. We come home with $123 a week. We don't even know how we are going to eat . . . how the kids are going to be fed."

One of the results of such scenarios was that poverty in America became increasingly a phenomenon experienced by adult women and their children in female-headed households. Between the 1950s and the late 1980s, the number of women and children receiving welfare assistance under Aid to Families with Dependent Children (AFDC) leapt from three to eleven million. Yet in only one state—Alaska—did AFDC payments and food stamps bring a family close to the poverty line. By the end of the 1980s, one in every four children in America was poor, and women comprised almost 70 percent of the adult poor. Most distressing of all given these economic circumstances the number of female-headed households continued to rise, increasing by 72 percent in the 1970s and by even more in the 1980s. The correlation with poverty was dramatic. If a child was born into a family with both parents present, he or she had only a one in twenty chance of being poor. If the child had a single parent who was male, the chances of being poor increased to one in ten. But if the parent were female, the chances were one in three. And the "feminization of poverty" was spreading, not diminishing. During the 1970s, the number of poor families with a man present declined by 25 percent, while the number of poor families headed by women increased 40 percent. The prospects seemed even more bleak when the mushrooming rise in teenage pregnancies was taken into account. One of every six children born in America during the 1970s had a teenage mother. Usually, the mother was unmarried, had dropped out of school in order to raise her children, and had little possibility of employment, except in the lowest-paying jobs that were available.

In all of this, the most striking reality was how race, class, and gender intersected to shape the experience of poverty. Black and Latina women were far more likely to get divorced than white women and far less likely to have ever gotten married in the first place. Although the number of white families headed by women had increased by nearly 100 percent, the actual percentage was still under 20 percent of all white families. Among blacks, however, the number of female-headed families had increased to nearly 60 percent of the total. For Puerto Rican families, the figure was over 40 percent. The overall poverty rate among blacks had increased to 36 percent in 1982, and Hispanic poverty had risen from 23 to 30 percent between 1972 and 1982. Much of this increase, in turn, reflected the impoverishment of women. More than half of all black and Hispanic homes headed by women fell below the poverty line.

For these women, the 1970s and 1980s represented a vicious cycle moving ever downward. If jobs were available, they paid a minimum wage. Marriage might be possible, but since the unemployment rate for minority teenagers was more than 50 percent, there was little material basis for building a family. Becoming pregnant and going on welfare represented another option, but there too, the road seemed to lead to ongoing impoverishment. Middle- and upper-class white women might be experiencing a new freedom, but almost none of the benefits they derived from women's new opportunities trickled down to the poor. For these women, race, class, and gender represented a triple whammy. Not only did the rhetoric of feminism sound distant and alien; the reality of life was getting worse, not better.

—— IV ——

One explanation for why the 1970s and 1980s were "the best of times, the worst of times" centers on the extent to which America was becoming much more a two-tiered society. The 1960s had spawned passionate crusades for social justice. With a degree of energy, collective mobilization, and ideological fervor not seen for more than a century, Americans from a variety of backgrounds had come together to struggle against racism, sexism, poverty, and war. Many of these movements had gone through similar stages of evolution. Beginning as moderate reform efforts, premised on the ability of social institutions to respond readily to proof of injustice, they had become rapidly radicalized as the depth of resistance to change became more obvious. By the end of each movement's history, some participants had become revolutionaries, some had dropped out, and some had joined in accepting whatever reforms had been achieved, choosing to work within the established order rather than try to overthrow it.

A key variable in all this, of course, was now how people in positions of power chose to respond. Would they give in to demands for reform? If so, by how much? Where would they draw the line? How much could change occur in favor of one side without generating even stronger demands for resistance by the other? Was it possible to find a middle way that would defuse the energy of insurgent groups without giving in entirely to their demands? What was the process by which change would occur? Must it be systemic, or could it be incremental, leaving basic structures in place?

When looking carefully at the experience of women during these decades, it seems clear that important reforms did take place, resulting in substantial elimination of barriers in law and custom that had denied women the freedom to pursue their own destinies. Just as the civil-rights movements led to the passage of public-accommodations laws, desegregation of many educational institutions, and destruction of Jim Crow, the women's rights movement brought a toppling of ancient barriers to women in the professions and support for a whole series of freedoms in personal behavior that had not been permitted before. Whether the issue was reproductive freedom, access to a career in corporate America, or greater flexibility of choice in one's mating or childbearing patterns, enormous changes had taken place. It would not be going too far to say that within the framework of the legal system at least, barriers to individual freedom based on race and gender had largely been eliminated.

What this meant, in reality, was that individual women and individual members of minority groups now had the opportunity to join the mainstream (a) as long as they had the economic base and educational qualifications for doing so; and (b) as long as they accepted the rules that governed mainstream institutions and agreed to operate within the prevailing norms of the status quo. Thus, large numbers of black Americans, including women, succeeded in getting college degrees in desegregated institutions and in joining the middle class through securing access to well-paid positions in corporate America. Similarly, large numbers of women, including some minorities, were able to enter business and professional schools, move into elite law firms and corporations, and create a life that combined professional achievement and personal fulfillment in a way that had never been available to their mothers and grandmothers.

In all of this, those in positions of power responded, albeit reluctantly, as long as basic structures remained intact. It was all right to admit blacks, Hispanics, or women into the corporate boardroom; it was not all right to abolish the boardroom or place blacks, Hispanics, or women in control. Reform was permissible; structural change was not.

In this context, the demands of liberal feminism were far more tolerable than those of radical feminism or of socialist-feminism. Liberal feminists wanted access for women to decent jobs, prestigious clubs, high-powered meetings; they wanted to abolish "male only" or "female only" job classifications; they sought the kind of self-determination for women as individuals that men had always had as individuals. And frequently, they asked for more radical changes as well. But it was possible for those with power to respond to the first set of demands because these were familiar requests, with compelling morality and logic behind them, and *they could be accepted without changing the rules of the game*, except in terms of defining who could play.

Radical feminists and socialist-feminists, by contrast, sought to redesign both the ballpark and the rules. Both insisted on placing collective priorities ahead of individual freedom of choice. In one case, it was all women *qua* women seeking to be treated as a class, with their own separatist institutions and values dedicated to ending patriarchy; in the other case, it was all oppressed people as a class seeking to destroy capitalism. But in both cases, the goal was radical transformation, not moderate accommodation.

In contradiction to the reform aspirations of the liberal feminists, the revolutionary demands of radical feminists and socialist-feminists were not absorbable. Basic structures would be challenged and changed. Power would be redistributed. The rules would be altered. And countless Americans—women and men—who were devoted to a different view of gender roles mobilized to resist these demands. Those in the opposition also organized to defeat the more frightening ideas of liberal feminists, or at least their version of these ideas. Hence, the ERA went down to defeat because anti-feminists said that it threatened to abolish all distinctions between the sexes, subvert the family, and sanction sexual deviancy. Still, people might resist the ERA and also be pleased that their own daughters could go to law school or become a bank manager.

In the end, however, victory for the goals of liberal feminism could occur without substantially altering the life and fortunes of women who were poor. Just as class became an increasingly powerful wall dividing middle-class blacks from poorer blacks, so did class (and race) become an increasingly powerful barrier dividing women. A well-off, highly educated and very successful career woman in New York, for example, could take advantage of the tax laws and with her equally well-off husband create a child-care arrangement for their children that was both good for the children and consistent with her and her spouse's ideas of an egalitarian marriage. They might even hire a "nanny" to take care of the children. But a poor woman could not take advantage of the tax laws and in many cases had no access to decent institutional child care, because governmentally supported day care was not universally available, regardless of ability to pay. Similarly, an economically comfortable woman could take advantage, at least until 1990, of the Supreme Court's decision giving individual women the freedom to terminate a pregnancy during the first two trimesters. But a poor woman living in a state that offered no medical aid for abortions might well find herself forced either to bear a child she did not wish to have or to seek illegal and dangerous help from others. In neither case did the poor woman have the *freedom* that was available to the economically secure woman; nor had feminism and its achievements made a significant improvement in her life.

Liberal feminism was not to blame for the emergence of such a two-tiered system, of course. Indeed, most liberal-feminist organizations strove mightily to pass legislation that would help the poor as well as the affluent. It would also not be fair to assume that any of the more transformative goals of radical feminists or socialist-feminists could have won sufficient support to be implemented. Nevertheless, it is important to recognize the political dynamics whereby some change does occur while other change does not and why that is so. It then becomes easier to understand the contradiction of why some women benefit enormously from change in a particular era while others find their circumstances becoming only more oppressive.

Ultimately, the paradox of these years being both the best and the worst of times is no paradox at all. It is rather the key to how American society has functioned in this era and a vantage point from which to better understand the persistent power of race and class—together with sex—to determine women's experience.

Conclusion

How does social change occur? What is the relation between social change and social reform? How does ideology affect the ways in which people live with each other or think about each other? Within the bounds of ideology itself, does it matter that people of diametrically opposed persuasions share certain thematic similarities—for example, that Phyllis Schlafly's pro-family movement shares with radical feminists the view that women are so different from men that they should never seek to exhibit the same behavior or hold the same values; or that the radical individualism of liberal feminists may be similar in outline to the anti-statist conservatism of *laissez-faire* anti-feminists. What does history tell us about the commonality or diversity that has prevailed in women's lives or about other commonalities such as race and class that serve as countervailing forces to gender? These and other questions like them have run throughout the preceding discussion, and although there are no definitive answers, it may be useful before closing to review some of what history tells us about these issues.

The first few questions on the relationship between social change and social reform are really variants of the question of whether attitudes determine behavior or vice versa. If one believes the former, then ideology is obviously crucial to any process of change, since people act according to their values and beliefs and will resist any behavior contrary to those values or beliefs. Hence, a change in society can come about only through persuading people that a given set of values is wrong and must be modified. The second position—far more skeptical—operates on the assumption that attitudes, especially those involving such emotional matters as race or sex almost never change except under compulsion and that behavior is a more likely source of change than attitudes. The sociologist Gordon Allport once observed about prejudice that "the masses of people do not become converts to [racial equality] in advance; rather they are converted by the *fait accompli*." Thus, white workers might lose some of their bias against racial minorities when forced to work alongside of them, but if the same workers had a choice beforehand, the contact would never occur, and the bias would remain intact.

Although the interplay of attitudes and behavior is far more complicated than the above paragraph might suggest, the distinction provides one useful device for understanding the recent history of American women. Clearly, there has been both enormous continuity and enormous change in women's experience. The continuity has perhaps been most evident in the persistence of traditional ideas in the dominant culture about women's primary role in society as mothers and homemakers, occupying a sphere distinct from men. Even when the ballot was won, allegedly reflecting a new *attitude* of sex equality, relationships between the sexes changed very little. Women might vote, but as long as gender roles were structured so that men were in control of the political process and women were to follow their lead on matters outside the home, the change did not really alter the status quo. Indeed, women's continuing ability to exercise political power in the 1920s and 1930s reflected the ongoing use of traditional ideas of women's sphere and of traditional women's networks. In the case of the vote, then, continuity rather than change seemed primary, illustrating the persistence of traditional attitudes.

In the area of employment, on the other hand, change stands out as more dominant—at least change in the aggregate and as defined by who performed labor outside the home. The increase in the female labor force represented a longitudinal pattern, and although absolute percentages of women who were gainfully employed remained fairly constant through 1940, the trends toward clerical and sales work and toward married women's employment were also obvious. Nonetheless, World War II provided a critical catalyst within this long-term process, disrupting traditional patterns of life and propelling both women and men into new activities that eventually affected some attitudes as well as much behavior.

The greatest change took place in the social compact about who could work. Prior to 1940, employment of middle-class married women had been frowned upon as unseemly, a violation of woman's place. Temporarily at least, the war made such attitudes irrelevant and caused women's employment to be recast as a national priority. As a result, more than six million women went to work, *three out of four of them married*. Most observers expected these women to go back home as soon as the fighting stopped, and under duress, some did; but once in the labor force, most of these women workers decided that they wanted to remain on the job. And at least in part because of that wartime experience, they did so, although their new postwar jobs were at lower pay and in more traditionally defined "women's work." The war had brought *no progress* toward economic equality between the sexes, but it had created a social legitimacy about the practice of married women working that carried over into the postwar years within the traditional framework of sex segregation and second-class jobs.

In the years after World War II, married women's employment behavior continued to change dramatically, partly as a response to inflation and rising family aspirations to join the middle class, but also partly because of a desire by many women to maintain the identity they had established outside the home. In the interwar decade it was rare for a middle-class wife or mother to work. Forty years later, nearly two-thirds of all such women were employed, with the highest rates of labor-force participation occurring among college graduates from affluent families. More than 55 percent of all mothers with children under six and more than 70 percent of those with children six to seventeen were in the work force. If the nation—including women—had been asked in 1939 whether it desired, or would tolerate, such a far-reaching change, the answer would undoubtedly have been no. But behavior bypassed public attitudes; change was absorbed into the existing value structure; and a new pattern of gender-role activity became an accomplished fact. The war, in short, was an event that accelerated a long-term process and helped to make conceivable new patterns of behavior among women.

But social change did not mean social reform, nor did it signify intentionality on the part of those with power in the society. As we have seen, all the structural barriers to equality remained in place. Women were still paid less, even in the war when government policy said otherwise; they were segregated—increasingly—into "women's work," especially in the clerical, sales, and service fields; and to an ever growing degree, they bore the brunt of the country's social problems, whether divorce, impoverishment, teenage pregnancy, or domestic violence.

To be sure, employment itself served as an engine of change—some of it positive—in women's lives. By the mid-1980s, nearly 60 percent of women said they liked their jobs and preferred to be working rather than at home. In 1970 some 43 percent of women said being a homemaker was one of the two or three most enjoyable things about being a woman; that figure had plummeted to 8 percent by 1983. Conversely, the number of women who said that their careers, jobs, and paychecks, were most enjoyable had climbed from 9 percent in 1970 to 26 percent in 1983. Women seemed to enjoy their work, to value the social companionship it brought, and to appreciate the bargaining power it sometimes gave them in their family relationships.

Still, there was no causal connection between the dramatic change in women's employment patterns and the status of women in society. Arguably, that status had deteriorated rather than improved. Average wages went down, poverty rates went up, discrimination remained. Whether the issue was rape, spouse abuse, sexual harassment on the job, or the simple fact that women were clustered in all the lowest-paying jobs, the evidence was overwhelming that employment by itself had not brought either liberation or equality to women.

However, social change may have set the stage for movements toward social reform. Rarely does social insurgency take place in a situation characterized by total oppression. More often, it occurs where some changes have already started and where those changes have helped create a new framework of experience within which to hear and respond to the demand for reform. Stated another way, ideology requires a base in material reality that can be used as a point of departure for raising consciousness about the existence of a problem and the presence of alternative programs to deal with the problem. The woman's movement of the post-1920 era, for the most part, lacked that base, except where women operating out of the Progressive-era tradition of women's separate sphere could connect to distinctive women's concerns. Most women, however, had no experience that permitted them to see the immediate relevance of feminist ideas—especially those of the National Woman's Party—to their own lives. During the post-World War II years, however, a different cycle of behavior was set in motion, and a new set of expectations concerning women's sphere began to evolve. The altered content of women's lives helped to highlight the disparity between myth and reality and to provide an incentive for considering new norms that might more appropriately speak to women's condition. Thus, the behavioral changes that took place in women's lives may not have led to the feminist revival of the 1960s and 1970s, but they helped prepare the ground for that revival.

How, then, do we understand the relationship between ideology and social practice? In large part, the answer seems to be that ideological visions help to give direction and energy to change, but not in a manner independent of that change or of larger social structures and values. Thus, for example, the presence of the women's rights and civil-rights movements of the 1960s exerted a substantial influence on the content of legislation, executive action, and judicial decisions in the 1960s and 1970s. Similarly, these movements played a pivotal role in altering the mind-sets of an entire generation of young women. A woman college student at an elite university in the 1980s grew up with a set of expectations and images of self that were radically different from those of her mother when she was at college in the 1950s. And feminism was largely responsible for that. "There was a new me inside my head," one feminist said in the 1970s, "and I could never again be what I was before."

Yet feminism in all its varieties could not determine what social change would occur or how much of that change would reflect politically intentional goals. Partly, that was due to the fact that feminists themselves differed so substantially on their analyses and goals; partly, to the way American society operated to channel and control movements for change; and partly, to the profound divisions that existed both among women themselves and among women and men about how to live and with what values. Perhaps above all, it was because of the strength of other social forces—such as race and class— to obliterate any possibility of women forming a global sisterhood to act for a common purpose.

Clearly, a variety of feminist movements emerged in the 1960s and 1970s in response to the changes that were occurring in women's lives and in the society generally. To a remarkable degree, these varieties replicated differences that had existed in the women's movements of the nineteenth and early twentieth centuries. The natural-rights individualism of liberal feminists in the 1960s and 1970s bore a striking similarity to the philosophy that dominated the Seneca Falls Declaration of 1848 and remained a primary theme of suffragists in the 1910s and of the National Woman's Party in the years after 1920. Seeking above all to eradicate sex as a category of differential treatment under the law, this individualism was premised on women joining with men in an integrated society where every person would be judged according to individual merit. There were parallels as well between radical feminists (with their contention that women were totally different from men and needed to have their own separatist, woman-defined institutions) and the nineteenth-century and twentieth-century women activists who formed the settlement houses and used their own sense of women's separate sphere to construct a distinctive political agenda. But in contrast to the radical feminists of the 1960s and 1970s, the nineteenth- and twentieth-century advocates of women's separate sphere never questioned the broader structure of society or named men—and patriarchy—as the enemy to be overthrown. Socialist-feminists of both eras perhaps had the most in common, given their shared Marxist ideology; yet there, too, socialist-feminists of the 1960s and 1970s were more revolutionary in their goals and perhaps more ready to acknowledge and deal with racism.

What remained most similar, however, was the parallel way in which the social, political, and economic institutions of the dominant culture dealt with the different feminist insurgences. The power to define an idea as deviant or beyond the pale is one of the critical means by which power is perpetuated in any society. This is why—among other things—the media is so important in today's society. If a certain point of view can be labeled as extremist or totally ludicrous, it becomes very difficult for supporters of that idea to win

an audience or a group of followers. On the other hand, the more familiar—
or the closer to dominant values—a cluster of ideas is, the more difficult it is
to rule it out of order.

There have been two sets of taboos, in particular, that people in positions
of power have been able to use to control debate. The first has to do with
separatism. Americans have always been taught to think of themselves as a
society of individuals who, whatever their backgrounds, share a common
loyalty and experience as Americans and to abjure any group identification
that might place a higher priority on being part of a collective group with
loyalties or an identity different from mainstream society's. Even though in
practice we have always used group labels to rationalize and enforce discrimination—whether against "dagos," "wops," "mics," "kikes," or "niggers"—
we have also responded vigorously, and even viciously, to those who attempt
to use their own group identity as an organizing base for self-defense or self-
assertion; historically, we have displayed animosity to Jewish "clannishness"
or to Italian-American "families" or to Black Power. It has been all right for
women to talk about a separate sphere, as long as it is subservient to and
consistent with men's rule, but talk about women as a force by themselves
generates a degree of fear and trembling. When we add to this syndrome the
issue of sexuality, we have perhaps the ultimate phobia. "Faggot" and "dyke"
are among the strongest words in the English language, and people tagged
with such labels become almost automatically "untouchables" in the political
discourse of the land.

The second taboo has been Bolshevism or communism. Just as we have
been taught that America is a land of individuals with no prior or supreme
group identity, so we have been taught that we are a nation without classes
that offers equal opportunity. Radicals who talk about class as the fundamental reality of capitalist society, or even about achieving substantive equality of condition between people of different backgrounds, automatically
become subversive. Whether these be advocates of the French Revolution's
"liberté, egalité and fraternité," mid-nineteenth-century utopian Owenites,
the Industrial Workers of the World (the "wobblies"), or Communists in the
twentieth century, such individuals have been persecuted, even deported, as
"un-American" people seeking to subvert and destroy all that has made the
country great by fabricating the false specter of class warfare as an issue with
which Americans should deal.

Each of these taboos has been used effectively to dismiss forms of feminism that seek radical change. During the nineteenth century, the utopian
aspirations of Victoria Woodhull and her allies were defined as unrespectable
by virtue of Woodhull's espousal of free love and the "radical" nature of her
goals. Radical feminists in the late 1960s and 1970s were struck down by the

double-edged sword of being both defenders of separatism and advocates of lesbianism. Groups like New York Radical Women were not only attacking the hegemony of patriarchy by urging women to be totally independent of men socially, culturally, and politically but also urging women to abolish the reign of heterosexuality by leaving the nuclear family. Socialist-feminists, in turn, were defined as un-American because allegedly they believed in the foreign idea that class was primary in American society and that capitalism must be overthrown. Both socialist-feminists and radical feminists made the cultural error of advocating "collectivist" identities and programs, whether gender or class-based; and in response, the people who exercised power in America curtly dismissed them. They were, literally, beyond the spectrum of permissible political discourse, their ideas sufficiently alien to the American "system" to be denounced as subversive.

For the same reasons, however, it was more difficult to dismiss liberal feminism. Its focus on gaining equal opportunity for women as individuals was completely consistent with "the American Creed." Liberal feminists did not seek to destroy or transform the American way of life or the nation's dominant social or economic institutions; they wished only to join those institutions on a basis of equal rights. Instead of aspiring to separate institutions run and controlled by women, liberal feminists wanted to have a voice in determining the fate of existing institutions, still controlled by men. Rather than overthrow capitalism, liberal feminists wanted to see women enter the corporate boardrooms. It was difficult, if not impossible, for national leaders to rule such ideas out of bounds; instead, it was easier to accommodate liberal-feminist demands, at least to the point of the most easily absorbed concessions. The pool of talent would be broadened; some women—and representatives of minorities—could join the structure of power; and everything else would remain the same.

On the other hand, when the individualism of liberal feminism went too far, it ran into trouble as well. The threat of women becoming *exactly like men* sufficiently alienated enough Americans—women and men—that a powerful countermovement developed to limit women's freedom. On such issues as the ERA and abortion, a large majority of Americans supported a liberal-feminist position. But enough conservatives remained committed to a more traditional definition of women's "separate sphere" that further political advances for feminism seemed very much in doubt.

Our postwar experience has shown, in particular, the power of race and class to shape women's experience and divide women—and men—from each other. Each ethnic and racial group in America has its own values and distinctive cultural traditions. Many of these place different priorities on women's roles and behavior than one would find in middle- or upper-class white

Protestant communities. Yet all too often, feminist groups have ignored or disregarded these cultural differences, preferring to assert a monolithic view of gender roles based on relatively narrow cultural and class experiences. More important, race and class have combined with gender to polarize dramatically the economic opportunities and life chances faced by women. Whether the issue be wages, job availability, pregnancy, abortion rights, housing, or relationships with men, women who are poor, black, or Latina share a set of experiences that have very little in common with women who are of the middle class, well-educated, and white. Even middle-class black or Hispanic women will live differently from their white middle-class, "sisters."

Thus race, gender, and class continue to intersect in ways that make inconceivable the kind of gender solidarity that has always been at the heart of most feminist appeals. Each source of inequality is so dependent upon and interrelated with the rest that progress on one single source of oppression will not address the overall structure of inequality that persists. If nothing else, the histories of the civil-rights and women's movements confirm the difficulty of winning equality for those whose material circumstances are such that they cannot take advantage of legal victories in the fight for equal opportunity.

The future, therefore, looks very much like the more recent past, with the best of times continuing to coexist with the worst of times. Social change will continue in gender roles, but only for an elite minority will that mean social progress as well. For others—statistically the majority—the structural barriers of race and class will remain. The ideology of liberal individualism will enable many women to expand—up to a point—the advances that they have won over the past thirty years. But even those advances will occur within a framework of cultural attitudes and control that limit how much change will occur.

Gender roles have altered significantly during the twentieth century, and new opportunities now exist for women whose aspirations in the past would have been circumscribed by the ideology of hearth and home. For those changes, both historical events and feminist movements deserve credit. It would be wrong, however, to underestimate how persistent and powerful have been the structural forces that have divided—and continue to divide—women and keep them in their "place." Only when a new set of social changes—and a new movement able to encompass women's diversity—becomes a reality will there emerge the kind of society where equality can exist, not only with regard to sex but with regard to class and race as well. The dream of equality persists—so, too, do the obstacles to its realization.

Bibliographical Essay

THE ORIGINAL EDITION of *The American Woman*, of which the present volume is a substantial revision, contains a complete set of footnotes. These are omitted here primarily because many of the citations in the 1972 edition were to government archives, such us the Women's Bureau Papers, that subsequently have been moved to a new location and thoroughly reclassified. (They are now at the National Archives and appear in a dramatically different form and arrangement from when I saw them—in dusty, uncatalogued cartons—at the Federal Record Center in Suitland, Maryland, during the years from 1968 to 1971.) Since it was virtually impossible to relocate the old material in its new setting, I regretfully decided to substitute a bibliographical essay for the original footnotes. For those sections that have not been altered, the former notes may remain useful. I have also appended a complete list of the manuscript collections used in both books. What follows is a selective discussion of the books and articles most relevant to the issues discussed in the new volume. As much as possible, the bibliographical essay follows the narrative progression of the new book.

For those interested in a general survey of women's history in America, the best place to begin is with a series of overviews. The most recent and up-to-date is Sara Evans, *Born for Liberty: A History of Women in America* (New York, 1989). Other texts include Nancy Woloch, *Women and the American Experience* (New York, 1984), and Mary Ryan, *Womanhood in America: From Colonial Times to the Present* (New York, 1979). On the twentieth century, see Lois Banner, *Women in the Modern World* (New York, 1975). Anthologies that contain material on this entire history include those by Nancy Hewitt, *Women, Families and Communities: Readings in Ameri-*

can History, two volumes, (Chicago, 1989); Linda Kerber and Jane DeHart, *Women's America: Refocusing the Past*, 3rd ed. (New York, 1990); and Nancy Cott and Elizabeth Pleck, *A Heritage of Her Own* (New York, 1977).

There are also a number of books in American women's history that extend beyond a particular subject or time period and that are useful in providing a backdrop for any specific scholarly work. Gerda Lerner, *The Majority Finds Its Past* (New York, 1980), offers an excellent introduction to the conceptual issues of women's history while providing examples of how women's history has evolved in one person's work. (See also Lerner's *The Creation of Patriarchy*). Anne Firor Scott's *Making the Invisible Visible* (Chicago, 1984) traces the contribution of women to shaping public institutions in America, even during periods when, for the most part, women were denied public roles. Her first book, *The Southern Lady: From Pedestal to Politics* (Chicago, 1971), is another classic work in women's history. Alice Kessler-Harris provides an excellent framework for tracing the evolving economic roles of women in *Out to Work: A History of Wage-Earning Women in the United States* (New York, 1983); John D'Emilio and Estelle Freedman offer a similarly valuable overview of the issue of sexuality in their book, *Intimate Matters* (New York, 1988); and Carl Degler does the same for the topic of women and family life in *At Odds: Women and the Family in America from the Revolution to the Present* (New York, 1980).

For those seeking to understand the context out of which 19th-century gender roles developed, the best places to start are Mary Beth Norton, *Liberty's Daughters: The Revolutionary Experience of American Women, 1750–1800* (Boston, 1980); Linda Kerber, *Women of the Republic: Intellect and Ideology in Revolutionary America* (Chapel Hill, 1980); and Nancy Cott, *The Bonds of Womanhood* (New Haven, 1977). Each of these books, for the most part, treats white women. For a view of black women's experience in the 19th century, see Deborah White, *Aren't I a Woman: Female Slaves in the Plantation South* (New York, 1985); Herbert Gutman, *The Black Family in Slavery and Freedom* (New York, 1976); Jacqueline Jones, *Labor of Love, Labor of Sorrow* (New York, 1986); and Paula Giddings, *When and Where I Enter: The Impact of Black Women on Race and Sex in America* (New York, 1984).

The evolving reform activity of white women is treated in a number of books: Barbara Lee Epstein, *The Politics of Domesticity: Women, Evangelism and Temperance in Nineteenth-Century America* (Middletown, Conn., 1981); Ruth Bordin, *Woman and Temperance: The Quest for Power and Liberty, 1873–1900* (New York, 1977); Keith E. Melder, *Beginnings of Sisterhood: The American Woman's Rights Movement, 1800–1850* (New York, 1977); and Karen Blair, *The Clubwoman as Feminist: True Womanhood Redefined* (New York, 1980). Nancy Hewitt explores the importance of class and status differences within the club movement in *Women's Activism and Social Change: Rochester, New York, 1822–1872* (Ithaca, 1984), while Carroll Smith-Rosenberg offers insights into the rich diversity of the entire period in *Disorderly Conduct: Visions of Gender in Victorian America* (New York, 1985)—a collection of her articles on subjects ranging from Jacksonian women to the "female world of love and ritual."

The world of women and gainful employment is the focus of Thomas Dublin, *Women at Work: The Transformation of Work and Community in Lowell, Massachusetts, 1826–1860* (New York, 1979). The life and culture of working-class women occupies Christine Stansell in *City of Women: Sex and Class in New York, 1789–1860* (New York, 1986). Kathy Peiss carries some of the same themes forward in *Cheap Amusements: Working Women and Leisure in Turn-of-the-Century New York* (New York, 1986).

The debate over politics and culture in women's history is effectively articulated in a forum by Ellen DuBois, Mari Jo Buhle, Temma Kaplan, Gerda Lerner, and Carroll Smith-Rosenberg in *Feminist Studies* 6, no. 1 (Spring 1980) entitled "Politics and Culture in Women's History: A Symposium." The settlement-house movement offered one way in which middle-class white women merged culture and politics. Among the voluminous writings on women in the Progressive era are Kathryn Kish Sklar, "Hull House in the 1890s: A Community of Women Reformers," *Signs* 10, no. 41 (1985), as well as Sklar's forthcoming biography of Florence Kelley; Allen F. Davis, *Spearheads for Reform: The Social Settlements and the Progressive Movement, 1890–1914* (New York, 1967); Allen F. Davis, *An American Heroine* (New York, 1975); and Blanche Wiesen Cook, "Female Support Networks and Political Activism: Lillian Wald, Crystal Eastman, Emma Goldman," in Cott and Pleck, *A Heritage of Her Own.*

The framework for linking women's reform activities to politics is most clearly presented in Paula Baker's pathbreaking article, "The Domestication of Politics: Women and American Political Society, 1780–1920," *American Historical Review* 89 (June 1984); and Suzanne Lebsock, "Across the Great Divide: Women and Politics, 1890–1920," in Louise Tilly and Patricia Gurin, eds., *Women, Politics and Change in Twentieth-Century America* (New York, 1990).

The classic work on woman suffrage remains Eleanor Flexner, *Century of Struggle*, rev. ed., (Cambridge, 1975). Other important studies of suffrage include Anne F. Scott and Andrew M. Scott, *One Half the People* (Urbana, 1975); Ellen Carol DuBois, *Feminism and Suffrage: The Emergence of an Independent Women's Movement in America, 1848–1860* (Ithaca, 1978); Steven Buechler, *The Transformation of the Woman Suffrage Movement: The Case of Illinois, 1850–1920* (New Brunswick, 1986); Sherna Gluck, ed., *From*

Parlor to Prison: Five American Suffragists Talk About Their Lives (New York, 1976); Aileen Kraditor, *The Ideas of the Woman Suffrage Movement, 1890–1920* (New York, 1965); and Kraditor, *Up From the Pedestal: Selected Writings in the History of Feminism* (Chicago, 1970). See also William L. O'Neill, *Everyone Was Brave* (Chicago, 1969). For a collection of suffrage documents, see Mari Jo Buhle and Paul Buhle, eds., *The Concise History of Woman Suffrage, Selections from the Classic Work of Stanton, Anthony, Gage and Harper* (Urbana, 1978). See also Maud Wood Park, *Front Door Lobby* (Boston, 1960).

One of the leading feminists of the late 19th and early 20th centuries (though not an ardent suffragist) was Charlotte Perkins Gilman. Her *Women and Economics* (1898) was reissued in 1970 with an introduction by Carl Degler. She is also the subject of two recent biographies: Mary Hill, *Charlotte Perkins Gilman: A Radical Feminist* (Philadelphia, 1983); and Ann Lane, *Charlotte Perkins Gilman* (New York, 1990). Mari Jo Buhle writes about *Women and American Socialism* (Urbana, 1981), while Ruth Bordin's *Frances Willard: A Biography* (Chapel Hill, 1986) describes the life of one woman leader who became a socialist. In *Beyond Separate Spheres: Intellectual Roots of Modern Feminism* (New Haven, 1982), Rosalind Rosenberg explores how female intellectuals were changing their world at the turn of the century. Rosalyn Terborg-Penn and Sharon Harley, eds., *The Afro-American Woman* (Port Washington, 1978), present a series of articles on black women, including their involvement in and response to woman suffrage, while Evelyn Brooks Higginbotham addresses the issue of how African-American women have been left out of women's history in "Beyond the Sound of Silence: Afro-American Women's History," *Gender and History* 1, no. 1 (Spring 1989).

The whole issue of continuity versus discontinuity around the 19th Amendment is the focus of Nancy Cott's article in Tilly and Gurin, *Women, Politics and Change in Twentieth-Century America,* as well as in her excellent survey, *The Grounding of Modern Feminism* (New Haven, 1987). There are a series of good books on women, politics, and reform during the 1920s and 1930s. These include James Stanley Lemons, *The Woman Citizen* (Urbana, 1973); Clarke Chambers, *Seedtime of Reform* (Chicago, 1969); Susan Ware, *Beyond Suffrage* (Cambridge, 1978); Elizabeth Perry, *Belle Moskowitz* (New York, 1987); Susan Ware, *Holding Their Own: Women During the Great Depression* (Boston, 1983); and Jacquelyn Dowd Hall, *Revolt Against Chivalry: Jessie Daniel Ames and the Women's Campaign Against Lynching* (New York, 1979). Eleanor Roosevelt is the subject of a series of essays in Joan Hoff-Wilson and Marjorie Lightman, eds., *Without Precedent* (Bloomington, 1984). See also Joseph Lash, *Eleanor and Franklin* (New York, 1973).

Susan Ware has written about Molly Dewson in *Partners* (New Haven, 1988). See also the collection of articles in Joan Jensen and Lois Scharf, eds., *Decades of Discontent* (Boston, 1983). For examples of political-science writing on voter turnout, see Angus Campbell et al., *The American Voter* (New York, 1964).

The history of the ERA is brilliantly covered in Cott's *The Grounding of Modern Feminism*. Other books that deal with feminism in this period include Judith Schwartz, *Radical Feminists of Heterodoxy: Greenwich Village, 1912–1940* (Lebanon, N.H., 1982); June Sochen, *The New Woman in Greenwich Village, 1910–1920* (New York, 1972); and Susan D. Becker, *The Origins of the Equal Rights Amendment: American Feminism Between the Wars* (New York, 1981). A pivotal article for understanding the success or failure of women's organizations during the 1920s and 1930s is Estelle Freedman, "Separatism as Strategy: Female Institution Building and American Feminism, 1870–1930," *Feminist Studies* 5 (Fall 1979).

An enormous amount of work has recently been done on the history of women and work. Glenna Matthews, *"Just a Housewife": The Rise and Fall of Domesticity in America* (New York, 1987), provides an overview of values and attitudes toward one kind of work. Domestic work itself is the topic of David Katzman, *Seven Days a Week: Women and Domestic Service in Industrializing America* (Urbana, 1981). Lois Rita Helmbold writes about similar issues of race and class in "Beyond the Family Economy: Black and White Working-Class Women During the Great Depression," *Feminist Studies* (Fall 1987), and in her forthcoming book on the same subject. A series of excellent books have dealt with the intersection of ethnicity, gender, and class. These include Sarah Deutsch, *No Separate Refuge: Culture, Class and Gender on an Anglo-Hispanic Frontier in the American Southwest, 1880–1940* (New York, 1987); Dolores Janiewski, *Sisterhood Denied: Race, Gender and Class in a New South Community* (Philadelphia, 1985); Julia Kirk Blackwelder, *Women of the Depression: Caste and Culture in San Antonio, 1929–39* (College Station, Tx., 1984); and Vicki Ruiz, *Cannery Women, Cannery Lives: Mexican Women, Unionization, and the California Food Processing Industry, 1930–1950* (Albuquerque, 1987). A number of books deal with specific occupations or categories of employment. These include Susan Porter Benson, *Counter-Cultures: Saleswomen, Managers and Customers in American Department Stores: 1890–1940* (Urbana, 1986); and Margery Davis, *Woman's Place is at the Typewriter: Office Work and Office Workers, 1870–1930* (Philadelphia, 1982). Judith Sealander examines the history of the Women's Bureau in *As Minority Becomes Majority: Federal Reaction to the Phenomenon of Women in the Work Force, 1920–1963* (Westport, 1983).

General accounts of women in the labor force include Alice Kessler-Harris,

Out to Work; Leslie Woodcock Tentler, *Wage-Earning Women: Industrial Work and Family Life in the United States, 1900–1930* (New York, 1979); Barbara Mayer Wertheimer, *We Were There: The Story of Working Women in America* (New York, 1987); Lynn Weiner, *From Working Girl to Working Mother: The Female Labor Force in the United States, 1820–1980* (Chapel Hill, 1985); Susan Estabrook Kennedy, *If All We Did Was to Weep at Home: A History of Working-Class White Women in America* (Indianapolis, 1979); and Julia A. Mathaei, *An Economic History of Women in America* (New York, 1982).

Some historians have focused specifically on issues of work and family. These include Lois Scharf, *To Work and To Wed: Female Employment, Feminism and the Great Depression* (Westport, 1980); Winifred Wandersee, *Women's Work and Family Values, 1920–1940* (Cambridge, 1981); and Ruth Schwartz Cowan, *More Work for Mother: The Ironies of Household Technology from the Open Hearth to the Microwave* (New York, 1983). Judith Smith has written about ethnic women and families in *Family Connections: A History of Italian and Jewish Immigrant Lives in Providence, Rhode Island, 1900–1940* (Philadelphia, 1985). The World War I experience of women is dealt with in Maurine Weiner Greenwald, *Women, War and Work: The Impact of World War I on Women Workers in the United States* (Westport, 1980); and Barbara Steinson, *American Women's Activism in World War I* (New York, 1982).

The topic of women in the professions and in higher education has also merited substantial attention. Regina Morantz-Sanchez has explored the lives of women physicians in *Sympathy and Science: Women Physicians in American Medicine* (New York, 1985). Taking a somewhat different approach is Mary Roth Walsh, *Doctors Wanted, No Women Need Apply: Sexual Barriers in the Medical Profession, 1835–1975* (New Haven, 1977). Margaret Rossiter has written about *Women Scientists in America: Struggles and Strategies to 1940* (Baltimore, 1982). The history of women in higher education is the subject of Barbara Solomon's *In The Company of Women* (Cambridge, 1987).

Historians have also written widely about women and the labor movement. Susan Levine's *Labor's True Woman* (Philadelphia, 1984) examines carpet weavers in the Gilded Age. Nancy Schrom Dye carefully examines the strengths and weaknesses of the WTUL in *As Equals and as Sisters* (New York, 1976), while Susan Glenn looks at the garment workers in *Daughter of The Shtetl: Jewish Immigrant Women in the American Garment Industry, 1880–1920* (Ithaca, 1990). See also Nancy Schrom Dye, "Creating a Feminist Alliance: Sisterhood and Class Conflict in the New York Women's Trade Union League, 1903–1914," *Feminist Studies* 2, no. 2/3 (1975). A good survey is Philip Foner's *Women and the American Labor Movement After 1914*

(New York, 1980). Alice Kessler-Harris raises some of the key issues in her article, "Problems of Coalition-Building: Women and Trade Unions in the 1920s," in Ruth Milkman, ed., *Women, Work and Protest* (Boston, 1985), and addresses them further in "Gender Ideology in Historical Reconstruction: A Case Study from the 1930s," *Gender and History* 1, no. 1 (Spring 1989). See also Jacquelyn Dowd Hall, "Gender and Labor Militancy in the Appalachian South," *Journal of American History* 73 (September 1986).

Various books have dealt with manners and morals, with Freedman and D'Emilio's *Intimate Matters* being the best place to begin. The issue of birth control is the subject of numerous studies, including Linda Gordon, *Woman's Body, Woman's Right: A Social History of Birth Control in America* (Middlesex, England, 1977); James Reed, *From Private Vice to Public Virtue: The Birth Control Movement and American Society Since 1830* (New York, 1978); and David Kennedy, *Birth Control in America: The Career of Margaret Sanger* (New Haven, 1970). See also Sheila Rothman, *Woman's Proper Place: A History of Changing Ideals and Practices, 1870 to the Present* (New York, 1978).

On sexual matters and courtship patterns, see Jonathan Katz, *Gay/Lesbian Almanac* (New York, 1983); Ruth Rosen, *The Lost Sisterhood: Prostitution in America, 1900–1918* (Baltimore, 1982); Joanne Meyerowitz, *Women Adrift: Independent Wage-Earners in Chicago, 1880–1930* (Chicago, 1988); Ann Snitow, Christine Stansell, and Sharon Thompson, eds., *Powers of Desire: The Politics of Sexuality* (New York, 1983); Ellen K. Rothman, *Hands and Hearts: A History of Courtship in America* (New York, 1984); and Blanche Wiesen Cook, "'Women Alone Stir My Imagination': Lesbianism and the Cultural Tradition," *Signs* 4 (Summer 1979). On youth generally during these years, see Paula Fass, *The Damned and the Beautiful: American Youth in the 1920s* (New York, 1977).

Historians have done an extraordinary job exploring the issues surrounding women's experience during the World War II decade. The best books include Karen Anderson, *Wartime Women: Sex Roles, Family Relations and the Status of Women During World War II* (Westport, 1981); Susan Hartmann, *The Homefront and Beyond: American Women in the 1940s* (Boston, 1982); Ruth Milkman, *Gender at Work: The Dynamics of Job Segregation by Sex During World War II* (Urbana, 1987); and Leila Rupp, *Mobilizing Women for War* (Princeton, 1978). Other important books include D'Ann Campbell, *Women at War with America: Private Lives in a Patriotic Era* (Cambridge, 1984); Maureen Honey, *Creating Rosie the Riveter: Class, Gender, and Propaganda During World War II* (Lincoln, 1984); and Sherna Gluck, *Rosie the Riveter Revisited: Women, the War, and Social Change* (Boston, 1987). Important articles include Alan Clive, "Women Workers in

World War II: Michigan as a Test Case," *Labor History* (Winter 1987); Karen Anderson, "Last Hired, First Fired: Black Women Workers During World War II," *Journal of American History* (June 1982); Ruth Milkman, "Redefining Women's Work: The Sexual Division of Labor in the Auto Industry During World War II," *Feminist Studies* 8 (Summer 1982); Valerie Matsumoto, "Japanese-American Women During World War II," *Frontiers* 8 (1984); Mary Schweitzer, "World War II and Female Labor-Force Participation Rates," *Journal of Economic History* 40 (March 1980); Nancy Gabin, "'They Have Placed a Penalty on Womanhood': The Protest Actions of Women Auto Workers in Detroit-Area UAW Locals, 1945–47," *Feminist Studies* 8, no. 2 (Summer 1982); and Gabin, "Women Workers and the UAW in the Post-World War II Period, 1945–54," *Labor History* 21 (Winter 1979–80).

The post-World War II era has yet to be explored fully. Some of the best books are contemporary to the time. See, for example, Mirra Komarovsky, *Blue-Collar Marriage* (New York, 1964), with a new edition published in 1987; Alva Myrdal and Viola Klein, *Women's Two Roles: Home and Work* (London, 1956); Mirra Komarovsky, *Women and the Modern World* (Boston, 1953); National Manpower Council, *Womanpower* (New York, 1957); National Manpower Council, *Work in the Lives of Married Women* (New York, 1957); and Barbara Cross, ed., *The Educated Woman in America* (New York, 1965). On two black women who played major roles during the 1950s, see David J. Garrow, ed., *The Montgomery Bus Boycott and the Women Who Started It: The Memoirs of JoAnn Gibson Robinson* (Knoxville, 1987); and Daisy Bates, *The Long Shadow of Little Rock: A Memoir* (New York, 1963).

The best overview of the postwar years is Elaine Tyler May, *Homeward Bound* (New York, 1988). See also Eugenia Kaledin, *Mothers and More: American Women in the 1950s* (Boston, 1984); Joan Huber, ed., *Changing Women in a Changing Society* (Chicago, 1983); and Helena Z. Lopata, *Occupation: Housewife* (New York, 1971).

Books that deal with various aspects of women's lives in the 1960s and 1970s include Lillian B. Rubin, *Worlds of Pain: Life in the Working-Class Family* (New York, 1976); Barbara Ehrenreich, *The Hearts of Men: American Dreams and the Flight from Commitment* (Garden City, 1983); Mary Aikin Rothschild, *A Case of Black and White: Northern Volunteers and the Southern 'Freedom Summers'* (Westport, 1982); and Cynthia Fuchs Epstein, *Woman's Place: Options and Limits in Professional Careers* (New York, 1970).

The revival of feminism has been the subject of numerous books, most of them very good. Betty Friedan's *The Feminine Mystique* (New York,

1963) represents one starting place for assessing the movement. Friedan's sequel, *It Changed My Life* (New York, 1975), traces her own evolving ideas on the movement. Other books by activists include Kate Millett, *Sexual Politics* (New York, 1969); Shulamith Firestone, *The Dialectic of Sex: The Case for Feminist Revolution* (New York, 1971); Germaine Greer, *The Female Eunuch* (New York, 1971); and various newspapers of the movement, including *Off Our Backs* and *Notes From the First Year*. An interesting example of a feminist publication that sold millions of copies is the Boston Health Collective, *Our Bodies, Ourselves* (Boston, 1973), and subsequent editions.

The best historical assessment of the women's liberation movement remains Sara Evans, *Personal Politics: The Origins of Women's Liberation in the Civil Rights Movement* (New York, 1979). Jo Freeman's *The Politics of Women's Liberation* (New York, 1975) deals more with the women's rights segment of the movement and its origins in various state commissions on the status of women. Cynthia Harrison examines the historical antecedents of feminism among women politicians and officeholders in *Prelude to Feminism* (Berkeley, 1987). Leila Rupp and Verta Taylor focus on the history of the National Woman's Party in *Survival in the Doldrums: The American Women's Rights Movement, 1945 to the 1960s* (New York, 1987). See also Judith Hole and Ellen Levine, *Rebirth of Feminism* (New York, 1971). M. Rivka Polatnick explores efforts to cross racial barriers in the movement in *Strategies for Women's Liberation: A Study of a Black and a White Group of the 1960s* (Philadelphia, 1987).

The best view of relations between men's roles and women's is Peter Filene, *Him/Her/Self*, 2nd ed. (Baltimore, 1987). Also on men, see Filene, ed., *Men in the Middle* (Englewood Cliffs, 1981); and Joseph Pleck, *Men and Masculinity* (New York, 1975). The theoretical argument for women's moral development being different from men's is presented in Carol Gilligan, *In a Different Voice: Psychological Theory and Women's Development* (Cambridge, 1982). On theory generally, see Charlotte Bunch, *Passionate Politics: Feminist Theory in Action* (New York, 1987), as well as the Bunch papers at the Schlesinger Library at Radcliffe. Feminist issues in religion are discussed in Mary Daly, *Beyond God the Father* (Boston, 1973); and Rosemary Radford Reuther, *Sexism and God Talk: Toward a Feminist Theology* (Philadelphia, 1980). The role of feminist scholarship in reshaping the history of traditional disciplines is explored in Ellen Carol DuBois et al., *Feminist Scholarship: Kindling in the Groves of Academe* (Urbana, 1985). The best book on the differences between liberal and radical feminism is Zillah Eisenstein, *The Radical Future of Liberal Feminism* (Boston, 1981).

The fate of the Equal Rights Amendment is the focus of numerous books. Donald Mathews and Jane DeHart explore the cultural politics of the amendment battle in *Cultural Fundamentalism and the ERA* (New York, 1990). Jane Mansbridge looks at the Illinois battle in *Why We Lost the ERA* (Chicago, 1986); Mary Frances Berry explores the legal and political issues in *Why the ERA Failed: Politics, Women's Rights and the Amending Process* (New York, 1986); and Joan Hoff-Wilson brings together various perspectives in her edited volume, *Rights of Passage: The Past and Future of the ERA* (Bloomington, 1986).

The issue of abortion is discussed in depth in Rosalind Pollack Petchesky, *Abortion and Women's Choice: The State, Sexuality and Reproductive Freedom* (New York, 1984). The right-wing response to feminism and abortion rights is the topic of Andrea Dworkin, *Right-Wing Women* (New York, 1983); Alan Crawford, *Thunder on the Right* (New York, 1980); and Rebecca Klatch, *Women on the Right* (Philadelphia, 1989).

Some of the major issues of the 1970s and 1980s were the impact of divorce, the feminization of poverty, labor segmentation by gender, and comparable worth. Winifred Wandersee's *On The Move: American Women in the 1970s* (Boston, 1988) is a good overview. See also Lenore J. Wietzman, *The Divorce Revolution: The Unexpected Social Consequences for Women and Children in America* (New York, 1985); ' Louise Kapp Howe, *Pink-Collar Workers: Inside the World of Women's Work* (New York, 1977); Diana Pearce, "The Feminization of Poverty: Women, Work and Welfare," *Urban and Social Change Review* 11 (February 1978); Karin Stallard, Barbara Ehrenreich, and Holly Sklar, *Poverty in the American Dream: Women and Children First* (Boston, 1983); and Sara Evans and Barbara Nelson, *Wage Justice: Comparable Worth and the Paradox of Technocratic Reform* (Chicago, 1989). For updates on women's status, see the annual series on *The American Woman*, edited by Sara Rix, which thus far includes volumes on 1987–88, and 1988–89.

One of the problems throughout the history of the women's movement has been a failure to include the perspective of minority and poor women. Reflecting that perspective are a series of books including bell hooks, *Talking Back: Thinking Feminism, Thinking Black* (Boston, 1989); bell hooks, *Ain't I a Woman: Black Women and Feminism* (Boston, 1981); Gloria Hull et al., *All the Women Are White, All the Blacks are Men, But Some of Us Are Brave* (New York, 1982); Angela Davis, *Woman, Race and Class* (New York, 1981); Alice Walker, *In Search of our Mother's Gardens* (San Diego, 1982); Michele Wallace, *Black Macho and the Myth of the Superwoman* (New York, 1978); and Toni Cade Bambara, ed., *The Black Woman* (New York, 1975).

Manuscript Collections

American Association of University Women Papers, Arthur and Elizabeth Schlesinger Library on the History of Women in America, Radcliffe College, Cambridge, Mass.

Grace and Edith Abbott Papers, University of Chicago Library, Chicago

Mary Anderson Papers, Schlesinger Library, Radcliffe College

Caroline Babcock-Olive Hurlburt Papers, Schlesinger Library, Radcliffe College

Mary Beard Papers, Sophia Smith Collection, Smith College Library, Northampton, Massachusetts

Dorothy Kirchwey Brown Papers, Schlesinger Library, Radcliffe College

Sophonisba P. Breckinridge Papers, Library of Congress, Washington, D.C.

Charlotte Bunch Papers, Schlesinger Library, Radcliffe College

Carrie Chapman Catt Papers, Sophia Smith Collection, Smith College Library

Child Care Parents Association Papers, Schlesinger Library, Radcliffe College

Democratic National Committee, Women's Division Papers, Franklin D. Roosevelt Library, Hyde Park, New York

Mary Dewson Papers, Franklin D. Roosevelt Library

Mary Dewson Papers, Schlesinger Library, Radcliffe College

Ethel Dreier Papers, Sophia Smith Collection, Smith College Library

Federal Works Administration Archives, National Archives, Washington, D.C.

Edna Gellhorn Papers, Schlesinger Library, Radcliffe College

Virginia Gildersleeve Papers, Special Collections, Columbia University Library

Alice Hamilton Papers, Schlesinger Library, Radcliffe College

Elinore Herrick Papers, Schlesinger Library, Radcliffe College

Institute of Women's Professional Relations Papers, Schlesinger Library, Radcliffe College

International Federation of Working Women Papers, Schlesinger Library, Radcliffe College

Florence Kitchelt Papers, Schlesinger Library, Radcliffe College

Alma Lutz Papers, Schlesinger Library, Radcliffe College

Lucy Randolph Mason Papers, William Perkins Library, Duke University, Durham, North Carolina

Mary McDowell Papers, Chicago Historical Society, Chicago, Illinois

Emma Guffey Miller Papers, Schlesinger Library, Radcliffe College

Morgan-Howe Family Papers, Schlesinger Library, Radcliffe College

National League of Women Voters Papers, Library of Congress

National Organization for Woman Papers, Schlesinger Library, Radcliffe College

National Women's Party Papers, Wisconsin Historical Society

National Women's Trade Union League Papers, Library of Congress

Agnes Nestor Papers, Chicago Historical Society

Katherine Norris Papers, Schlesinger Library, Radcliffe College

Mary T. Norton Papers, Rutgers University Library, New Brunswick, New Jersey

Office of Community Welfare Services Archives, National Archives

Leonora O'Reilly Papers, Schlesinger Library, Radcliffe College
Frances Perkins Papers, Franklin D. Roosevelt Library
Frances Perkins Papers, Schlesinger Library, Radcliffe College
Mabel Reif Putman Papers, Schlesinger Library, Radcliffe College
Raymond Robins Papers, Wisconsin Historical Society
Edith Rockwood Papers, Schlesinger Library, Radcliffe College
Franklin Delano Roosevelt Papers, Franklin D. Roosevelt Library
Josephine Schain Papers, Sophia Smith Collection, Smith College Library
Belle Sherwin Papers, Schlesinger Library, Radcliffe College
Hattie Smith Papers, Schlesinger Library, Radcliffe College
Hilda Smith Papers, Schlesinger Library, Radcliffe College
Hilda Smith Papers, Franklin D. Roosevelt Library
Jane Norman Smith Papers, Schlesinger Library, Radcliffe College
Southern School for Workers Papers, William Perkins Library, Duke University
Doris Stevens Papers, Schlesinger Library, Radcliffe College
Marion Talbot Papers, University of Chicago Library
Elizabeth Hewes Tilton Papers, Schlesinger Library, Radcliffe College
United Auto Workers Papers, Local 95, Wisconsin Historical Society
United Auto Workers Papers, Local 121, Wisconsin Historical Society
Marguerite Wells Papers, Schlesinger Library, Radcliffe College
Mary Winslow Papers, Schlesinger Library, Radcliffe College
Mary Winsor Papers, Schlesinger Library, Radcliffe College
Women's Advisory Committee Archives, National Archives
Women's Bureau Archives, Federal Record Center, Suitland, Maryland
Women's Joint Congressional Committee Papers, Library of Congress
James Madison Wood Papers, Oral History Collection, Columbia University
Ellen Woodward Papers, Schlesinger Library, Radcliffe College
Works Progress Administration Archives, National Archives

Index